The Value of Values

Management on the Cutting Edge series

Abbie Lundberg, series editor

Published in cooperation with *MIT Sloan Management Review*

Marco Bertini and Oded Koenigsberg, *The Ends Game: How Smart Companies Stop Selling Products and Start Delivering Value*

Christian Stadler, Julia Hautz, Kurt Matzler, and Stephan Friedrich von den Eichen, *Open Strategy: Mastering Disruption from Outside the C-Suite*

Gerald Kane, Rich Nanda, Anh Nguyen Phillips, and Jonathan Copulsky, *The Transformation Myth: Leading Your Organization through Uncertain Times*

Ron Adner, *Winning the Right Game: How to Disrupt, Defend, and Deliver in a Changing World*

Satish Nambisan and Yadong Luo, *The Digital Multinational: Navigating the New Normal in Global Business*

Ravin Jesuthasan and John W. Boudreau, *Work without Jobs: How to Reboot Your Organization's Work Operating System*

Mohan Subramaniam, *The Future of Competitive Strategy: Unleashing the Power of Data and Digital Ecosystems*

Chris B. Bingham and Rory M. McDonald, *Productive Tensions: How Every Leader Can Tackle Innovation's Toughest Trade-Offs*

Thomas H. Davenport and Steven M. Miller, *Working with AI: Real Stories of Human-Machine Collaboration*

Ravi Sarathy, *Enterprise Strategy for Blockchain: Lessons in Disruption from Fintech, Supply Chains, and Consumer Industries*

Lynda Gratton, *Redesigning Work: How to Transform Your Organization and Make Hybrid Work for Everyone*

John Horn, *Inside the Competitor's Mindset: How to Predict Their Next Move and Position Yourself for Success*

Elizabeth J. Altman, David Kiron, Jeff Schwartz, and Robin Jones, *Workforce Ecosystems: Reaching Strategic Goals with People, Partners, and Technologies*

Barbara H. Wixom, Cynthia M. Beath, and Leslie Owens, *Data Is Everybody's Business: The Fundamentals of Data Monetization*

Eric Siegel, *The AI Playbook: Mastering the Rare Art of Machine Learning Deployment*

Malia C. Lazu, *From Intention to Impact: A Practical Guide to Diversity, Equity, and Inclusion*

Daniel Aronson, *The Value of Values: How Leaders Can Grow Their Businesses and Enhance Their Careers by Doing the Right Thing*

MITSloan
Management Review

The Value of Values

How Leaders Can Grow Their
Businesses and Enhance
Their Careers by Doing the
Right Thing

Daniel Aronson

The MIT Press
Cambridge, Massachusetts
London, England

The MIT Press would like to thank the anonymous peer reviewers who provided comments on drafts of this book. The generous work of academic experts is essential for establishing the authority and quality of our publications. We acknowledge with gratitude the contributions of these otherwise uncredited readers.

This book was set in ITC Stone Serif Std and ITC Stone Sans Std by New Best-set Typesetters Ltd. Printed and bound in the United States of America.

Library of Congress Cataloging-in-Publication Data

Names: Aronson, Daniel, author.
Title: The value of values : how leaders can grow their businesses and enhance their
    careers by doing the right thing / Daniel Aronson.
Description: Cambridge, Massachusetts : The MIT Press, [2024] | Series:
    Management on the cutting edge | Includes bibliographical references and index.
Identifiers: LCCN 2023008798 (print) | LCCN 2023008799 (ebook) |
    ISBN 9780262048385 (hardcover) | ISBN 9780262375801 (epub) |
    ISBN 9780262375818 (pdf)
Subjects: LCSH: Success in business. | Business planning. | Leadership.
Classification: LCC HF5386 .A763 2024 (print) | LCC HF5386 (ebook) |
    DDC 650.1—dc23/eng/20230912
LC record available at https://lccn.loc.gov/2023008798
LC ebook record available at https://lccn.loc.gov/2023008799

10 9 8 7 6 5 4 3 2 1

Contents

Series Foreword

The world does not lack for management ideas. Thousands of researchers, practitioners, and other experts produce tens of thousands of articles, books, papers, posts, and podcasts each year. But only a scant few promise to truly move the needle on practice, and fewer still dare to reach into the future of what management will become. It is this rare breed of idea—meaningful to practice, grounded in evidence, and *built for the future*—that we seek to present in this series.

Abbie Lundberg
Editor in chief
MIT Sloan Management Review

1 Introduction

Why This Book?

I conceive that [a] great part of the miseries of mankind are brought upon them by false estimates they have made of the value of things.

—Ben Franklin[1]

What if you knew you were missing a tremendous source of power, profit, and competitive advantage in your business—and in your own performance? What if that source of power was easily available to you, something you could tap into with little additional investment? And what if it created a real advantage for you and your company because, despite its availability and power, nearly everyone else was overlooking it too?

This power source exists. You unleash it when you *act on values*. Skeptical? Good. You should be. Often, when someone says they see something no one else does, *they're* wrong.

So let me prove the power of values to you. Over the course of this book, I'll make my case so you can decide for yourself. I believe you'll see the power that values-based action can unleash—and that you'll choose to harness it.

Three Key Organizing Questions: Why Values, Why Quantify Them, and Why Now?

I'll start by addressing three key questions here, questions that will continue to resonate throughout the book:

- Why focus on values—aren't there plenty of other things that matter in business?
- Why quantify values—does quantification really matter?
- Why now—values have been around, and have been discussed, for thousands of years, so why talk about this now?

Why Values?

This book is about values for one simple reason: because they matter. Everyone knows that our traits, how we act, have value. However, values are often relegated to the realm of fables instead of finance. This means that their business value is underestimated or even missed altogether.

Here's a simple illustration: being honest is both inherently good and helpful in business dealings. It makes others more likely to trust us, to want to do business with us, and to act honestly in return. That means honesty has a *commercial* value in addition to its ethical value.

We recognize honesty's importance intuitively, even teaching it to our children. We read them *The Boy Who Cried Wolf* to show that being dishonest means others are less likely to believe you the next time. In fact, the story illustrates two very important points at once: first, that this lesson is important enough to prioritize teaching it to our children, and second, that even something as foundational as honesty is seen as belonging in stories, not spreadsheets.

But this is an example of impaired vision. In fact, if we look just a tiny bit below the surface, the financial cost of the boy's dishonesty in the story immediately comes into focus. After all, what is the consequence of the boy's dishonesty? It's the loss of his family's entire flock. What if we calculated the loss caused by the boy crying wolf and found it was dramatically more than the savings from grazing patterns optimized by artificial intelligence (AI), the productivity gained by feeding the sheep a high-growth diet, and the revenue increases from consultant-recommended wool-marketing strategies—combined?

If we did that calculation, that is undoubtedly what we would find. And yet, using AI to optimize grazing, or using a special diet so that the sheep grow faster, or hiring a marketing consultant—all of these things would clearly be considered business decisions. If these are all dwarfed by the loss stemming from the boy's dishonesty, then how can we treat that as less of a business factor?

It's not just bad actions—like crying wolf—that have commercial effects. There is also a very strong affirmative case for acting on values. For example, one hundred-billion-dollar company I worked with discovered that the financial return on investment (ROI) of acting on the firm's values, and making sure customers knew about that, was much higher than previously thought. In fact, it was many times higher than the ROI from traditional investments such as upgraded technology or new marketing campaigns. Yet the importance of technology and marketing were clearly understood as key areas of the business, while the importance of values was vastly underestimated.

It's not enough, when discussing values, to describe risks to a company's reputation, or an executive's desire to leave a positive legacy, or leaders wanting their children to be proud of the work they do. Those things are all important! But they are rarely—if ever—entered in spreadsheets or used to determine which actions have the highest ROI.

All the while, there's enormous attention paid to increasing efficiency, profitability, productivity, customer loyalty, all the standard things widely understood to help the bottom line. What if you treated values as a key business driver—like information technology (IT), innovation, mobile technology, and so on—looking concretely at what matters to the bottom line using the power of numbers? Throughout the book, I'll show you just how powerful that would be.

Why Quantify Values?

Why talk about the benefits that come from acting on values? Shouldn't realizing values be its own reward?

Yes. You should do the right thing because it's the right thing to do. But that doesn't mean doing so also doesn't have other benefits. It also doesn't mean that underestimating the ROI of values-based actions isn't a problem; in fact, drawing on interviews with three thousand chief executive officers (CEOs), IBM and Oxford Economics found that "unclear ROI and economic benefits" was the top challenge for CEOs when it came to achieving environmental sustainability objectives.[2]

There's a perception that acting on values doesn't produce business value and therefore you can't afford to put your values into action. But quantifying the benefits of values shows that not only is this untrue but it's also *exactly backward*. Not only can you afford to act on values, but if you want to maximize your success, you can't afford *not* to—and the penalty for not doing so is growing.

Another big reason to quantify values is that virtually all areas of a business use numbers to make their case. As the chief financial officer of a multibillion-dollar company once said to me, "Only two departments come into my office and ask for money with no numbers: HR and sustainability." Not bringing numbers hurts credibility, and it also leads people to deprioritize values-related issues.

The idea that decision makers prioritize considerations that have a monetary value attached to them, and that they give more weight to environmental and social issues when their impacts are expressed in financial terms, makes sense. Therefore, it's not surprising that researchers found just that.[3] One of the researchers' conclusions was that all environmental and social impacts of a decision should be monetized to the extent possible to ensure that decision makers weigh all impacts appropriately.

Over twenty-five years ago, a vice president (VP) at a major pharmaceutical company told me it was impossible to measure the benefit—to the world and to his company—of a corporate program that donated medicine in Africa. "It's a shame," he said, "because that would be really helpful." This statement is the beginning of the answer to the question of why we should quantify values—because quantifying their value helps companies do better financially and also do more good in the world. I took the VP's comments as a challenge and determined I would make quantification work. I had to think differently and to look at things in a new light—both of which I'll show you how to do over the course of this book—but it was absolutely doable.

In the quarter century since that conversation, I've quantified over $2 billion in financial benefit from values-based initiatives, and I've worked with companies that had annual revenues as low as a few million dollars and as high as $100 billion. In addition, my company, Valutus, has collected over half a million data points, on four continents, showing how customers respond when products include values-based attributes and how much that's worth. We've also created tools that help customers do more, and faster, to quantify and capture the value of values.

In short, my experience has been that quantifying values-based considerations is both quite possible—in nearly three decades of doing so, I haven't yet run into a case where it wasn't—and also very beneficial. I wrote this book because every day that goes by without doing more to act on your values is a waste: your business is less profitable, you are less successful, and the world benefits less than it should from your company. Everyone loses.

Why Now?

The influence of values on your customers, employees, and even the world around you is already extensive, and it's exploding. Before, customers might've only had a few choices about what products to buy or who to buy from, but now that isn't true.

Before, employees might have only been able to choose between a few local employers, but that has changed dramatically—not only can they move more easily, but many of them can work for a company far away without having to move at all. Before, the vastness of the world and its resources might have seemed almost endless, and countries far away much less important, but that has all begun to change—changes that will only accelerate.

That isn't to say that values haven't had clear value before—they have. Almost two thousand years ago, Roman emperor Marcus Aurelius saw the benefits that come from acting on values. In his *Meditations*, he wrote, "Have I done something for the common good? Then I share in the benefits."[4]

But as powerful as values were thousands of years ago, hundreds of years ago, and decades ago, they are more powerful now—and their power is only growing. As you go through the book, you will see that "values lenses" enable you to see more clearly some of the biggest changes that are transforming business and the world. They unlock innovation, efficiency, and smarts in a way that is dramatically more important than it was when the world was less connected and business was less competitive.

And, in a time when products, technologies, and markets are becoming less differentiated, it will become clear that values are a source of untapped competitive advantage. As you will see, these are not theoretical or potential factors—they are concrete forces creating real effects, with quantifiable financial results.

What You'll Get from This Book

When you're done with this book, you'll see the world differently, and you'll see both the risks and the opportunities you had missed. I'll take you on a tour of familiar territory but with new lenses—values lenses—so that what you see is new.

You'll see how values change people's behavior, both those outside your company (e.g., customers) and those within it (employees). And it will be clear how these changes interact with the external changes in the world, creating opportunities for tremendous benefit—or tremendous loss. You'll see that not only can you afford to act on your values, but in fact you can't afford not to—at least not for long.

That's because *where people are, values matter*—and, as illustrated throughout the book, they matter now more than ever.

Which Values?

This book will focus on values that:

- relate to doing good for the world and those who live in it,
- are key parts of the conversation about the role of business, and
- are the subject of skepticism about their business value.

Many of the examples I'll provide are about social and environmental efforts such as combating the climate crisis, assisting those who have been out of the workforce in getting jobs, or creating an inclusive environment for employees from different backgrounds.

There are certainly plenty of other values—thousands of years of philosophers, religious leaders, and business gurus have made sure of that. These other values include some that are more clearly commercial and some that are more clearly personal or religious. However, in these pages, the focus will be on values that are directed outward, toward the world and those who live in it. As an example of the difference between the kinds of values that will be discussed and those that won't, here is one of each—both from the exact same company, fast food restaurant chain Chick-fil-A.

It's well-known that Chick-fil-A restaurants are closed on Sundays, a decision the founder, Truett Cathy, made based on his religious beliefs. As a 2009 company press release explained, the decision was "a testament to his faith in God. Within the first week of business at his Dwarf Grill restaurant in Hapeville, Ga. more than 60 years ago, Cathy knew that he would not deal with money on the 'Lord's Day.'"[5] While this decision clearly reflected Cathy's personal values, it wasn't about doing (earthly) good for the world and those in it, so decisions like this won't be the focus of this book.

Chick-fil-A also makes polo shirts worn by restaurant employees out of recycled plastic bottles (rPET) as part of its environmental programs.[6] Unlike the decision to be closed on Sundays, this is the kind of values-based action that will be covered in the book because it is externally oriented, relating to doing good for the world and others.

These types of decisions are especially important when those values are both key parts of the conversation about the role of business and are the subject of skepticism about their business value. Take the concept of corporate social responsibility (CSR) for example. CSR is both a very significant part of the conversation about the role of business—such as whether businesses should serve only shareholders or a broader set of stakeholders—and has been a subject of controversy for over half a century. The same is now true for corporate sustainability; for environmental, social, and governance (ESG) investing; and for other environmental and social efforts.

This book addresses these kinds of values—outward-looking, part of conversations about the role of business, and the subject of uncertainty or skepticism about their business benefits. It especially addresses that exact skepticism: the question of whether such values have business value.

Not One Penny

Sometimes, the belief that values are peripheral to the "real" work of the company is stated explicitly. Discussing whether to buy an environmentally sustainable product, one buyer said bluntly: "We're as green a company as there is out there. But if I have to spend even one more penny for this, I'm not going for it."[7]

Now imagine replacing the "green" language with something else like, "We are as customer-focused a company as there is, but if I have to spend even one more penny for something that helps to please customers, I'm not going for it." How about, "We are as innovative a company as there is, but if we have to spend even one more penny on innovation, we won't do it." Doesn't compute, right?

It's intuitively clear that customer service and innovation are important for the business and are therefore important and worthwhile investments. Apparently, sustainable decisions are not intuitive, however. Many companies think of taking the environment into consideration as an optional "nice to have," rather than as something that's core to the business.

That's another big part of the motivation behind this book: to demonstrate exactly why and how values must be a key part of strategy, operations, planning, recruitment, and so many more activities. Because once executives and their companies understand where to look, investing in values will become the same intuitive, *must-have* decision as in these other core functions. At that point, it will be clear that *not* investing in values is just as short-sighted as refusing to invest in any critical business function.

The CORE of This Book

I've structured what follows around the acronym CORE, referring to the four main areas in which values create business value: customers, operations, risk, and employees, followed by the fifth, more personal, domain of leadership. To give you a sense of what's to come, below I've listed two to four of the points each part will cover. (There's much, much more in the parts themselves, of course.)

The first part discusses why, as important as values have always been, they're even more important now. It covers the following:

- Leaders have known that values produce tangible benefits for thousands of years, but values matter even more now than they did then because, in a sense, we're already living in the future—a tense, risky future, one where the speed and scale of changes is rising.

- The clock speed of events is increasing—things that used to be considered "once-in-a-hundred-year events" are happening increasingly often, which is changing what customers expect from businesses.

- Political pressures are also on the rise; companies that want to be able to look back on this period with pride need to use values and courage to guide their actions.

The second part, the customers section, revolves around a simple truth: emotions and values affect what customers are aware of, what they buy, and what they say about you. Key points include:

- Emotions matter to customers—their decisions, their experiences, and more.
- Using over half a million data points, my company, Valutus, has shown that values-based attributes affect what customers prefer and how sensitive they are to price.
- This is why the answer to "who pays for acting on values?" is neither "you" nor "the customer." Instead, the answer is that your *competitors*, especially the values laggards, are the ones who pay.
- Shared values are also a great way to increase trust, which brings even more benefits.

The operations section, part III, focuses on the many ways that values improve operations, such as reducing costs and improving decision-making:

- One of the most surprising benefits is how using values lenses changes what you look for and what you see.
- In a world of change and disruption, there's also the advantage of dealing better with both: shared values make for faster decisions, resilient teams, and an increased ability to prosper during challenging times.

The risk section, part IV, covers the risk-related benefits of values:

- Values lenses help you see risks that would otherwise be missed.
- Putting more weight on values helps prevent problems, and shared values help respond to those that do happen.

Part V, the employees section, explores the obvious—but insufficiently appreciated—fact that people want to work for companies that share their values:

- Good employees are crucial to a business's success, and values matter for attracting and keeping them and will matter even more in the future.
- Values also help speed the attraction of talent—which has quantifiable financial benefit—and help protect you against the cost of a bad hire.

The leadership section, part VI, adds a personal layer to the benefits of acting on values. The previous parts focus on company benefits, but that's not the full extent of the benefits created—acting on values also helps you in your leadership journey:

- It helps you get more of the credit you deserve for your accomplishments, makes you more persuasive, and, even when your audience doesn't share your positions, can help lower opposition.
- When you lead a team with values, the team works better together, collaborates more across boundaries, and performs better.

The coda, part VII, concludes the book with a discussion of what to do next, including how to see more, do more, and say more. It touches on some of the challenges that you may face and provides strategies for dealing with them:

- Using values lenses to see more risks and opportunities—for you, your company, and the world.
- When you see that you can use values to create more innovative products, find more customers, reduce key risks, and attract the best people, doing more becomes obvious.
- Saying more is how you get the full benefit out of your values-based actions and how you amplify your impact by helping inspire others.
- There are challenges to doing and saying more, just like there are for any change or new initiative. There is the challenge of newness, the challenge of resources, of credibility, and of ROI. But whether you face one, two, three, or even all of them, they can all be overcome.

That's just a taste of what's to come. Before we dive in further, however, there's one bedrock concept I need to illustrate for all the rest to make sense: submerged value.

2   Submerged Value

Look beneath the surface; let not the . . . quality of a thing nor its worth escape thee.

—Roman emperor Marcus Aurelius[1]

Maybe you've heard people say that there aren't $100 bills lying around because if there were, others would have picked them up already. Of course, in general, that's true—but not always! I was walking with a group once, on my way to a lunch meeting in Las Vegas, when one of the people I was with saw a bill on the floor. She walked over and picked it up: a $100 bill.

Of course, this doesn't happen often (although it did happen to me again, this time in the New York area). One reason it doesn't happen a lot is that a $100 bill is pretty easy to spot and its value is evident, which means it doesn't remain unclaimed for long.

It matters that the value of a bill is obvious. No one picks up a $100 bill and says, "I don't know if this is really worth anything" and then throws it back on the ground. But in other cases, sometimes value is there for the taking but is not so easily seen.

Why Don't Executives See the Value of Values?

It is the theory that decides what we can observe.

—Albert Einstein[2]

You might well wonder, given all the current attention to values, and the controversies over CSR and sustainability, how such a storehouse of business benefits could possibly remain untapped. The answer is simple: most of the value of values is hidden or, as I've come to call it, *submerged*, and executives don't know how to look for it. Since they don't see it, it doesn't get included in their calculations of benefit, which means benefits are greatly underestimated.

A team from a European manufacturing company once asked me for help making the business case for reducing waste in its factories. They couldn't demonstrate, to the satisfaction of the finance department, that the benefits would generate a good ROI. I asked what they were including when calculating the return on waste reduction, and they offered only two factors: lower waste-removal costs, which, at between $0.05 and $0.10 a pound ($0.11 to $0.22 per kilo), represented a modest savings; and less wasted material, which would enable the company to reduce purchases of key inputs—a noticeable savings but not enough in this case.

While these two points are real and useful, the company was missing nearly two dozen other value areas. It hadn't occurred to the team that buying less material also meant the following:

- No one had to process additional purchase orders, pay additional invoices, put the extra material in the inventory system, take it off the boat and put it in the truck, or take it off the truck and use a forklift to put it in the warehouse.

- Less warehouse space was needed, which lowered heating, cooling, and insurance costs.

- In addition, no one ever got hurt moving material that they never bought to begin with; plus, material that doesn't get purchased need not be tracked and rotated, and it also doesn't require certification or compliance with handling and storage requirements.

- Wasting less also means there's less waste material to take out of the inventory system, put back on the forklift, put back on a truck, and pay someone to take away.

- During this whole process, unpurchased material doesn't consume working capital and also doesn't raise inventory levels, which prevents many other potential problems such as reduced flexibility and lower productivity.[3]

Note that none of these benefits are intangible or "fluffy." There's nothing intangible about having to heat, cool, and insure warehouse space, nor is there anything softheaded about the cost of someone getting hurt moving inventory or the expense that comes from increased working capital. They're real, concrete benefits; they're just submerged.

One financial services company quantified these costs for a commodity the firm bought (literally) tons of; these additional costs were about three times larger than the initial purchase price. That means the total cost of ownership was four times as much as previously thought.

That's a big difference, but it's by no means out of the ordinary. In fact, for the organizations Valutus has worked with, it's on the low end. We typically find submerged value is four times to ten times as much as visible value and sometimes much more.

Returning to the case of that European manufacturer, quantifying submerged value completely changes the equation. Consider the ROI on a project that cuts costs by four times as much as previously thought, all while reducing waste. That's a real return, the kind that shows that values do have value—if you know where to look.

An Example of Surfacing Submerged Value

A professional services firm I know took the lead on a "suits to succeed" clothing drive, collecting dress clothes to help people returning to the workforce get jobs. Employees donated suits, skirts, shoes, and other garments, and they also coordinated with other firms in their buildings asking them to do the same.

Not only did the firm and its partners collect an enormous amount of clothing, but working with other tenants led to several new contracts with clients they would not have talked to otherwise. Counting only these new relationships—and only additional contracts signed within four months of the event—the firm's leadership role in the clothing drive led to an ROI over 500%. And that climbed much higher if lifetime value was included.

Where People Are, Values Matter

In the previous example, you saw that submerged doesn't mean intangible. But this doesn't mean that submerged value doesn't include things like innovation, employee engagement, and customer loyalty. Far from it—in fact, these are additional major constituents of submerged value. As you'll see throughout the book, values matter to people in lots of ways, which means that wherever people are, values matter. Further, how much they matter will only increase in the future. The business value that comes from caring for the world and those who live in it will only continue to grow.

I'll offer more examples of submerged value throughout the book. For now, I will leave you with two key points:

- Submerged value can dramatically change the ROI of initiatives.
- While it matters for all kinds of initiatives, it is especially important for values-based ones. In quantifying billions of dollars' worth of value, I have found that submerged value typically exceeds visible value when it comes to social, environmental, community, and employee-related initiatives; in fact, it's frequently worth *four to ten times* as much.

I Now More than Ever

Values have always mattered. But today, many of the strongest trends and most powerful forces shaping the business environment are values-related—a changing climate, evolving social and political realities, and new customer expectations have made sure of that. This part introduces these forces and the pressure they are increasingly putting on businesses.

3 Closer to 2070 than 1970

We're closer to 2070 than 1970. Let that sink in.

When we talk about "the future," we should really be using the present tense. And "tense" is the right word to describe the present, with accelerating changes and challenges. What does this have to do with values? A lot.

It's been clear for literally thousands of years—Roman emperor Marcus Aurelius talked about it almost two thousand years ago—that values create value. But that has never been truer than it is today. Many of the tremendous shifts in the world, and many of the forces shaping the future that we're already living in, relate to values.

The interconnected forces reshaping the world came through clearly in research that Valutus conducted about which megatrends are likely to shape the current decade. We collected predictions about 2030 from thirty different sources, including consultants such as McKinsey, military intelligence organizations, European Union (EU) researchers, global accounting firms, and futurists.

We then reviewed these megatrends predictions to see what they had in common. Which issues will be most influential? One top issue was artificial intelligence. Another was demographic change, while the rise of populism was a third. However, climate was the single most cited megatrend across all these different analyses. Combining input from various organizations in different sectors located on different continents with different focus areas, climate rose to the top, superseding all of these other issues.

By the way, this outcome wasn't a result of choosing environmental, nonprofit, or scientific organizations; of these thirty organizations, 90 percent were not focused on sustainability, responsibility, values, or related issues. In fact, in 2021, the US Director of National Intelligence—not exactly an environmental nonprofit!—had this to say about the climate: "We in the Intelligence Community view climate change as an urgent national security priority."[1]

It wasn't just climate that made the list of top forces driving this decade. Resource scarcity and mass migration (substantially due to changes in the climate) also made the top ten, with inequality and renewable energy, while falling outside the top ten, also being important.

Concrete Changes

Climate and other issues aren't just abstractions or issues for the future. They're also finding increasingly unprecedented ways to disrupt the regular functioning of countries and economies. In 2022, for example, a Bloomberg article entitled, "A Hot, Deadly Summer Is Coming, with Frequent Blackouts" said that "Asia's heat wave has caused hours-long daily blackouts, putting more than 1 billion people at risk . . . Blackouts have been basically nationwide in Pakistan, Sri Lanka and Myanmar, home to a combined 300 million people. And in India, 16 of the nation's 28 states—home to more than 700 million people—have been grappling with outages of two to ten hours a day."[2]

Lest it seem this is not a US problem, the article also noted that six Texas power plants failed in May, before summer's full onslaught, causing Houston power prices to soar *twenty-two times* higher. And in Japan, over fourteen thousand people were hospitalized for heat stroke and heat exhaustion in a single week of that year alone.[3] The heat caused more air-conditioning use, stressing Tokyo's power grid and leading to calls for conservation to avoid blackouts. This meant both consumers and businesses had to cut their power consumption.[4]

Some of these problems may seem sporadic, once-in-a-decade, or once-in-a-century events. Sure, millions of Texans lost power, and in many cases access to safe drinking water, this thinking goes, but "only" for a few days. And only during a "hundred-year" weather event. However, the problem with taking comfort in the relative infrequency of these events is that they're becoming more frequent. The world has had "once-in-a-century" events much more often than that, and some things have happened that should not have been possible. Climate website Carbon Brief compiled a database of over five hundred extreme weather events where attribution studies had been done, and a dozen of them were "deemed virtually impossible without humanity's destabilization of the climate."[5]

Temperature records have existed for the last 140 years, since 1880. Yet we don't find a one-in-one-hundred chance of a new hottest year, or a one-in-twenty chance of seeing one of the five hottest years over that period. Instead, the six years from 2014-2020 were the six hottest years the world had ever seen. Two years later, that had changed: of the eight hottest years ever recorded, all were during the previous eight years.[6]

Beyond average temperature, the world is also seeing previously unheard-of extremes. In 2020, the record heat in parts of Siberia during the month of May was so remarkable that it reached five standard deviations above normal.[7] How often should we expect temperatures five standard deviations from normal? An answer might be: "If hypothetically you were able to live in that area for one hundred thousand years, statistically speaking you should only experience such an extreme period of temperatures one time."[8]

The number of occurrences of extreme weather have led to questions about "hundred year events." As Andy Pitman, Anna Ukkola, and Seth Westra of the University of New South Wales asked in 2021, "What is a 1-in-100-year weather event? And why do they keep happening so often?"[9] They concluded that "it is clear that with temperatures and heavy rainfall events becoming more extreme with global warming, we are likely to experience one-in-100 year events more often. We should not assume the events currently unfolding will not happen again for another 100 years. It's best to prepare for the possibility it will happen again very soon."[10]

A Single Summer

The summer of 2022 was so hot for so long that major Japanese insurers started selling heat stroke insurance—by the day—to cover the cost if the buyer needed hospitalization because of the heat. Europe, North America, and China saw their hottest summers (and Augusts) ever.[11] The commercially essential Rhine River in Germany became almost impassable for large ships because of low water levels,[12] and a large portion of Pakistan flooded (one government minister said one-third of the country), affecting thirty-three million people.[13]

The combination of changes in the climate and the La Niña weather phenomenon meant that, according to Bloomberg, the world was "hurtling toward $1 trillion in weather-related damages"[14] by the end of 2023. Scientists warned the world was approaching five major climate tipping points, such as changes to northern forests and the collapse of a critical North Atlantic Current.[15]

The commercial environment underwent changes as well. US automaker Ford announced a $50 billion investment plan in electric vehicles, and one of the largest purchasing organizations in the world, the US government, announced it was changing its procurement of steel, concrete, glass, and asphalt to help achieve its climate goals. Adding in new standards from the US Department of Transportation, that laid the groundwork for "98% of materials purchased by the federal government, across both the GSA and DOT, [to] be in service of decarbonizing our industrial sector and infrastructure and creating green jobs."[16]

Beyond climate, Bloomberg unveiled an Election Risk Index for the United States, exploring how vulnerable states were to election interference, including whether officials would even respect the results.[17] And, connecting climate and social developments, researchers in the US found that extreme temperatures are associated with hate speech on social media,[18] echoing the findings of an earlier study of forty-three million people in China.[19]

A new US law went into effect banning the importation of multiple categories of products from the Xinjiang region of China unless they can be shown not to involve slave labor,[20] while the EU drafted its own, similar legislation.[21] US inflation hit a forty-year peak in June,[22] while EU inflation was the highest on record and continued to rise through October.[23] All in a single summer.

The Clock Speed of Events

Values can become more top of mind based on events. This matters because today's events, and those of coming years, are going to be increasingly shaped by forces such as climate change, inequality, health, and skepticism about corporate power. Companies will be under more frequent pressure to express their values and to align with the values of their customers and employees.

Recall that our research on megatrends included many connected to values. When you combine that with more frequent manifestations of these issues (e.g., more frequent extreme weather events) and add perennial concerns such as how well a company treats its employees (made more top of mind by pandemics, economic upheaval, and other events), the picture is clear.

These issues are being increasingly translated into litigation as well. Take climate-related litigation: according to the UN, "in 2017, 884 climate change cases were brought in 24 countries. By the end of 2020, that number had nearly doubled, with at least 1,550 cases filed in 38 countries—39 including the European Union's court system."[24] By 2023, according to the Sabin Center for Climate Change Law at Columbia Law School, the number was over 2,800.[25] The rise in litigation isn't limited to emissions, either; plastic and biodiversity loss, among other topics, are also subjects for potential lawsuits.[26]

And many issues are coming faster than they used to, faster than we expected, or both. Whether it's potentially doubling the melting of ice sheets or substantial parts of the US coastline seeing sea level rise happen twice as fast since 2010 as before, events are speeding up, and businesses' reflexes must do the same.[27]

Other Pressures

Pressure on businesses can also come from geopolitical issues, whether diplomatic and economic contention or all-out war (such as Russia's invasion of Ukraine). Consider what happened after the Russian invasion of Ukraine in 2022: by June of that year, almost 85 percent of companies headquartered in the United States, Europe, and the United Kingdom had left Russia or scaled back their operations there. Of the 281 Fortune 500 companies that had been present in Russia before the war, nearly 70 percent either left or cut back.[28] As a McKinsey article said, "More than ever, core management choices are being shaped by a broad set of stakeholders beyond investors, including employees and customers."[29]

In the US, when the Supreme Court overruled the *Roe v Wade* decision that had undergirded the national right to abortion access, companies had to figure out what to do—such as whether to support employees who needed to reach another state to obtain an abortion. Some companies, such as Dick's Sporting Goods, announced a policy of reimbursing up to $4,000 for such travel expenses.[30] However, many legislators began drafting laws and using court filings to prevent employers from doing that[31] and making it a crime for residents to travel to another state to obtain an abortion.[32]

Other states moved to make simply providing information about how to obtain an abortion (e.g., having a website with that information) illegal.[33] Companies located in these states feared that such laws could inhibit their ability to recruit workers. As Eli Lilly, one of Indiana's largest employers put it after the state passed a near-total abortion ban, "We are concerned that this new law will hinder Lilly's—and Indiana's—ability to attract diverse scientific, engineering, and business talent."[34]

Only time will tell what happens to existing rights (and it may take many years to know the final outcome given that *Roe* was fifty years old when reversed), including whether some states go beyond abortion to outlawing same-sex marriages[35] and restricting access to contraception.[36] But just the potential for such restrictions can affect a company's ability to recruit and retain workers and to support its existing employees.

Even internal company investment and policy decisions are not off limits from new political pressure. As the *New York Times* noted in 2022, treasurers in nearly half the US states were pushing companies not to move away from fossil fuels. Some even punished those who do, such as West Virginia's treasurer, who barred several banks from government contracts with his state because they were reducing their investments in coal.[37]

Even public health and pandemic response are not immune from political pressures. In 2021, the governor of Florida, Republican Ron DeSantis, banned private businesses from requiring customers to show that they've been vaccinated against COVID.[38] Norwegian Cruise Line sued, and while it eventually won the right to determine what it requires of customers, the conflict was a stark example of the increasingly frequent collisions between political and business forces.

Nor did Norwegian's victory stop other companies from experiencing something similar. The following year, DeSantis and the Florida legislature retaliated against the Walt Disney Company for opposing passage of a law that restricted teachers' ability to discuss sexual orientation in the classroom. In a speech, he said that the company was "free to indulge in that type of views and ideology, but that's not consistent with our values in the state of Florida, so we took action and now, because of what we did, Disney is not going to have its own [local governing body] anymore."[39]

This type of occurrence isn't limited to DeSantis or Florida, either; it's part of business' new reality. As much as some companies and executives wish it otherwise, there's no escaping these forces—or the need to decide how to act on their values.

An Unavoidable Pressure Cooker

When you combine the pressures coming from changes in climate, society, and the economy with the increasing politicization of company decisions, it creates an ever more difficult situation for companies. But avoiding it isn't possible.

Whether it's the health of your customers or employees, the decision about which energy source should power your business, the policies you implement to support your employees, or your decisions around which countries to do business with, these choices are no longer under the radar. Employees and others expect you to express the company's values, investors want you to show that you're taking the dynamics of the future seriously, and some politicians want to legislate what you say or choose.

How do you decide what to do when some stakeholders expect you to speak up, but others say there will be consequences if you do? There is one sure way: your values. There will always be another conflict, always new challenges and realities to address. And there will always be evolving expectations from stakeholders. Sometimes, different stakeholders (such as different groups of customers) will even have conflicting demands. But your company can choose to remain true to its values—and to say so.

Where to Start

Values should be integrated into day-to-day choices as well, not just big decisions such as where to put a new factory. In fact, they should be part of the company's products and policies, and this should be done in a way that creates business benefit.

As an example, the leadership of a company in the health sector wanted to do more to realize the firm's purpose while also being more successful in the market and fending off competitors. My colleagues and I helped them see how infusing more of the company's values into products and marketing could create deeper connections with buyers and increase customer preference.

We started by having the team reflect on the organization's values—not just the ones in official documents but also those in the hearts and minds of employees. Out of twelve initially identified by groups of executives, managers, and line employees, compassion was the one that rose to the top. In particular, employees cared about people in service careers, who can be more susceptible to stress and burnout—and who often don't see those things happening until their physical or psychological health is affected.

Though the value of compassion was already reflected in the organization's work, the team identified it as one that they wanted to make more prominent and do even more to embed in their products and services. Together, we went through a process of clarifying how to do this:

- Whom the changes would benefit—for example, specific types of customers, important communities, society, and the business itself.

- Where these benefits would be seen—such as in the health of those in service careers, in their families' health, in their communities, and where there is societal need.

- When the greater integration of values would be clearest—such as in regular communications with those in service careers or when there were major life or community events (including natural disasters, which can place additional stress on everyone and especially those in service careers).

- How expanded compassion would be built into products, services, and policies—ranging from revised educational materials to new policies such as reducing fees when there was a major community event. These and other changes would be built into products and services, which would be modified to better support customers in service careers.

- Who they would work with on each initiative—some changes, such as changing policies on how to react to major community events or natural disasters, could be done within the company's four walls. But some, such as disaster recovery, community support, and health promotion activities, either required or greatly benefited from the involvement of others (such as suppliers, business partners, and community organizations).

This process generated dozens of candidates for changes, which were then prioritized. The prioritization process included internal factors, such as alignment with the company's purpose and capabilities, and external ones, such as which candidates produced the most competitive benefit.

As part of the competitive analysis, we conducted research to see which factors most affected customers' preference when they were given a choice between the company's offerings and those of competitors. Then the benefits were quantified financially, including under different scenarios, allowing the company to select the best options.

Issues May Change, but Values Don't Have To

When companies hold to their values, they can use them to make decisions that they are still proud of decades later. While specific political issues come and go (conflicts change, issues evolve), a consistent commitment to do good for the world and those who live in it provides steady guidance.

In the early 1950s, when IBM was exploring building factories in North Carolina and Kentucky, segregation was still legal in the United States. In 1953, company President Thomas Watson wrote Policy Letter #4 and circulated it to his managers, stating the company's position plainly: "It is the policy of this organization to hire people who have the personality, talent and background necessary to fill a given job, regardless of race, color or creed."[40]

The official history of IBM continues:

> Policy letter #4 conveyed without qualification that IBM would not comply with "separate but equal," an entrenched euphemism for sanctioned segregation in the US, and what would today be considered institutional racism. . . .
> In effect, Watson was publicly stating not only the ethical but the business case for diversity, forcing the governors in North Carolina and Kentucky to decide between racial segregation and an influx of job opportunities along with their associated tax revenue. Three years later, black and white IBMers worked and ate together in the company's new plants in Raleigh, North Carolina, and Lexington, Kentucky.[41]

This is a case when the cost involved in acting on values wasn't primarily monetary. IBM did get to build its new facilities, and it didn't have to pay more to do so. Yet there was a cost—the cost of using some political capital with the state and perhaps losing some customers who favored segregation—and acting as it did required courage. But the company stuck to its values and made a decision they can look back on with pride.

II CORE Customers

One day, my daughter really made it clear to me how much the backstory of an experience matters. I served her dinner, and she took a bite and said, "This is pretty good." I asked *how good*, and she said she would rate it a five or six. She then told me that I should make the dish the way her mom makes it. "Oh," I said, "your mom did make this." She blinked, paused, and took another bite. "Actually, this is really good," she said. "I'd give it a nine or a ten."

As my daughter made clear, people use emotion as well as (or in place of) logic when experiencing the world—and when making decisions. Companies understandably spend a lot of time on their value proposition, the benefits they offer, and their competitive positioning, and they should.

But human factors such as emotion, identification, belonging, connection, and values matter too. In fact, values matter much more than most people think. How and when this is true is the topic of this section.

4 Customers' Emotions, Experiences, and Behavior

Purpose is the aim around which we structure our lives.
—Richard Leider[1]

Values, Identity, and Expression

It's well understood that customers prefer products that match their image of who they are—or who they want to be. They tend to choose brands that fit their self-image, and to signal who they are, as a "lifestyle beacon."[2] To put it simply, "in modern times people use consumer goods to display their values as well as their wealth."[3] This idea has been well understood for decades. In 1998, Russell Belk published a paper on this idea, titled "Possessions and the Extended Self" in the *Journal of Consumer Research*. A 2015 analysis found that it was arguably one of the most influential papers ever published in that journal.[4]

It's no surprise that this is also true for products that have environmental and social attributes. In fact, an analysis of young adult behavior published in 2023 shows that values impact purchasing choices in at least two different ways: individual values and peer identity.[5] One interesting thing about this finding is that it shows how multiple avenues for self-reinforcing growth in values-oriented purchasing could work. First, the increasing prominence of social and environmental values among individuals increases values-related purchasing decisions. Second, these choices are visible to others (e.g., those who see the individual driving an electric car), increasing others' perceptions of the importance their peers are placing on values. Third, this drives further increases in such purchasing behavior, starting the cycle again.

This is a dynamic that companies must consider if they want to find and persuade tomorrow's customers as well as today's. As research firm Ipsos put it in 2020, based on data from over twenty-two thousand individuals in thirty-three countries, "Brands will need to think much more holistically about their consumers and think about them as citizens as well, considering [much] more expansive consumer needs. Needs which range from those that impact 'me,' to those that impact 'my world,' to those that impact 'the world.' Brands then need to both innovate and communicate with their consumers based on this understanding."[6]

Finding Customers

Early in the customer acquisition process, you have to make it possible for potential customers to learn about you. Since they must find you to buy from you, making that process easier is important. Here again, values help. Values provide a different level of insight into customers, their needs, and what it takes to have a deeper mutual relationship. Understanding what's most important to them offers insight into what they're looking for, how they think, and where they might congregate.

And where is that most likely to be? Most likely it will be in places where they have common interests, sure, but also where they have common *values*: nonprofits, faith communities, groups dedicated to advancing their values, and media that report on the stories that potential customers care about. Knowing what they value helps map out where they are and, as we'll discuss later, break through the clutter to get their attention.

This remains true for almost any set of values. But the great thing about deeper values, such as doing good for the world and those who inhabit it, is that they touch people very differently than more mundane concerns. For this reason, they break through the clutter more powerfully. This creates competitive advantage as well, since far fewer of your competitors focus on these deep values—and, as a result, those who do tend to stand out. Companies catering to those who value things like convenience are numerous. The field is far more open when it comes to organizations offering to help you with deeper concerns, such as leaving a legacy.

Deep values also make it easier to know not only where to find customers, but also which channels to use to communicate with them. For example, values-based investors have their own conferences, publications, and specific media channels. Alternative-fuel vehicles do too, as do those involved in solar power and in advancing justice. Here, customers congregate on the basis of their shared values as well as their interests.

Being Found

As noted, values also help customers find you even without advertising, in places that resonate with their values. It's like placing a retail store in a high-traffic area instead of a low-traffic one or locating it near an area frequented by the types of customers you want. Knowing your potential customers' values and where they go to express them—in person or online—tells you where to place yourself so they will see you.

In the beginning, this positioning may seem like seeking a niche. But that's not right, since values positioning isn't like choosing a physical location. You can still serve your previous customers and markets so customers you find within a values niche add to your current base rather than replacing it.

Many big brands and companies like Procter and Gamble and Pepsi are already household names. Nonetheless, they sponsor events around values—such as environmental sustainability events[7]—so that customers who value those things see that they do too. For smaller brands there's another values benefit: being memorable. After gauging consumers' associations with brands, communications firm Porter Novelli asked them to reflect on their purchasing and decision-making processes. The company reported that "78 percent of respondents said they are more likely to remember a company that has a strong

Purpose"—where purpose was defined as a commitment to both making a profit and making a difference for society.[8]

1,500-fold Growth

Values-based market segments often start out small, only to rapidly grow much larger. Take values-based investing that includes ESG as decision factors. Such funds have grown from a small portion of the market to one that encompasses truly enormous sums. In fact, while ESG funds already total trillions in assets, in 2021 Bloomberg projected that ESG assets under management (AUM) could reach $50 trillion plus by 2025, representing over one-third of all AUM.[9] This growth came from a segment without a single related index until 1990. Thirty years after the first index launched, ESG indices had multiplied 1,500-fold.[10] (While there has been some pushback against ESG—more so in the US than in Europe—that is unlikely to prevent it from continuing to grow since environmental and social issues continue to increase in importance.)

Not all values-based markets grow as quickly as ESG investing has, but many run ahead of the market, making new customer acquisition much more rewarding in these areas. Some companies that started in growing niches have grown along with them. Whole Foods was just such a case. The first Whole Foods Market (WFM) opened in 1980 in what was then a niche market, natural foods. When Amazon acquired WFM thirty-seven years later, it paid $13.7 billion.[11] Natural foods were niche no longer, and WFM had ridden that wave.

Conversion to Customers

Of course, finding such values-based customers isn't enough by itself. You must also convert them into paying customers. Mainstream customers may hold values but may not prioritize them over concerns such as price, quality, or performance—in fact, a strong majority of potential customers don't. But the alignment of values may just be the straw that tips them into your customer base.

Consider your own experience of all the companies trying to get you to buy from them. The average person sees or hears hundreds or thousands of marketing messages each day.[12] As all companies know, breaking through that level of clutter is both difficult and expensive. It's far easier to stand out when your values and offerings are aligned with customers' values.

There are other ways to break through, such as using humor, creativity, or better jingles. But shared values add additional arrows to your quiver, and they're long-lasting differentiators. Knowledge of them endures beyond one season's ad campaign. As I'll discuss in depth later, this is part of values' contribution to long-term success.

The shared values approach has proven true for investments. There are thousands of investment vehicles, and more created every year, but few have real values at their core. This was especially true at the inception of values-based investing: a fund that had values and was open about them had a much easier time getting noticed. While ESG funds, like any, must perform well, their ability to attract attention is one reason why they've grown so much.

The same concept worked for Tesla. It's certainly possible that such an innovative vehicle would have garnered plenty of attention even if it were gasoline powered. But it was far less challenging to break through against the likes of Ferrari, Lamborghini, Bentley, and other well-known luxury brands, with electric rather than standard internal combustion engines. Ditto for personal care firms The Body Shop and Burt's Bees, which had an easier time breaking through using natural ingredients, responsible sourcing, recyclable packaging, and no animal testing. Both companies were distinctly different, and people who wanted something different—and shared their values—took notice.

Vocality

This willingness to talk about a company is something I call "vocality." General vocality is great, but can shared values increase customer vocality?

In its 2020 *Strength of Purpose* report, Zeno Group writes that "over the last year, more than 8 in 10 (82 percent) of consumers said they took action to support a company when they believed in its Purpose." Their actions included purchasing, posting positive reviews, and evangelizing their brand.[13]

Note that vocality isn't the same as whether people think highly of you. Of course, as shown by my daughter, the chances of a high rating increase when there's an emotional connection involved! But leave that aside for a moment and consider what happens just after you receive a high rating.

Imagine two different customers, both of whom are very satisfied with your products and services, rating you a ten out of ten. Both are likely to be loyal and to purchase from you. But what about customers' willingness to tell others what they think of you? Now imagine that the first customer rates you a ten out of ten but is quiet about it. Meanwhile, the second customer is equally enthusiastic and vocal to boot, urging friends and family to buy from you, gushing on social media, seeking out review sites to spread the good word, and talking you up at work.

Clearly, the vocal customer is more valuable and is more likely to bring others into your orbit. But is their vocality affected at all by whether they share your values?

Research by Porter Novelli found that 76 percent of respondents would tell their friends and family about a purpose-driven company (defined as "organizations that are committed to both making money and making a positive impact on the world."[14]), and 73 percent would share information or stories about the company, while the same number would defend the company if others spoke badly of it.[15] It's no surprise that personal recommendations are more believable than advertisements. If you're like most people, you're much, much more likely to believe a recommendation from people you know and trust than from paid actors, influencers, or media personalities.

Recommendations are strongly at play in now-ubiquitous online reviews. Studies have shown that such reviews and recommendations, even from strangers, affect the purchase intentions and behaviors of customers, with higher-star reviews getting much more in sales than lower ones. And this persuasion has real consequences. A 2020 study of Amazon merchants, for example, found that 1 additional star, such as a rating of 4.5 rather than 3.5 stars, increased conversion rates by about 20 percent, while a 2-star differential increased them close to 50 percent.[16] Separate research showed that a 1-star increase in Yelp ratings led to a 5 to 9 percent increase in revenue for the studied businesses.[17]

The effect of word of mouth is so powerful that many firms offer rewards for those who email or text their friends about the company or products. In 2022, Instacart, the grocery delivery company, offered customers up to $1,000 total in referral bonuses,[18] and many firms offer payments for referring employees.[19]

Vocality benefits aren't limited to your customers. One $100 billion firm I worked with found that when the company communicated its values (and values-based actions) to retail staff, employees became far more vocal with customers. One executive told me he'd rarely, if ever, seen anything like it.

Customers' Expectations

Research by Edelman, a public relations consultancy firm, said that whether customers trust a brand to do what's right—for the company and for society—was either a deal breaker or deciding factor in buying decisions 81 percent of the time. 72 percent of consumers said the same about values, while 71 percent felt the same specifically about environmental impact.[20]

As it turns out, consumers expect companies to be catalysts in these areas: more than three-fourths of consumers surveyed feel that a brand should work to inspire its customers. For example, brands can encourage customers to be healthier, make better financial decisions, and be more involved in environmental and social issues.[21]

Such expectations are on the rise all over the world. Surveying fourteen thousand people in fourteen countries in 2022, Edelman found that on average 77 percent of people believe improving societal issues is a primary business function, and 59 percent say that addressing geopolitics (e.g., the Russian invasion of Ukraine) should be a top priority for business.[22]

Now More than Ever: Events as Triggers

When people are triggered by events, they back their values with actions, even at personal expense to themselves. For example, new parents reconsider their purchasing behavior as they think about buying the best, highest-quality, safest, and least toxic products for their children. They may not have cared as much before, but now that they have kids, they look for safety, natural content, and so forth because their value of taking care of their family, once activated, comes first.

This is one of the reasons that values continue to matter more and more—as mentioned earlier, there are more changes in the world, happening faster, which means a greater number of events that can change people's beliefs and behaviors. For example, a 2021 research review found that personally living through a natural disaster is associated with higher levels of concern about changes to the climate.[23]

It's not just climate; the same is true for many other issues. When North Carolina passed a law barring antidiscrimination protections for LGBTQ+ people, boycotts and pressure ensued. Eighty CEOs, and large numbers of companies, condemned the law and many made it clear that they would reduce their spending in North Carolina. Governors in New York, Washington, and Vermont banned most official state travel to North Carolina.[24]

Similarly, consumers are willing to boycott products and pressure other companies to boycott those who don't support their values. When television host Tucker Carlson, who then had a show on the Fox News cable channel, said immigration "makes our country poorer, and dirtier, and more divided," over a dozen advertisers pulled their spots from his show.[25] After he endorsed the White supremacist "replacement" theory in 2021,[26] his show had very few big-brand advertisers left.

The following is one example of why: on June 9, 2020, a customer tweeted at the T-Mobile CEO that he was dropping the company if Carlson's statements were "the type of message [the company] support[s]." The reply was from the account of T-Mobile CEO Mike Sievert, who said, "We don't advertise on that show and won't."[27]

Political power ebbs and flows: not every event triggers a reaction, and not every boycott succeeds in changing the behavior of the target company. But cumulatively, events demand attention and response. Pressure can build over time—and it can be dramatically accelerated by events. As just one example, IBM found in 2021 that 93 percent of global consumers said that COVID-19 had influenced their views on sustainability.[28]

How much can events accelerate change? A lot. As Oliver Wright, managing director and head of Accenture's global consumer goods practice, said in 2020, "While we have been seeing [ethical consumption] trends for some time, what's surprising is the scale and pace—compressing into a matter of weeks changes that would likely have taken years."[29] Partly as a result of this acceleration, in 2022 IBM found that purpose-driven consumers, who choose products and brands based on how well they align to their values, became the largest segment of consumers across all product categories.[30]

Doing, Not Just Saying

In theory, there is no difference between theory and practice; in practice there is.

—Yogi Berra[31]

Sometimes people say that consumers care about these issues only when there is no cost, but that isn't so. For consumers, the primary cost of pressuring advertisers is in taking the time to make their voices heard and asking companies to stop supporting things like Carlson's show. However, this is still a definite cost! In fact, the awareness that time and action entail costs is a core driver for many brands that focus on ease and convenience.

Customers may also incur monetary costs to have their values reflected in their purchasing behavior. Many surveys have asked consumers if they'd be willing to pay more to buy from a company that supports their values, and the answer is yes. A majority of respondents (59 percent) to the Meyocks Mentor Branding Survey said they prefer a brand that advocates for something they believe in or feel strongly about, while 72 percent of eighteen- to thirty-four-year-olds agreed.[32]

If you're thinking, "it's possible people say they choose products and companies based on values when in fact they don't," I don't blame you. I wondered about that too, so, wanting to nail it down, Valutus conducted research on it. We queried hundreds of thousands of consumers to see how they responded to companies and products that embody values.

To avoid asking people, "Would you choose a more sustainable or ethical product?"—because people will sometimes tell you what they think you want to hear or what they wish were true—we presented them with a choice of two products to see which one they preferred. First, we tested baseline products and then those with an environmental or social attribute.

What happened? Preference went up for the product with an environmental or social attribute (compared to the base case), often by 25 percent or more. In fact, preference even went up (though not by as much) when the price of the values-related product went up as much as 10 percent.

As of this writing, we have collected well over half a million data points this way. In the vast majority of our experiments, values-based attributes:

- Change what people choose. The change is normally between 5 and 25 percent, though it can be much greater (in some cases exceeding 90 percent).

- Change both customer preference and price sensitivity, lowering the effect of price increases on customer choice.

- Have a greater effect for new or unknown products, which may be one reason why new entrants in many markets are trying to differentiate themselves along the values dimension.

- Have both upside and downside effects such that a product that trails the competition in preference has more to gain from values-based attributes, while an already strong product has more to lose from falling behind on values.

- Provide a bigger boost when the competitive set is bigger so that when a consumer is choosing among two products, the effect of values is strong, but when they are choosing among three, four, or six different competitors, the effect of values is proportionately stronger.

More about Skepticism of Consumer Results

As alluded to above, common objections to existing data on consumer preferences for products that embody values, such as sustainable or responsible products, stem from directly asking people questions about values. If you ask, "Would you buy a sustainable product over one that isn't sustainable?" there are two legitimate potential confounding factors, which skeptics (both well-intentioned and not) often point out.

The first is desirability bias, in which people will tell you what they think you want to hear or what presents them in the best light.[33] This means people may wonder if respondents who said they would prefer the environmentally or socially responsible product were telling the truth or if some of them were saying what they thought they "should" say.

The second is what I call the "New Year's resolution" bias. This is where people respond by telling you what they wish were true of themselves, not necessarily what actually is true. Someone who states a New Year's resolution may not be consciously lying even if they don't achieve their goal. They may firmly believe that this is the year they finally get into shape, for example, but we know that most people don't end up accomplishing their New Year's resolutions. So, we want to find out not what people think will affect their actions but rather what actually does.

To address both objections—and to generate results that show causation, not just correlation—at Valutus, our experiments are designed not to ask people what they think they would do but to present them with options and see which they choose.

The Stern School of Business at New York University (NYU) also found support for the customer effects of values. The school worked with Circana (formerly IRI), which collects sales from retailers, to study more than seventy-one thousand products over a four-year period. Together, they discovered that products explicitly marketed as having some kind of sustainability or responsibility benefit made up much more than a proportional share of market growth.

In 2022, NYU reported that, while sustainably-marketed products were about one-sixth (17 percent) of total sales, they accounted for almost a third of the total growth in the thousands of product categories studied. In fact, sustainably-marketed products grew 2.7 times as fast as conventionally marketed ones over the six years from 2015 to 2021.[34]

McKinsey and Nielsen IQ came to a similar conclusion in 2023, after studying over 600,000 individual products representing over $400 billion in annual revenues. They found that products making ESG-related claims averaged more cumulative growth over the previous five years than products that didn't and also accounted for 56 percent of all growth, even though they were a minority of the products studied.[35]

While the extent of the difference is impressive—as is the data collected—in some ways the results are intuitive. Making products less toxic, safer to manufacture, and more sustainable is the right thing to do for employees and the community, and should anyone be surprised if consumers preferred the nontoxic brand? Even when it's not the top concern of buyers, it matters.

This is especially true for some consumers, such as parents. Research by Mintel found that parents are more likely than nonparents to purchase personal care products that are natural or organic. Products included "hand and body lotion (53 percent of parents versus 34 percent of nonparents), facial skincare (51 percent of parents versus 32 percent of nonparents), haircare (50 percent of parents versus 34 percent of nonparents), and body cleansing products (48 percent of parents versus 34 percent of nonparents)."[36]

Habits and Relationships

Beyond the possibility that customers will pay to live in alignment with their values, there's also the role of values in building a deeper, longer-term relationship between you and them. I'll look at two aspects of customer relationships in particular: those involving habits and those that involve emotion. In this discussion, habits, often partly unconscious, will include customers' purchasing routines, while emotions will refer to their feelings about you.

Our brains are habit-forming machines, and quite a bit of work has been put into understanding how people form, and change, habits. Why are habits so important? For one thing, some types of goods are strongly related to habits. People tend to buy the same deodorant, shampoo, and similar products once they find one that works for them. That's why there's so much marketing attention paid to first-year college students, who may be buying such things themselves for the first time. Marketers know that if you get to people early, you have a chance of keeping them for a long time, whereas getting them to change habits later is very, very difficult.

Habitual customers are also less sensitive to price changes than other types of customers. Habit creation is also important because it cuts through a lot of the information challenges that people have. When someone has a habit, they search less for alternatives, so they're harder for competitors to steal away. They also buy more regularly and predictably, which means they provide a nice, consistent flow of revenue and profit.

Emotions and Relationships

Another avenue to building a strong relationship, and one related to habits, is creating an emotional connection. Whether by the "personality" of the brand, by its design, or by the sentiments in the advertising—upbeat, scary, confident—companies try to establish emotional bonds with customers.

The human brain is not only a habit-forming machine but also an emotion-processing one. It's evident that long before children have any rational or logical associations with things, they have emotional ones. Similarly, there's evidence that even adults make decisions unconsciously. Subsequently, emotion is engaged, and only then does the brain create logical justifications for choices.[37] This is true in many domains, especially when it comes to loyalty. As Brand Keys says, "We estimate that on average the consumer decision loyalty process is 70% emotional and 30% rational."[38]

This unconscious decisions-to-emotions-to-justifications process is very powerful, for good or ill. It can generate an immediate reaction that closes off rational thought and openness to new ideas, or it can create a bond with a company that is very difficult for a competitor to break.

Another example is Ben & Jerry's, a brand that has been famous since its founding as much for social advocacy as for innovative, whimsically named flavors. Although it has been around for a very long time, the company gained renewed currency after the murder of George Floyd.

Hundreds of companies put out statements affirming that Black lives do matter and decrying what happened. However, very few of those companies' statements got the attention or traction of that put out by Ben & Jerry's, titled "Silence Is NOT an Option."[39] The statement pulled no punches and let the world know exactly where the company stood on the issue. It began with "The murder of George Floyd was the result of inhumane police brutality," referenced the company's public support for the Black Lives Matter movement, and went on to list four concrete steps the president, Congress, and the US Department of Justice could take to prevent similar issues in future. This clear statement of the company's values received 1.3 billion media impressions, 1.2 million mentions, and 3.5 million page views.[40]

Ben & Jerry's CEO Jostein Solheim says sales were never the point, stressing that the company's campaigns have neither hurt nor helped demand during his eight years running the company. He told *Business-Week* that he traces the fundamental appeal of its pints to indulgent flavors as well as to carefully timed price reductions and product releases.

Solheim believes the company's expressions of principle serve to solidify its long-term ties with fans. "Loyalty is pretty valuable in this business," he says "If we share values on climate, same sex marriage rights, racism, I think that's a deeper bond than sugar and fat."[41]

What do you get when you know your customers better, have an emotional connection with them, and they develop the habit of buying from you? Loyal customers—and profitable ones.

5 Trust and Customer Economics

If you want more loyal customers, you're not alone. Everyone does—they're much more profitable. According to a report by Brand Keys, a loyalty increase of just 7 percent can boost lifetime profits per customer by as much as 85 percent. An increase of only 3 percent is equivalent to a 10 percent across-the-board cost-reduction program, depending on the sector.[1]

And a powerful way to get such loyalty is through trust. Not surprisingly, trust drives loyalty, "with 62% of consumers stating they are loyal to brands they can trust."[2] (That makes sense; would you be loyal to a brand you couldn't?)

Expectations are changing. Even before COVID-19, Brand Keys found that almost half (47 percent) of categories had new leaders in 2019, the vast majority because of changes in how customers saw them. That is "three times the normal rate we see. Of that, 90% of those shifts were due to changes in consumer trust perceptions."[3] Ethics matter. Values matter. And keeping your word matters.

You might expect people to trust a company based mainly on competence: how professional they are or how good the product is. Yet, while competence certainly matters, it's not the essential factor influencing trust. You might want to trust an expert's judgment, and you might in fact trust their expertise. But do you trust *them*? You trust them only if you trust their character, who they are down deep.

This is just as true for companies, perhaps more. As Edelman notes in describing the results of their 2020 Trust Barometer, ethics-related dimensions are three times more important than competence in building trust. How good a company is at what it does explains 24 percent of its trust score, but the ethical dimensions of its behavior—purpose, integrity, and dependability—are off the charts at 76 percent![4] "Stakeholder expectations," Edelman continues, "have risen. Consumers expect the brands they buy to reflect their values and beliefs."[5]

You might say to yourself, sure, more trust is good, but is openness about values a good way to increase peoples' belief in your ethics and integrity? What about people who don't believe your values statements or who are skeptical even when they see what looks like ethical behavior? These are good questions. When Valutus researched whether people believed firms that tout their products and services as better for the environment, we found that about a quarter of respondents didn't, perhaps because some companies have engaged in "greenwashing" in the past.

Trust and Standing for Something

Nonetheless, when respondents were asked to think about a company with an environmental or social purpose, they were more likely to trust that company, about 15 points more likely, despite about a third of respondents saying climate leadership doesn't change their trust in a company one way or the other. (The gains from the other two-thirds were enough to make the overall increase in trust quite significant.) In other words, it's valuable for a company to lead on the issue of climate even when some people are unsure how sincere it is. The act of assuming leadership is beneficial in spite of that skepticism.

This finding makes intuitive sense, like the old saying, "If you stand for nothing, you'll fall for anything." It seems reasonable for people to apply the same maxim to companies. If a business really doesn't stand for anything, if it lacks or doesn't communicate any values, it suggests a willingness to consider going outside the lines to make a little more money. Show them you care about something. Be more transparent, more open than competitors. Share that there's more to you than profit margins—and even if they're skeptical, trust goes up.

People like honesty and transparency. As University of Houston professor Brené Brown says, "We love seeing raw truth and openness in other people."[6] Perhaps this dynamic, applied to business, is why researchers at Porter Novelli found that "about 3 in 4 respondents (77%) claim to feel a stronger emotional connection with Purpose-driven brands."[7] And yet, even though ethics generates trust better, most companies still don't put their values out there. More than 80 percent of the six hundred plus companies Edelman analyzed got higher marks for competence than they did for the more influential dimension of ethics.[8]

How Customers Feel

If it's true that customers trust companies that simply have values, how much more likely are they to trust companies whose values align with their own? A lot more. The research makes clear that shared values are a key ingredient for trust.[9]

According to the Arthur W. Page Society, there are three core dynamics of trust:

- Mutuality—that is, based upon shared values or interests.
- Balance of power—where risks and opportunities are shared by parties.
- Trust safeguards—that limit vulnerability in the context of power imbalances.[10]

Shared interests, of course, help create trust. They're often a great way to kick-start the trust process. People find trust easier when they see that you have a reason to do what they want and that it benefits you too. But what happens when those interests change? Where customers and company do not fully align on interests, there's another way to add trust: shared values.

Imagine you're talking to a salesperson who says, "We want this to feel like a good deal for you as well as us. Let's find a point where you're happy with the value you get and we're happy with the price you pay." Would that encourage you to trust them? For most people, the answer is yes.

One kind of shared value is commercial honesty, such as an honest negotiation and a fair price. But it turns out that people judge companies by deeper values, not just transactional ones. Research Valutus conducted showed that customers were more likely to trust a company that had committed to being an environmental leader, a value that has nothing to do with buying or selling.

It's *possible* that a company would be a genuine advocate for the environment yet be perfectly willing to cheat its customers. But people believe, quite rationally, that it's less likely when a company displays shared values. After all, environmental leadership is neither required nor easy.

That's why people see environmental leaders and recognize the work they've put in for something other than their direct financial interests. No wonder 90 percent of respondents said they'd be more likely to trust companies that actively try to make a difference.[11] As Michael Weissman, CEO of The Values Institute, says, "Shared values bond us," and they're the gateway to trust.[12]

David Horsager, author of *The Trust Edge*, identified eight pillars for trust. Of these, the second is "compassion . . . People put faith in those who care beyond themselves," while the third is "character . . . People notice those who do what's right over what's easy." In other words, living your values—such as caring beyond yourself and doing what's right even when it's not easy—are key pillars of creating and sustaining trust.

The Economics of Customer Relationships

Let's turn to the economics of customer relationships. We've seen how customers are more likely to trust you if you share values with them. But what happens after you win a new customer?

There are two customer-related justifications for acting on values that you frequently hear: first, that people will pay more for a product that aligns with their values and, second, that acting with some modicum of values is only "table stakes," a bare minimum without which potential customers will not consider the company. It turns out that neither of these assertions has to be true to create customer-related value from values.

The first assertion is that people are willing to pay more for a sustainable product. That may be true for at least some people. They're willing to pay more for better design or a fancier name or a specific color, so why not pay more for something that's more sustainable or in line with their personal values? However, while it's great if people are willing to pay more, it's not necessary. In addition, a willingness to pay more is often conflated with the idea that people *must* be willing to pay more for values to create benefit or that willingness to accept a higher price is the main source of a company's payback for acting on values.

However, neither is correct. In fact, talking too much about willingness to pay more can produce the impression that acting on values is something that only appeals to elites. Paying more for something with environmental or social benefit sounds like buying a hundred-thousand-dollar electric car: it's something only a small fraction of people can do. This impression is unfortunate, and it's incorrect. Everyone has values, and everyone's behavior can be affected by actions that are either in concert with, or opposed to, their values. A customer's action may not be paying more or buying more, yet customers may do other things, such as being more vocal or more loyal. Those types of customer actions also matter.

The second assertion you sometimes hear is that not acting on values is a dealbreaker for certain people. They consider you only if you act in a strongly value-based way. This is occasionally true: a vegetarian won't consider buying food if it contains meat, nor would someone keeping kosher or halal consider products containing pork. There are two key factors that make this so clear-cut:

- A very bright line between the acceptable and unacceptable and clear definitions of what's on each side of that line.
- Accepted information about which side of the line something falls on, such as a definitive answer as to whether a product contains pork or not.

However, customers don't have to adopt this absolute, yes-or-no approach for there to be customer-related benefits from acting on your values. If embodying values is a differentiated "feature" of a product, one that increases preference for it (such as by 10 percent), that's more than enough to create a very substantial benefit.

To be concrete about this, in most cases, companies embody a mixture of good things and bad, and products do too. More importantly, the purchase decision includes many other factors, such as price and performance. Therefore, the purchase decision comes down to comparing multiple options (one of which is not purchasing from any of the competitors at all, putting off buying entirely) and determining which option to choose.

Product A might be made by a company that seems mostly OK but has some flaws, product B by a firm known as a leader in acting on values, and product C by an outfit that's unknown. Adding to that, product A might come in the right color or style, B may be harder to find, and C might be less expensive.

All these factors will be weighed, with levels of importance varying by customer. One customer might choose product A, even though the company isn't known as a leader, because the product itself is more to their liking, while another chooses C because it's less expensive. All of this is quite unavoidable—and is completely OK! The key is that both companies and products are judged *at least partially* by whether they align with customers' values. That is, values matter—not, in most cases, to the exclusion of everything else, but they do matter.

Here's one way they can matter: Valutus research shows that customers are more willing to give a new company a chance when the company (or product) is more aligned with their values than what the customer is currently buying. This is true for business-to-business (B2B) buyers as well; purchasers responsible for buying for both large companies and small ones told us that values alignment matters. Another frequent benefit is that customers can become loyal faster and reach a higher level of eventual loyalty. A third non-price benefit is vocality;

as discussed previously, customers are often more willing to tell other people about their positive experiences with the product.

Once someone buys from you, does acting on your values help you keep them? How do you make that relationship more profitable? Does it mean they become better champions for you, helping you to acquire even more customers? All these affect the lifetime value of a customer—their economic value to you over the time that they remain your customer.

Profitable Customers

Beyond getting customers in general, you want *profitable* ones. Some are more profitable than others, so you want to both attract the more profitable ones and make your existing customers more profitable over the lifetime of your relationship with them. ("Lifetime value" refers to their value from the time of their first purchase until they stop buying from you altogether. Their "lifetime" could be a single purchase. If they return after a long absence, that purchase begins their second "customer lifetime.")

It's a straightforward concept: how much money you earn from a customer, from when you first try to attract them until they cease buying from you. But sometimes there are items that get missed in thinking about it.

Xynraso Scientific

I'll illustrate with the example of a company I worked with. To preserve confidentiality, I won't use the company's real name, instead calling it Xynraso Scientific. I've also modified the numbers in this example slightly (though only slightly) to protect the firm's identity.

Xynraso is a B2B company primarily selling to customers in science-heavy industries. For this example, we'll look at one of the company's product lines. The average order for customers of this product line is

---

The Basics of Customer Lifetime Value

If you're already familiar with the basic ingredients in customer lifetime value, feel free to skip this. If not, here are a few fundamentals that will help you follow the discussion in this chapter.

Cost to acquire: This is the amount you have to spend to convert someone from prospect to paying customer. When we discussed being considered and chosen by prospects earlier, we didn't talk about the economics of it. Now, let's expand on that idea to talk about how acquiring a customer is a big part of the economics of the business. That is, if it costs too much to acquire a customer and you don't make much off them while they are your customer, then you may actually lose money on them.

Average revenue per sale: A customer who buys only a few things is generally worth less than one who buys a lot each time they shop. Of course, profitability partly depends on how often they buy, which is our next element.

Sales per year: How many different times does a customer buy from you in an average year? If you multiply this together with average revenue per sale, you end up with the amount of money that customer spends with you in an average year.

---

a bit over $500; on average, a customer orders from Xynraso about once a month, making (in round numbers) average annual revenue per customer (12 × $500 = $6,000). The company has twenty thousand of these customers, making revenue from this product line about $120 million per year.

Xynraso's cost of goods sold (COGS) is 50 percent, which makes its gross margin (revenue minus COGS) also 50 percent. This means the cost of the items in the order is $250, leaving $250 of the $500 total to cover expenses such as research and design (R&D), administration, advertising, sales costs, insurance, debt payments, and other needs. A typical customer buys from Xynraso once a month and typically stays a customer for about two years (i.e., their customer lifetime is about twenty-four months).

To maintain the 50 percent margin for this product line, Xynraso has to stay at the forefront of the market in terms of technology, which requires significant R&D investment. I'll use $10 million per year for this expense, which is just over 8 percent of revenue.

Cost to serve is the cost to meet the customer's needs, not related to any specific order. For example, if a customer calls Xynraso because there was something wrong with the way the charge went through, the cost of handling that call and fixing the issue would be part of the cost to serve that customer. (This is different from the cost of the items that the customer buys, the $250 mentioned earlier.)

Some customers have a higher cost to serve because they need more help solving problems or they call your customer service desk more often. Other customers have a lower cost. Although it's hard to pin this down exactly, to be conservative I'll say that the cost to serve the customer is $500 per year on average.

Putting that all together, we get an average sales per year of $6,000, and an average lifetime of two years, which equals $12,000 in revenue. Of the $12,000 in sales, $6,000 is gross margin on those sales (revenue minus COGS). Then there is $1,000 for the cost to serve that customer for two years (at $500 per year). That leaves $5,000 to cover everything else.

It's difficult to pin down the total cost of getting a new customer—marketing, sales visits, and so on—especially given that Xynraso sales reps offer other products and services, not just from this product line. To again be conservative, I'll use a value of $1,000, which means that Xynraso spends $10 million annually on the marketing, sales, and other activities needed to acquire ten thousand customers each year.

Since the average customer stays for two years, that results in the twenty thousand customers mentioned earlier. (Note that this $10 million is an annual expenditure, but Xynraso spends this money only once during each customer's lifetime. As mentioned above, each of these ten thousand newly acquired customers then remains with the company for two years.)

This brings up another, more commonly overlooked, part of the equation: a customer's effect on other customers and potential customers through word of mouth. This, too, is difficult to pin down in this case, so I won't include it in the final calculations below. However, the intuition behind this effect is straightforward: if a customer costs $1,000 to acquire but they tell their colleagues about Xynraso, and as a result that leads to an additional Xynraso customer, that lowers the acquisition cost to $500 ($1,000 spent, as before, but resulting in two customers instead of one).

Customers also can have other effects on those they know. For example, they could influence other customers to buy more often or to purchase more when they do buy. If they influence their friends, family, and officemates to switch from buying one delivery a month to two deliveries a month, then that effect would make it worth paying more to acquire that customer. This effect on the behavior of others is part of the customer's lifetime value.

I've gone through this description of customer lifetime value because it turns out that acting on values can have an effect at several different places during the customer's journey, thereby changing their lifetime value.

Values and Lifetime Value

Acting on values can help you reach more customers, get them to purchase from you, and increase their lifetime value. To see why that's the case, let's look at the value Xynraso receives from each customer over the customer's lifetime. In order not to get too deep in the weeds of accounting, we'll use operating income (OI) so we can exclude taxes and income that isn't related to the product line (e.g., rental income). To keep things simpler, we will include R&D expenses, but we won't deal with depreciation of buildings and other assets. (In accounting terms, this means our measure is like operating income before depreciation and amortization except that we're including R&D expenses, which in some cases include depreciation and amortization.)

In our Xynraso example, revenue of $6,000 per customer per year multiplied by 20,000 customers yields $120 million in annual revenue, as discussed above. From that, we need to subtract COGS ($60 million), cost to serve ($500 × 20,000 customers, or $10 million), customer acquisition cost ($1,000 × 10,000 newly acquired customers, or $10 million), and R&D expense ($10 million). Doing so leaves our calculation of OI at $30 million per year.

Although customer acquisition went up, we couldn't do experiments like those mentioned earlier, so we can't attribute all of the increase to shared values (the overall market was also growing at the same time). To estimate the benefit, you could take the bottom end of the 10 to 25 percent gain we've seen in the experiments covered previously. At a 10 percent gain, that increases customers to eleven thousand per year, meaning that Xynraso has twenty-two thousand customers on average at any given time, since each of those eleven thousand newly acquired customers stays for two years. With no changes to customer spending, that increases OI to $35 million per year, a 17 percent increase since revenue increases to $132 million, gross profit increases to $66 million, and acquisition cost and R&D stay the same—but having more customers means total cost to serve rises to $11 million.

The next part of the analysis was to determine if customers who share Xynraso's values (which we'll define as engaging with the company's environmental and social programs) purchased more; they did. In this case, revenue per sale was 2 percent higher compared to a control group of similar customers. Keeping everything else the same means that, according to our calculation, OI increases to $31.2 million, an improvement of 4 percent, double the percentage increase in revenue per sale. (If we also include the previous increase in customer preference, OI becomes over $35 million, an increase of 18 percent.)

A values match with customers can also affect the number of sales per year, but since we didn't track that separately in this case, I'll leave it aside for now. (Incidentally, because cost to serve is often partially driven by the number of sales, we'd want to increase the cost to serve if we increased sales frequency.)

More frequent purchases have other benefits as well, such as smoothing out cash flow, with more frequent infusions of revenue, and they also keep you more top of mind for customers. I haven't included these benefits in our example, but they can provide additional value.

Margin

The next factor to examine is margin per sale. Here the key question is, "What kinds of products do customers buy, and how profitable are they?" Many businesses have certain products that are very profitable and others that are less so. If you've been to a movie theater and paid for popcorn, you know what I'm talking about. The popcorn is marked up 900 percent,[13] whereas the movie ticket itself has a far lower profit margin.[14]

I've been using 50 percent as the gross margin per sale for Xynraso. But customers who share the company's values also buy more of the company's higher-margin products and services, which further changes the economics. About one-third of customers changed their purchases enough to increase the average margin by 15 percent, which meant the average margin rose by 5 percent (one-third of 15 percent), from 50 to 52.5 percent.

By itself, this 5 percent increase in margin would change the result of our OI calculation by 10 percent. When we add in the changes we've discussed previously, the result is an increase in our OI number to over $38 million per year, almost 30 percent more than the original figure.

One thing I want to make clear is that while some customers will in fact pay more for the more environmentally friendly or more values-based option, that's not necessarily the source of the increased margin. One of your higher-margin products might *save* the customer money that they're currently spending elsewhere.

A simple example here is food waste. Recall that when supermarkets have food waste, they also have financial waste. If they can't sell something they've paid for, it hits their bottom line negatively in multiple ways. This dynamic means that when a supermarket undertakes an effort to reduce food waste because of its environmental footprint, it also increases the margin on its perishable goods. On average, about 10 percent of groceries are thrown out without being sold, according to some estimates, with the percentage being higher for fresh fruits and vegetables.[15]

Spoiler Alert

Spoiler Alert was founded in 2015 "to power the waste-free economy"[16] by a pair of entrepreneurs (one of whom is a friend and former colleague of mine) who met at the MIT Sloan School of Management. In taking on the challenge of reducing food waste, they also set out to capture economic value that was being wasted—as the company points out, food waste is a major drain on profitability in addition to being an environmental and social issue.

By 2022, the company counted numerous top global food and beverage companies (including Nestlé, Kraft Heinz, Campbell Soup Company, and Danone North America) as clients and, in January 2022, the company passed another milestone as it facilitated the sale of over two million cases of excess inventory in a single month. This both reduced waste and benefitted its clients: according to Danone North America's Camila Leal, the company has seen both reductions in waste and better returns on its markdown sales program[17]—capturing additional value for the company.

If a supermarket earns a 15 percent margin on one category of perishable products and it reduces waste from 10 to 8 percent, what is the effect on its financials? Under reasonable assumptions, it would yield about a 40 percent improvement in gross profit. In other words, this increase in sustainability raises profits by reducing "deadweight" losses that don't benefit anyone: the food that gets purchased and thrown away.

This can happen in other areas too, such as taking better care of your employees' health by improving indoor air quality in your offices. As Lawrence Berkeley National Laboratory notes, "performance (speed and accuracy) of typical office tasks improves with increased ventilation rate." They note that the reduction of indoor pollutants is associated with "approximately 4% to 16% increases in the performance (speed or accuracy) of selected office work tasks" such as typing and call center tasks.[18] To the extent that such improvements decrease errors and cost to serve, they also increase margins.

Stepping back from the specifics, increasing the margin per sale is quite valuable from a financial perspective—no matter how you do it.

Loyalty and Lifetime

The next factor to address is the average customer lifetime. For Xynraso, the average customer lifetime is two years. But what happens when a customer becomes more loyal because they realize that you share their values? Additional loyalty extends their customer lifetime and therefore the total value of having them as a customer.

We looked at the average customer lifetime of the most profitable segment of customers at Xynraso, which grew by over 12 percent, from two years to a little under 27 months. If this were to hold for all customer segments (we didn't look at all of them), it would mean an

---

Who Pays?

Companies sometimes ask, "Who should pay for the cost of our environmental and social efforts? Should we raise prices so the customer pays, or should we keep prices the same and pay for the changes out of our margin?" At Valutus, our answer is that neither you nor the customer should pay—your competitors should.

As Xynraso found out, improving your own performance, and making sure customers know that, increases customer preference for your offerings. That means you can do things such as take market share from the competition or sell more higher-margin products. (You could also discover you have more flexibility to raise prices, as customer price sensitivity declines, but for now I'll leave that possibility aside.)

This means you're making more money and your customers are not paying more. Who is paying? Competitors, particularly those that are lagging behind you in their environmental and social performance, are paying. They are seeing their customer preference decline, leading to consequences such as reduced sales, lower margin, or the need to spend more on promotions. This is exactly as it should be—those who are not keeping up in terms of acting on values also shoulder the resulting costs.

increase of 30 percent in OI. The reason for this is that increasing customer longevity increases the total number of customers at any given time—from 20,000 to a bit over 22,000. (If you acquire 10,000 customers per year but keep them for about twenty-seven months instead of twenty-four, you end up with around 22,400 customers.) This naturally increases revenue and improves financial results. And, undoubtedly, longer lifetimes only compound the benefits of the higher margins mentioned above.

Of course, there are plenty of other factors that can increase customer lifetime (e.g., customer service, ease-of-use), and a smart company will work on those also. Acting on values is a complement, not a substitute, for these other improvements.

Where to Start

Understand key customer groups and look for where they share your values. Take advantage of the customer intimacy benefits of values: get to know them, their communities, and their events. Get to know how they think and, more importantly, how they feel.

The healthcare organization I mentioned earlier did just this. Employees talked to customers directly, sought input from salespeople about what they were hearing, and went to events with customers and asked what mattered to them. They used "voice of the customer" data and reports on the experiences of customers along with external benchmarks.

Then look for ways to incorporate the values shared by your company and customers. The healthcare organization focused on deepening emotional connections with customers and prospects through doing more to incorporate its values in its offerings. Values could provide the foundation for meeting customer needs that weren't being adequately addressed in the marketplace.

The company realized that its offerings already embodied some of its core values, but other strongly held values either weren't incorporated or were not obvious to customers and prospects. For example, there was already deep concern about the health of people who were in service careers, and there were already some efforts to help them be physically and mentally healthier. But the company's offerings didn't make this

clear to customers, which meant that even organizations with a lot of service career workers (e.g., educational institutions) didn't see this focus—
and therefore it didn't change which provider they preferred. Nor was
this concern as clear to the service professionals themselves as it could
have been, so their health didn't benefit as much as it could have.

Based on the values the team chose to focus on, they came up with
concrete ways to expand how these values were reflected in products
and services. Examples included templates, targeted rebates, guided assistance, more information about work-life balance, and greater financial
incentives for healthy behaviors.

After finding ways to incorporate values, test your ideas. You can use
experiments, interviews, focus groups, or other research. However you
do it, make sure to test your understanding of what customers want to
see and hear from you. Putting values into action isn't about a marketing
slogan or a flavor of the month. It's important and requires effort, so it's
crucial to get it right. It's worth it.

The company then tested these ideas with customers to see which
ones resonated the most. It found two specific ideas that raised customer
preference by between 14 and 20 percent. These results were combined
with internal prioritization factors (e.g., their ease of implementation and
the strength of their connection to the company's values) to determine
which ideas to pursue first.

Working for Customers

Reaping all these benefits isn't automatic, of course. One reason is that
realizing the full customer-related benefit of acting on values requires
multiple actions to ensure customers are aware of what you're doing.
This can mean incorporating new messages into marketing and giving
salespeople new talking points, for example, and those don't happen
overnight. However, as Xynraso found out, there's benefit from each
customer who becomes aware, and they frequently help you spread the
word by evangelizing.

Another reason is that your competitors are also doing more. This
means that as you improve your environmental and social performance,
part of that improvement goes to simply preventing you from falling

behind. As an illustration, Valutus researched the environmental and social performance of two hundred food and beverage companies. Over a three-year period, we found that, first, average performance increased. Second, the gap between the leaders and the laggards dropped, as the laggards made increasing efforts to catch up. As your competitors and your industry improve, the differentiation you get from improving is reduced, and you'll have to work harder to stay ahead.

However, that doesn't decrease the value of putting your values into action. You can't stop your competitors from improving their performance, which means that if you don't improve also, *they* become the ones who benefit from values-based differentiation. For one very well-known brand, Valutus found that the penalty for being a laggard was a 15 percent drop in customer preference, enabling competitors to pick off customers who had previously preferred the company's product.

You can either be the beneficiary of these changes or you can watch as your competitors are. But either way, someone is going to reap the benefit of better alignment with their customers' values.

III CORE Operations

A European manufacturer discovered that they could increase the efficiency of their cleaning process, reducing the required water, cleaning solvents, and time. The water and cleaning agent reductions had environmental benefits, and the reduction in required materials generated financial savings. But the big surprise was the value of the time savings. The hours previously spent on the inefficient process could instead be used for something far more useful—in fact, *fifty times* more financially valuable. Seeing the potential for an environmental benefit had unlocked a tremendous financial ROI as well.

This is not unusual. Acting on values provides real benefits in critical operational areas, making your organization more efficient, more innovative, and ultimately more successful. That's what this part is about.

6 More Efficient

Being more efficient, trimming the use of raw materials, lowering emissions from energy, and reducing or eliminating pollution and waste are all actions that reduce costs and improve the bottom line—while also expressing the value of protecting the environment. But even in such obvious areas, changes that *should* happen sometimes don't. It's the corporate equivalent of the fact that even people who know that eating less and exercising more would make them healthier often don't act on that.

Here's where the values-thinking perspective shift comes in handy. The view through values lenses offers such useful opportunities to cut waste, energy, and raw material use that even companies with a laser focus on expenses are often surprised.

IT manufacturing giant Cisco found this out after installing 1,500 energy sensors in one of its Asian manufacturing facilities in 2015 and measuring the plant's total energy use for the first time, finding ways to cut it by 30 percent. Cisco's senior VP of supply chain, John Kern said, "We always manage costs so closely, but we weren't really measuring energy—we didn't know how much we spent!"[1]

Something similar happened at oil refiner Valero, which, using cheap energy meters and some specialized software, captured $120 million in energy savings in just the first year.[2] Now, these are companies with plenty of sharp people and thousands of tech experts. But their focus had been elsewhere, so they hadn't seen these savings before—until their people began looking through values lenses.

A strong focus on expenses—even when you're fully aware that energy represents one of the largest variable costs for a manufacturer— isn't always enough to realize these savings opportunities. But when values lenses are on, such opportunities become clear.

Values Lenses

Seeing things through the prism of values helps you by:

- Orienting you toward the future: Because so many values-related issues touch on the future—those related to children, of course, but also climate, health, and others—thinking about them helps you look beyond the near-term.

- Emphasizing otherwise-overlooked factors: Because doing good for people naturally encourages you to think about those who are more vulnerable, you become aware of things that are often overlooked (since the vulnerable are more likely to be affected by them)—an awareness that helps reduce blind spots.

- Dealing with areas that are becoming more important: Because of changes in the world and societies, topics where values play a big role—such as social equality, climate, education, and others—are becoming even more prominent, which means you're more prepared for big-picture issues that are increasingly strong.

- Helping you to connect with your own—and, often, others'—core motivations and beliefs: People who are more connected and aware of their own values are less easily thrown off course.

To put on your values lenses, first bring your values to the fore, clari- fying how you want to benefit the world and those in it. For example, you might choose to help solve the climate crisis or to reduce poverty (or something else).

Second, look deeply at that issue along three dimensions: its inputs, its signs / metrics, and its outputs. That is, use values to inform *what you look at and where you focus*. Continuing the climate example:

- You would go beyond elements such as GHGs and see inputs like the growing demand for goods as incomes rise, the energy intensity of producing those goods, and the competition (economic and political) from different sources of energy.

- When it comes to signs, you would look not just at average temperatures but also at extremes, at the frequency and strength of extreme weather, and the "wet bulb" index (a combination of temperature and humidity).

- When it comes to outputs, you would see increases in the cost and disruption caused by extreme weather, more rapid changes in energy and production technology, and greater intensity of political activity—particularly by actors who think they are losing the competitive battle.

Third, look at the places where people are most vulnerable to the problems the issue entails and also the places where the situation is most ripe for change. That is, let values also guide *where you look*.

- Who is most vulnerable to changes in the climate? One answer is those who work outdoors in hot areas, where air temperatures around workers can reach heat index values of over 125 degrees Fahrenheit (52 Celsius),[3] especially in developing countries.

- Where is the situation most ripe for change? One place is where operational conditions are best for alternative energy (such as strong sunlight for solar panels and few cloudy days) and so are competitive conditions (few or expensive incumbent sources of energy), such as in parts of Africa.

Putting all of this together, values would help change *what you see*, bringing into focus things you might not notice otherwise, such as:

- Places where you can both reduce vulnerabilities in your supply chain and also help workers who are at elevated risk from rising temperatures.

- How changes to the climate could upend the competitive environment while also changing which humanitarian issues are most pressing.

Olympic Hurdlers

The examples above of how companies saved money through environmental efficiency are not isolated cases. In the middle of the last decade, a report by the We Mean Business Coalition examined more than 1,400 companies that had invested in lowering carbon emissions. The coalition found that the most aggressive—those that set emissions targets in line with climate science—averaged an internal rate of return (IRR) of 27 percent.[4]

As it happens, the average hurdle rate—the rate of return required for an investment to be approved—for large companies in the S&P 500 is about 15 percent (and this rate has been relatively stable since the mid-1990s[5]). This makes 27 percent about double the return that's typically required. An area with even greater returns is industrial process energy, that is, the energy for manufacturing or activities other than lighting and heating facilities. In the United States, the average IRR for improvements was 81 percent in 2014[6]—more than five times the average hurdle rate.

This is not something that only works with major redesigns, either. How about turning off lights, lowering air-conditioning intensity, using climate controls only where and when needed, and sealing doors and windows against drafts? These are low-tech, simple solutions that save energy and money. Most require very little investment, but unless executives have their values lenses on, they often overlook these opportunities. When they do see them, however, the IRR of small changes is quite high. Over a two-year period, the average reported return was 88 percent,[7] nearly six times the typical hurdle rate.

The returns just listed only capture the visible value of the changes discussed; the submerged value is even greater. Consider that energy availability is becoming a bigger risk with blackouts, brownouts, and increasing demand on tired electric grids (more on this in the section on risk, part IV). This risk is crucial in places where the grid is in worse condition and energy is less consistent, such as in developing economies like India.

It stands to reason, then, that lowering energy consumption means reducing vulnerability if something goes wrong with the power supply since you need to draw less power from the grid. A common strategy is to purchase and run diesel generators when the grid fails or power drops—and you need fewer expensive generators when your operations are more energy efficient.

Wasted Value

If part of the discipline of operations is reducing unnecessary costs, then values-based action provides real operational and financial benefits. As I detailed above, using less energy for production or heating, ventilating, and air-conditioning creates very positive returns indeed. And the same reasoning applies to raw materials, unneeded space, and other types of waste.

To illustrate, I'll look specifically at companies that have been quite aggressive in reducing their waste to landfill, such as Unilever and Pfizer, as a means to reduce their environmental impact. Both companies have a number of "zero waste to landfill" facilities—hundreds, in the case of Unilever[8]—meaning they've reduced the waste leaving their facilities to almost nothing.[9] And they're not alone; Nike managed to divert 99.9 percent of its manufacturing waste away from landfills, to be either recycled or converted into energy,[10] as long ago as their 2018 fiscal year.

There are several ways to achieve these results, with some used in concert. One is to redesign products or processes so less waste is produced. One of many illustrations is a 3M plant in Brookings, South Dakota. Over a decade ago, the facility replaced a vapor incinerator with new equipment that not only captured more vapor but also recovered more of the heat from incinerating it, reducing natural gas consumption by 84 percent.[11] Thousands of similar projects are why 3M credits its company-wide Pollution Prevention Pays program with saving over $2 billion[12] and preventing over three billion pounds of pollution.[13] (The financial savings are likely significantly understated due to 3M's policy of counting only first-year savings.)

Waste Not

While all the above efforts are great, there's no way to eliminate *all* excess material. Is there a values-based opportunity here? After all, if you just toss the material, you pay to have it removed and get nothing in return. If, however, you recycle it then you extract some value from it.

Recycling material matters a lot also; as one example, a decade ago General Motors began making more than $1 billion annually from recycling waste, including steel.[14] While waste reduction is better, there's still plenty of value to be gained from recycling. Then there's the matter of submerged value. As I listed earlier in the book, there's a long, long list of cost reductions and gains from simply reducing material waste. If done right, waste reduction produces significant visible savings and revenue, significant submerged value, and significant environmental benefits.

And there's still more value to be captured. Driving down waste leads to operational efficiencies. All sorts of steps are saved when less material is coming in and when processes are streamlined to ensure less waste is going out. These steps chew up precious time. Simply put, "reducing waste universally implies reducing *time*."[15]

I saw this in person when working with a European firm using large amounts of water, energy, and detergent to clean pharmaceutical production equipment. The company looked at how to reduce water consumption and in doing so realized that there were cleaning steps that could be reduced or eliminated. This change reduced water and energy consumption, but it didn't end there: the productivity of both the employees and the capital equipment went up.

The time employees had spent washing and drying vats was now available for more valuable tasks. It now took less time to switch from producing one compound to another, which meant the expensive equipment and highly trained personnel spent less time out of production. For the same amount of effort, the company could produce more products in less time and generate more revenue.

The (Submerged) Value of Water

IBM wanted to reduce water use in semiconductor manufacturing. Eventually, the company lowered water use by 29 percent at one of its factories, saving millions of gallons—and millions of dollars—in the process. What's interesting is why and how this happened.

Compared to other resources, water is dirt cheap. It *seems* cheap, anyway, at under a penny a gallon (about 3.8 liters) for commercial use. Its *value*, however, is far higher. For IBM, that value included all the processing needed to produce top-notch semiconductors: exceptionally pure water was required. Beyond that, "IBM's utility plant creates nine custom varieties of water. Each variety of water costs 4, 5, or 10 times more than the cost of the raw water itself."[16]

If the postproduction water were simply discharged, much of this added value would be wasted. The local river system would accept some exceptionally clean water, the utility would pump in more of the raw stuff, and the factory would start processing the water again. What a waste.

In addition to not being ultra-pure, the water coming in from outside was cold, and that was also a problem: "Water comes into IBM Burlington cold from Lake Champlain and the Champlain Water District. It's so cold that it has to be warmed up before the staff can turn it into ultrapure water. Meanwhile, the factory has thirteen massive, two-story-tall chillers using huge quantities of electricity to produce cold water [for cooling equipment], even in winter."[17]

The point was that IBM had been spending (cold) hard cash to warm some water for manufacturing while spending more to cool other water down. Realizing that water, though cheap, was not free, IBM saw potential for savings on its water bill—three-quarters of a million dollars a year, it turned out. As Eric Berliner, IBM's water and environmental manager, said in an interview, "When you start to think how we think . . . you don't see water in the pipes. You see dollar signs."[18]

As a result of seeing things differently, IBM built new pipes that used the cold-water intake for cooling, thereby warming it for production processing. This lowered the cost of warming, the cost of cooling, and used far less water in the bargain. A win-win-win.

Looking at things differently led to creating new piping systems to take advantage of existing water temperatures, saving money. But now, the submerged value really kicked in: "Cutting water use saved an additional $600,000 in chemical and filtration costs each year, plus an additional $2.3 million in electricity and energy costs. For every dollar that IBM Burlington cut from its basic water bill, it saved $4 more."[19]

Values Lenses and Packaging

Staples, one of the largest office supply retailers in the world, also runs one of the planet's biggest e-commerce sites. The company wanted to reduce its products' sustainability impact by reducing paper and plastic as well as addressing various other issues. Part of doing this was a changed packaging process and a system to place each product in the right size package, so a small product no longer came in a medium box with extra bubble wrap. It now had a smaller box that fit much better.

The change worked. In the initial years of the program's operation, filler material use ("void fill") was reduced approximately 60 percent,

---

The ROI of Better Lenses—and a Phone Call

A retail chain was receiving crates of individually packaged products that were among its most theft-prone items (I'll call them "TPIs"). To prevent this, store staff were asked to remove these TPIs from their individual boxes and stash them behind the counter.

Meanwhile, the company's sustainability officer, while working on material reduction, asked the manufacturer to deliver each TPI without its customary box. This led to packaging materials being dramatically reduced, just as was hoped.

But the change also produced several unexpected (submerged) results. First, a lot of time was saved now that staff didn't have to open all those boxes or break them down for recycling when they were empty. And more products now fit into shipping containers of the same size, reducing shipping costs. The first two actions alone netted the company millions in labor savings.

The manufacturer, too, saved on shipping since more items now fit in the same size shipping container.

and total packaging weight fell by 8 percent. Corrugated cardboard use dipped by 15 percent in US operations.[20] Well done, reduction team. But what about submerged value? The change increased cube efficiency on trucks by 30 percent.[21] Better cube efficiency creates cost reductions in areas such as transportation, warehousing, material handling, and carrying inventory.[22]

Small and Diverse Suppliers

As a different example of using values-based actions to lower costs, consider a company that has a program to increase purchasing from small businesses, companies owned by minorities or women or veterans, or companies located in areas that aren't doing well economically. Such supplier diversity programs not only help these suppliers grow, and the communities where they are located succeed, but they also benefit the company doing the purchasing.

As Simha Mummalaneni and Jonathan Z. Zhang note in MIT's *Sloan Management Review* special collection on procurement, "A stream of academic research has demonstrated that supplier diversity initiatives can quite substantially reduce the buyer's purchasing costs in a wide variety of industry settings. Such initiatives were shown to save $45 million in the radio spectrum industry, reduce expenditures in the logging industry by 10%, trim Montreal's snow removal costs by 6%, and most recently, cut Virginia's government procurement expenditures by 12%."[23]

How does this work? It starts by reducing the power of any one supplier in terms of providing what that company buys. Suppliers with less competition for the customer's business can become more comfortable and do less to constrain prices over time. In this way, less competition can lead to prices that are higher than they would otherwise be, even when what the company is buying would naturally decline in price— and reducing a supplier's power reduces this temptation. Suppliers realize they need to compete to continue being the supplier of record and therefore work harder to retain business. They may become more responsive and more innovative and sweat even harder to wring efficiencies out of the system, all of which benefits you as their customer.[24]

That very flexibility can make supply chains themselves more adaptable operationally. One thing COVID taught the world is that both businesses and individuals are much more vulnerable to disruption than previously thought. Often, small businesses can get back up and running sooner (although they don't always have the same financial cushion, which, in the case of a disruption, can mean you need to be flexible financially). The result of this is a more flexible and innovative supply chain and more protection against future risks.

Finally, minority- and women-owned businesses offer another potential advantage. As your customer base becomes more diverse, a supply chain that mirrors this may be more attuned to those changes. As such, they can provide valuable information, products, and services to meet these changing interests. A diverse supplier base acts as a kind of insurance policy, reducing risk and mitigating the consequences of mistakes.

Values, Capital Efficiency, and Stock Price

So far, I've been talking about lowering more traditional kinds of costs, such as procurement and energy. But another part of operational excellence is managing the company's cost of capital, which is how much it has to pay to acquire financing (whether through borrowing or issuing stock). For public companies, this includes managing perceptions that affect stock price, which both lowers cost of capital and increases the company's return to shareholders.

As it happens, addressing energy issues more broadly helps with both of these. Andrew Winston, George Favaloro, and Tim Healy note in *Harvard Business Review* that "an apparel-sector analyst report . . . Morgan Stanley raised its stock price targets for Nike, Hanes brands, and VF because they outperformed peers with a 'better and more effective sustainability strategy.'"[25]

Seventy senior executives at forty-three global investing firms—including the three biggest—said in interviews that ESG issues mattered to them. In fact, ESG was, according to research leads Robert Eccles and Svetlana Klimenko, "almost universally top of mind for these executives." They were convinced by their own companies' integration of ESG into investment decisions that "corporate leaders will soon be held accountable by shareholders for ESG performance—if they aren't already."[26] Indeed, it wasn't much later that the US Securities and Exchange Commission proposed a new reporting rule for public companies, one requiring emissions data to be collected and reported within the following two years.[27]

Investors weren't waiting for regulation, however. A team from Lazard Asset Management—working with experts from Harvard, MIT, Columbia, and Imperial College London—studied over sixteen thousand stocks over the period from 2016 to 2020 and found that investors were already beginning to incorporate GHG emissions into their valuations. An increase in emissions was associated with a decline in the company's price-to-earnings multiple (P/E multiple)—at the high end, a 10 percent increase in a large European industrial company's emissions came with an 18 percent reduction in their P/E multiple.[28] While the average company's P/E reduction was lower than this, the study showed that investors were already penalizing companies that emit more GHGs, even before changes in rules and regulation, let alone a widespread price on carbon or similar possible actions.

7 More Innovative

Someone once told me that acting on values is not just about defining what you want but also clarifying what you're *not* willing to accept. In other words, values can constrain the options you're willing to tolerate, and acting on values forces the elimination of unacceptable actions.

Values that prioritize caring for the environment constrain the use or manufacture of products destructive to the environment or constrain doing business with companies vying to drill in the Arctic. Values regarding the dignity of life constrain a company from accepting modern slavery in its supply chain. You might think that constraining what is acceptable would squash innovation. But since necessity truly does beget invention, the reverse is true. Constraints actually *promote* creativity.[1]

I once conducted a years-long experiment exploring the effect of constraints on personal creativity by asking groups I was leading to write poems in sixty seconds. In one variation, I told them to write a haiku, one of the most restrictive types of poems, with specific rules governing the number of lines and syllables per line. In another variant, there was no instruction to use the haiku form: they could structure the poem as they liked.

The haiku group accomplished more in sixty seconds than the free-form poets. They were more likely to end up with a poem they liked, and they found the task less stressful—even though the haiku form was very constraining. In other words, more constraints made it easier, rather than harder, to be creative.

Catalytic Constraints

The same dynamic holds true at the corporate level. Grappling with sustainability, and trying on sustainability lenses, fuels innovation.

At a large company, I led a team looking at the intersection of sustainability and innovation. We looked at top leaders in both areas and found that being a sustainability leader actually increased the likelihood of being an innovation leader as well. While it was rare to be an innovation leader (someone in the top 2 percent of companies for innovation performance), it was much more common to be an innovation leader if you were also a sustainability leader. In fact, sustainability leaders were more than 400 percent more likely to be innovation leaders.[2] This was certainly a surprise—to the company, the team, and even to me. I had expected some improvement from the connection, but the magnitude of the effect surprised me.

We also wondered if this was correlation without causation or if other factors could explain the results, but neither hypothesis checked out. The conclusion that sustainability performance enhances innovation was the best explanation.[3]

How many companies want to compete better through innovation? A lot. The value of sustainability, even unintentionally, is a prime mover of innovation.

Viewing a company through sustainability-colored glasses encourages a very different perspective. I have since had the opportunity to do this work with other clients, not just for sustainability but for values more broadly. We found the results to be the same—focusing on values led to seeing different opportunities and possibilities and to creating innovative services and products. In one case, a client, reflecting on the company's values, generated more than a dozen innovative takes on its existing product lines.

This relationship between constraints and innovation is reflected in advertising legend David Ogilvy's dictum about the project requirements marketers call "briefs." "Give me," Ogilvy said, "the freedom of a tight brief."[4]

Inspiring Innovation

Beyond providing constraints, values can also serve as inspiration. In my experience, this is especially true when the goal is both measured and concrete. Apparel companies, for example, use "pattern efficiency" improvements to reduce the amount of wasted fabric from manufacturing, which makes it a great measure to use. If a particular pattern encourages more waste, it has a lower pattern efficiency. Knowing this, designers can create patterns with high efficiency.

Pattern efficiency offers a pleasant choice: manufacture the same number of garments with less fabric—a cost savings—or make more garments with the same amount of fabric, increasing production without spending more on material. Both are obviously beneficial, but it also matters whether there is additional improvement—and thus additional value—created by a values-based effort to reduce waste.

Nike has been hammering away at this. The company's desire to increase pattern efficiency led to a truly innovative design for the Atsuma running shoe: the Swoosh logo on one side was mirrored by negative space on the other, so the two sides can be cut from the same piece of material without creating waste.[5] Would this design innovation exist unless Nike was searching for waste reduction? It seems unlikely. Though the company understood the economic value of pattern efficiency and had plenty of top-notch designers, this solution hadn't appeared previously.

This isn't Nike's only waste-reduction innovation: Flyknit is a manufacturing innovation that greatly reduces waste and material use. Using a knitted fabric made in one piece, rather than by cutting, Flyknit uppers generate 60 percent less scrap versus typical shoes.[6] The material contains 90 percent recycled content as well.[7] Flyknit uppers are also lighter than those made the traditional way, which is beneficial for athletic performance—a core element of Nike's brand.

Values, Innovation, and Willingness to Work with Others

Values-motivated employees are more innovative, with heightened levels of personal creativity and greater willingness to partner with others to bring changes to life. Feeling part of a larger, important effort changes how people behave. As Harvard professor Rebecca Henderson says, "the sense of being part of something greater than yourself can lead to high levels of engagement, high levels of creativity, and the willingness to partner across functional and product boundaries within a company."[8]

This finding appears to hold true across countries and cultures as well. In 2017, Chin-Lung Lin and Shih-Kuan Chiu analyzed information from more than three hundred subjects at Taiwanese companies with strong CSR programs. Their results suggested that CSR correlated positively with innovation at the individual, team, and organizational levels. They concluded that the "results showed that strategic thinking of shared values had a significant and positive effect on CSR strategies . . . and CSR activities [are] correlated positively with IB [innovative behavior]."[9]

Beyond Constraints

For some, values alone can be a great source of inspiration and innovation.

In their book *Dare to Inspire*, authors Allison Holzer, Sandra Spataro, and Jen G. Baron lay out their model defining three main pathways to inspiration. They write that "looking inward and connecting to your own values, purpose, and personal why is a powerhouse source of inspiration—in fact, out of all the engines of inspiration, it may be the most potent of all."[10]

An illustration of this pathway in action is the experience of Meril Sakaria, chief technology officer of the global retail unit of Tata Consultancy Services, a firm with over $30 billion in revenue and upwards of 500,000 employees. She writes the following:

> My passion for innovation began as a student when I participated in a school competition. Inspired by the vision of empowering people with disabilities to live a life of dignity, my team and I created an award-winning prototype of an automated room for self-care for the physically challenged. The key to this innovation? A shared goal that inspired us. I've learned that as humans, we are often drawn toward objectives and initiatives that have a purpose that elevates and excites us. This sense of purpose is the basis of creating a culture of innovation.[11]

Strong values not only help inspire new ideas; they also help to inspire persistence when tackling a problem. People work harder and bring more of their true capacity to a task when it is related to their values, which improves problem-solving and is critical for innovation and change. As management great Peter Drucker wrote, "in innovation, as in any other endeavor, there is talent, there is ingenuity, and there is knowledge. But when all is said and done, what innovation requires is hard, focused, purposeful work. If diligence, persistence, and commitment are lacking, talent, ingenuity, and knowledge are of no avail."[12]

The reason for this is that a lot of failures arise when an organization starts doing something and then stops before the job is complete. In fact, Harvard Business School professor Rosabeth Moss Kanter has seen this problem so often that she coined Kanter's law: "Everything can look like a failure in the middle." She writes that "there are numerous roadblocks, obstacles, and surprises on the journey to change, and each one tempts us to give up. Give up prematurely, and the change effort is automatically a failure. Find a way around the obstacles, perhaps by making some tweaks in the plan, and keep going. Persistence and perseverance are essential to successful innovation and change."[13]

Diversity and Innovation

When a team of researchers examined over six million scientific papers published over a period of twenty years, they found that teams with both men and women produced work that was both more novel and more influential (highly cited) than those comprised of only one gender. That is, publications by mixed-gender teams outperform those from all-male and all-female teams. They were up to 7 percent more likely to produce a novel paper and over 14 percent more likely to produce a heavily cited one.[14] The researchers also found that gender *equality* has an impact. That is, the closer a team is to 50 percent women and 50 percent men, the stronger the benefits.

Mixed-gender teams are significantly less common than they should be—less than they would be if team formation were random, and certainly much less common than they should be given that they produce superior results. The research team hypothesized that "the under-representation of gender-diverse teams may reflect research showing that women receive less credit for their successes than do men team-mates, which in turn inhibits the formation of gender-diverse teams and women's success in receiving grants, prizes, and promotions."[15] In other words, encouraging gender-diverse teams creates commercially beneficial outcomes while also better allocating credit for successes.

In 2011, Cristian Dezso of the University of Maryland and David Ross of the University of Florida published an updated examination of the executive management teams of the top 1,500 S&P companies. Drawing on fifteen years of data, they found that companies with an innovation-focused strategy had an average of $42 million higher firm value when women were represented in the top management ranks.[16] One notable point about this result is that for many of the years for which they had data, there were very few female top executives at the companies studied. As an illustration, in 2006, their last year of data, "only 30 percent had even a single woman among their top managers."[17] As it happens, updated research has not only reinforced these findings but has also found even broader and higher levels of benefit.

Although the evidence for the effect of racial and ethnic diversity on innovation is more mixed than for gender diversity, the overall evidence points to a positive relationship. (Even if there were no relationship, of course, company efforts to increase racial and ethnic diversity would make sense as expressions of the values of inclusivity and equality—and firms would also reap the decision-making benefits of diversity.)

As one example of the evidence pointing in the direction of innovation benefits, consulting firm Boston Consulting Group (BCG) and the Technical University of Munich set out to see if there were business benefits from management teams with more women and people from other industries, companies, and countries (defined as having been born in another country or having parents who were). Studying 171 German, Swiss, and Austrian companies, they found a connection between such diversity and innovation in particular. The data showed a clear relationship between the diversity of companies' management teams and the revenues they received from innovative products and services.[18]

The positive effect they found was statistically significant, got stronger when organizations were more complex, and also rose as companies got larger. However, there was a threshold effect—for example, with the benefits only appearing when over 20 percent of managers were women. As the study authors wrote, "Having a high percentage of female employees doesn't do anything for innovation, the study shows, if only a small number of women are managers."

When BCG published a follow-up study a year later, using data from ten times as many companies (over 1,700), the company again found a strong innovation benefit: "The biggest takeaway we found is a strong and statistically significant correlation between the diversity of management teams and overall innovation. Companies that reported above-average diversity on their management teams also reported innovation revenue that was 19 percentage points higher than that of companies with below-average leadership diversity—45% of total revenue versus just 26%."[19]

In a study of the ethnic backgrounds of US-based authors of 2.5 million scientific papers (similar to the one mentioned above that focused on gender), Harvard Professor Richard B. Freeman and Wei Huang, who was a Harvard PhD candidate at the time, explored the relationship between author diversity and the impact of the papers. Freeman and Huang found that more diverse author teams saw their papers get published in more prestigious journals and receive 5 to 10 percent more citations.[20]

However, the effects of diversity don't only depend on individuals' background, such as gender, ethnicity, or country of birth. Even adding differences in thinking styles (cognitive diversity) doesn't complete the innovation picture; it's also essential to consider *policies* and the way companies engage with diversity. Just having people from different backgrounds isn't enough to get the full benefit; companies also need to have the right policies and cultures. As one study that looked at this specifically found, "using new product announcements, patents, and patent citations as measures of corporate innovation, we find that corporate policies that promote more pro-diversity cultures, specifically treatment of women and minorities, enhance future innovative efficiency."[21]

The role of culture and policy may help explain the divergence between studies that find diversity benefits and those that don't. For example, you might not find a benefit of team diversity without also building a supportive culture.

Another possible explanation comes from research that looked at both inherent diversity, which the researchers defined as coming from traits you are born with, "such as gender, ethnicity, and sexual orientation," and acquired diversity, which comes from experience, "such as working in another country . . . [or] selling to female consumers."[22] The researchers found that companies with both kinds of diversity, which they called "2-D diversity," had better innovative performance. Specifically, they found that "companies with 2-D diversity out-innovate and out-perform others. Employees at these companies are 45% likelier to report that their firm's market share grew over the previous year and 70% likelier to report that the firm captured a new market."[23]

Research by Deloitte concurred that

> high-performing teams are both cognitively *and* demographically diverse. By cognitive diversity, we are referring to educational and functional diversity, as well as diversity in the mental frameworks that people use to solve problems. . . . Demographic diversity, for its part, helps teams tap into knowledge and networks specific to a particular demographic group. More broadly, it can help elicit cognitive diversity through its indirect effect on personal behaviors and group dynamics: For example, racial diversity stimulates curiosity, and gender balance facilitates conversational turn-taking.[24]

This raises the possibility that researchers who find different results when testing for diversity's effect on innovation might (unintentionally) be examining different situations—some in which there is just one kind of diversity, and some that have both inherent and acquired diversity. Maybe joining both kinds of diversity with the right organizational policies and culture would produce consistent innovation benefits and, with it, a consensus about diversity's effect on innovation.

Business Model Innovation

A restaurant start-up I worked with wanted to increase its social impact by helping long-term unemployed people reenter the workforce. But the company realized that additional skills and resources, such as time management and transportation assistance, were needed if it was going to help people get back into the workforce. The firm built those needs into its hiring and training processes and expanded its training programs to better prepare candidates. (By the way, the start-up didn't try to do this alone; it partnered with organizations dedicated to assisting individuals transitioning into the workforce.)

Values-based innovation cuts across many areas of operations, but it's worth examining on its own terms as well. Asking how you can do more to promote your values, and how you can do less that isn't in line with them, will open new avenues of exploration. You are likely to find that values-based constraints and perspectives yield new insights and creative ideas—that you, too, benefit from "the freedom of a tight brief."

The restaurant company's training program was successful both in giving new employees the skills they needed and in delivering the types of cost savings we've been detailing: more loyal and motivated staff who stayed with the company longer. But there was a limit to how many people the restaurant alone could hire, especially when its staff members were more loyal and therefore stayed longer than the industry average.

Using creativity and innovation techniques, a new solution presented itself: train people in the company's excellent and proven program, and then offer other restaurants and hospitality companies the chance to hire program graduates. The start-up also earned a fee for this, opening an entirely new revenue stream. A local workforce development agency helped fund this expanded training program since it furthered the organization's objectives too. The restaurant firm helped far more people, cut its own costs, and took in more revenue, all because it looked for innovative ways to do more good.

Now More than Ever: Innovation

Innovation has been near the top of business priority lists for years, and there's no reason to think that will change. As an illustration, in 2021, Tata Consultancy Services asked more than 1,200 senior executives to choose the three most important aspects of their company's culture through the middle of the decade: "Between now and 2025, what do you anticipate will be the three most important aspects of your organization's culture (in ranking order)?"

Innovation came out on top.[25] Companies may not think their values and their diversity and inclusion strategies are connected to their innovation performance, but they are—and even more so now than in the past. As the participation of women and younger generations changes the workforce, missing the opportunity for more innovative work from mixed-gender teams becomes a greater loss.

This dovetails with the research mentioned earlier: after finding that gender-diverse teams produced better, more innovative scientific papers, the team wrote that "team gender balance is a phenomenon at the center of a confluence of changes in the composition of the workforce, innovation, fairness, and inclusion. In this sense, our findings provide a different lens on potential gender and teamwork synergies that correlate with the rate of scientific discoveries and inform opportunities in DEI initiatives."[26] Maybe that's why, in the research of Tata Consultancy Services, respondents' top priority after innovation was "diversity, inclusion, and equal opportunity."[27]

Inefficiencies are supposed to be fixed, and profit opportunities captured, in the natural course of business, with no values lenses required. But is that always the case?

IBM's semiconductor plant in Vermont, you recall, had been working against very efficient competitors for years. In fact, the facility had been operating for decades before the desire to reduce water consumption uncovered new efficiency opportunities. Grounding the examination of water use in the value of environmental protection enabled IBM to see a savings opportunity that had gone unnoticed for many years.

Groupthink

Acting on values helps make your company smarter in other ways as well, including by breaking up groupthink, a phenomenon that leads to worse decision-making. (The American Psychological Association defines groupthink as "a strong concurrence-seeking tendency that interferes with effective group decision making."[1])

Group decisions suffer when groups share blind spots, when group members assume others think as they do, and when a desire for conformity prevents individuals from raising objections or alternative points of view. Although many discussions of groupthink emphasize the pressure on individuals to conform, for the purposes of this chapter, the most interesting aspects of groupthink are the tendencies for group participants to think similarly (regardless of whether they feel the pressure to conform) and assume that others think the same way they do (even when that isn't true).

Consider the case of venture capital firms. Venture capitalists make decisions with clear financial results (the eventual value of their investments), and they have very strong incentives to maximize the returns their investments generate. This makes them good candidates for examining whether homogeneous or diverse decision makers make better, more profitable decisions.

Professor Paul Gompers spent years examining thousands of venture capitalists and tens of thousands of their investing decisions. The research he and his team conducted found that groupthink was surprisingly prominent: "Along all dimensions measured, the more similar the investment partners, the lower their investments' performance. For example, the success rate of acquisitions and IPOs was 11.5% lower, on average, for investments by partners with shared school backgrounds than for those by partners from different schools."[2]

Shared backgrounds (partners having attended the same schools, even if in different years) isn't something that gets a lot of attention, but that doesn't mean it doesn't matter. Though people from various backgrounds attend the same schools but take different classes from different instructors, the similarities in what they learn and how they're taught were enough to lower the quality of investment decisions.

REDI

While relatively few companies have values-based policies to increase the diversity of schools where they recruit, many do have policies to increase racial, ethnic, and gender diversity among managers. Having women and minorities underrepresented at the management and executive levels of the firm[3] simply doesn't sit right with many companies, so they attempt to change it.

This is, of course, the right reason for taking values-based actions: you should do the right thing because it's the right thing to do. Centering values, such as inclusivity and fairness, is essential. But that doesn't mean such actions don't also have business and financial consequences: they do. I call these financial consequences REDI—the return on equity, diversity, and inclusion.

Intuitively, if shared school background is important enough to matter to decision quality, you might think that shared ethnic and gender backgrounds would also have groupthink consequences—and thus that putting into practice values like equality, diversity, and inclusion would have business benefits. But do they?

In a word, yes. While shared schooling mattered, Gompers's team found that the effect of shared ethnicity was even stronger, reducing an investment's comparative success rate by 26.4 to 32.2 percent.[4] Their conclusion was that "diversity significantly improves financial performance on measures such as profitable investments at the individual portfolio-company level and overall fund returns."[5]

This isn't just the case for investment decisions; there is evidence that this same relationship holds at the company level. In fact, the connection to financial performance seems to be increasing over time. For example, McKinsey issued three different reports on the value of diversity in 2015, 2018, and again in 2020. In the last of these, the firm summed up a half decade of findings, with the most recent iteration encompassing over a thousand companies across fifteen countries: "Our latest report shows not only that the business case [for diversity] remains robust but also that the relationship between diversity on executive teams and the likelihood of financial outperformance has strengthened over time."[6]

The report found that companies in the top quartile for gender diversity on the executive team had a 25 percent greater chance of financially outperforming than those in the bottom quartile, a difference that had increased from 15 percent in their first analysis. Further, the researchers found a "dose-response" relationship between the percentage of women on the management team and performance: "the greater the representation, the higher the likelihood of outperformance. Companies with more than 30 percent women executives were more likely to outperform [than] companies where this percentage ranged from 10 to 30, and in turn these companies were more likely to outperform [than] those with even fewer women executives, or none at all. A substantial differential likelihood of outperformance—48%—separates the most from the least gender-diverse companies."[7]

This finding strengthens the case for the relationship being causal and points out the downside of not acting on values. While the difference between the top and bottom quartiles was 25 percent, notice that the gap nearly doubles to 48 percent for the most and least gender-diverse companies.

In 2021, Credit Suisse updated its Gender 3000 report, which analyzed over thirty-three thousand executives at more than three thousand companies in forty-six countries. The firm found "200 basis points [2 percentage points] of alpha generated by those companies displaying gender diversity above the average vs those below. ESG scores are also superior. Furthermore, the latest report highlights that the best-performing companies display superior diversity in both the boardroom and the C-Suite."[8]

Since alpha is "an investment strategy's ability to beat the market, or its 'edge,'"[9] companies with above-average gender diversity beat below-average firms in terms of stock market return by two full points. Given that the average long-term return on a stock is about 10 percent,[10] this bump of two points equals about a 20 percent performance premium for companies with more women executives.

Performance and Racial and Ethnic Diversity

Similarly, when examining racial and ethnic diversity, companies whose executive teams were in the top quartile for diversity were 36 percent more likely to outperform financially. That is, firms with more diverse executive teams were far more likely to have higher profitability, and this was the case for all three of McKinsey's analyses in 2015, 2018, and 2020.

There is disagreement about findings like McKinsey's,[11] and not all studies have had the same results. That's not surprising as so many factors influence financial performance—the overall economy, the regional economy, company strategy, quality of competitors, and how well a business executes. And there are so many ways to slice the market for a study, such as McKinsey's 1,500 global corporations, or firms listed in the S&P 500,[12] or even by sector or geography.

While there are many potential explanations for why studies differ on the effect of diversity on performance—different initial attitudes affect results, as do different management approaches—in many cases, just showing that diversity doesn't hurt financial performance is enough. This is as it should be; since inclusivity and fairness are important values in themselves, if a firm wants to pursue an important value and it doesn't hurt the company financially, then that makes sense. But if you look more deeply, a stronger financial case for diversifying management emerges. There are many factors impacting companies' overall financial performance, and these may overpower the beneficial effects of increased diversity. That isn't specific to diversity—those factors may also be stronger than a good marketing team or a high-quality sales force.

But the fact that good marketing and top salespeople don't guarantee you'll outperform your competitors if your products aren't great, or your tech is obsolete, or your competition is exceptionally good doesn't mean good marketing and top salespeople aren't good to have! If diversity improves team performance within a company, then it has business benefits even in cases where those benefits don't overcome the bottom-line effect of other factors.

Diversity and Team Performance: Conformity Effects

For the explanation of a relationship—such as that between diversity and increased performance—to be credible, it needs to fit the data. But that's not enough; it also needs to include a causal explanation, a reason why the relationship exists. With that in mind, what's the causal explanation for why more diverse groups and companies would perform better? One core reason is better decision-making. More diverse groups have different perspectives, and those different perspectives lead

---

The Importance of Design and Execution

Businesses have been trying to create more diverse, equitable workforces for years, with mixed success. (As just one example, the representation of women in the C-suite went from 20 percent in 2017 to 26 percent in 2022;[13] while an improvement, this is still far below their 48 percent share of entry-level employees.) Not everything that has been tried to improve the situation has worked—just like in any area of business. Some diversity programs don't work, and some can even backfire.[14]

Quite a few initiatives *do* work, however, and they can help to generate the benefits for innovation and decision making covered in this chapter. Centering inclusion,[15] focusing on a learning orientation,[16] encouraging involvement from managers,[17] aligning personal values with organizational ones,[18] and generally using evidence-based practices[19] are all ways to increase the likelihood your program succeeds.

---

to better decision-making by reducing groupthink and expanding the possibilities that get considered. That is, groups that have more diversity in thinking (more "cognitive diversity") make better decisions.

Of course, cognitive diversity doesn't only come from identity diversity—gender, ethnicity, and background—but the two, as Professor Scott Page of the University of Michigan says, "often go hand in hand. Two people belonging to different identity groups, or with different life experiences, also tend to acquire diverse cognitive tools."[20] This doesn't mean that any individual is smarter or more valuable because of the way they think. In fact, the point is that cognitive ability ("smarts") and diversity are different—and complementary—and this makes the outcomes of team thinking stronger.

As mentioned earlier, one way this happens is that diversity reduces groupthink, in part by reducing the pressure to conform. In fact, this pressure is one of the best-understood reasons why groupthink leads to worse decision-making. One example of this is a set of experiments conducted by a team led by Sarah E. Gaither of Duke and Evan P. Apfelbaum of the MIT Sloan School. The team wanted to see how subjects' tendency to conform changed depending on whether the group they were in was homogeneous or diverse. All subjects were told that their group was to recommend candidates for admission to college, but some subjects were placed in all-White groups, while others were assigned to diverse groups. In both cases, three planted confederates endorsed admitting clearly inferior college applicants, after which the subjects were asked which applicant they would select.

The experimenters wanted to know if the subjects would go along with the confederates' preference for the clearly weaker applicant or not. The results were clear: "Participants in diverse groups were significantly less likely to conform than those in homogeneous groups."[21] In fact, this was true even when the entire experiment was conducted online, with no in-person interaction at all.

The researchers suggested that this may not have been solely about feeling a conscious pressure to conform but also that group members seem more likely to trust the judgments of others who are superficially like them, even when those judgments are objectively poor, as in this case. As they wrote, "this evidence dovetails with recent work arguing that people become overly reliant on and responsive to others' decisions in homogeneous settings."[22]

And this is true even when the individuals are not part of a team, as shown by research involving small stock markets especially created for the experiment. After getting to know the other study participants, individuals were randomly assigned either to an ethnically homogeneous market or to a diverse one. The result was that "across markets and locations, market prices fit true values 58% better in diverse markets. . . . Specifically, in homogenous markets, overpricing is higher as traders are more likely to accept speculative prices. Their pricing errors are more correlated than in diverse markets. In addition, when bubbles burst, homogenous markets crash more severely."[23]

Diversity and Team Performance: Deliberation Effects

Diversity's positives go beyond reducing conformity; it also improves information processing and deliberation behavior. A study of two hundred participants led by Samuel Sommers placed participants on mock juries, some with all-White members and some with diverse members. Diverse groups containing both Black and White members performed better than all-White groups in several important areas. Diverse juries "deliberated longer, raised more facts about the case, and conducted broader and more wide-ranging deliberations. . . . They also made fewer factual errors in discussing evidence and when errors did occur, those errors were more likely to be corrected during the discussion."[24]

What caused the changes? It wasn't just the input of Black participants; there were also changes in the behavior of the White participants. As Sommers wrote, the difference "was not wholly attributable to the performance of Black participants, as Whites cited more case facts, made fewer errors, and were more amenable to discussions of racism when in diverse versus all-White groups."[25]

Obviously, more facts, fewer errors, and a greater willingness to discuss sensitive issues such as racism produce advantages when it comes to decision-making. But the advantages don't stop there. More diverse groups also process information differently and better.

Diversity and Team Performance: Information Processing

People react differently to the opinions of people they see as different from themselves compared to opinions voiced by those seen as being like them. In one case, when researchers tasked pairs of people with solving a murder mystery, participants behaved differently when they were told that the other member of their pair was from a different political party than they were.

Before meeting their partner, each person was told their partner's political affiliation, Republican or Democrat. Then they were informed about the case and were asked to write their thoughts on who committed the crime. Finally, they were told that their partner disagreed with them and to prepare for a meeting with that partner to decide who had committed the crime.

When the partner was of the same political affiliation, people prepared less thoroughly for the partner meeting; those who were told their partner supported a different party than they did prepared noticeably more thoroughly. These differences in preparation affected the quality of the final decisions; groups with differing party affiliations correctly identified the perpetrator far more often.[26]

If talking with someone with differing political views can change how people approach decisions, how about teaming up with someone from a different racial or ethnic background? In a study led by Anthony L. Antonio of Stanford, researchers found that hearing a dissenting opinion from someone of another race or ethnicity was perceived differently than dissent by a member of their own ethnicity—even when those opinions were identical. The researchers created groups of four students. Three White students read information about an issue and wrote two short essays about their position, one before a group discussion and one after. The fourth group member (unbeknownst to the other three) was part of the experiment and, during the group discussion, didn't convey their individual opinion but rather followed a specific script. In this way, the researchers could control the content of the fourth group member's contribution to the discussion.

Some of those planted group members were White and some were not. The researchers found that—even when the actual content was the same—what the fourth group member said was seen as more novel when coming from someone of a different ethnicity.[27] That is, to a significant degree, the other group members' judgments of the exact same opinion were affected by whether that opinion was voiced by someone who looked like them or not.

If diversity can affect how people perceive information, can it also affect group effort and performance? Researchers from the University of Illinois attempted to answer that question.[28] They wrote that "we put together three-person groups—some consisting of all white members, others with two white members and one nonwhite member—and had them perform a murder mystery exercise. We made sure that all group members shared a common set of information, but we also gave each member important clues that only he or she knew. To find out who committed the murder, the group members would have to share all the information they collectively possessed during discussion."[29]

This design added realism to the experiment as, in a real corporate setting, this would happen naturally: people are often added to teams precisely because of their unique perspectives. Of course, individuals with different perspectives are only valuable to the extent that the group takes advantage of those differences. Here there was a difference between the types of groups: the homogeneous groups perceived team members' information to be less unique and, relatedly, spent less time discussing the task.[30]

If these results seem similar to those of the mock jury experiments discussed earlier, they should. The same dynamic seems to be at play, where implicit assumptions lead homogeneous groups to less examination and deliberation. Or, as Professor Phillips put it, "being with similar others leads us to think we all hold the same information and share the same perspective."[31]

As you might imagine, then, "the groups with racial diversity significantly outperformed the groups with no racial diversity."[32] Teaming up with people of a different race led to inquiring more about what each knew and working longer on the task and thus led to better performance.

No doubt the presence of groups that deliberate better, use more information, and are less vulnerable to groupthink goes a long way toward explaining why more diverse companies perform better. Overall, we now know that—as the head of Novartis's investor relations group put it in 2021—diversity improves decision-making.[33]

Better Acquisitions

One way these better decisions show up is that companies with women in the boardroom make fewer acquisitions and pay lower prices when they do. One research team found that—in another example of diversity combating groupthink—female board members moderate the overconfidence of male directors and CEOs, resulting in better acquisition decisions. They said that "female participation in the boardroom attenuates the CEO's overconfident views about his firm's prospects as we find that male CEOs at firms with female directors are less likely to hold deep-in-the-money options," an indicator of overconfidence [34] No significant effects were found on the behavior of female CEOs.

Overconfident CEOs are not randomly distributed; they are more prevalent in some industries than others. When the team looked at those industries specifically, they found that "female directors are associated with less aggressive investment policies, better acquisition decisions, and improved financial performance for firms operating in industries with high overconfidence prevalence."[35]

Companies with women on their boards aren't *timid*, however, just more rational in their risk-taking. In fact, while such boards are more likely to be cautious in some areas, they are *more* likely to take risks in others.[36] After scrutinizing a decade and a half of S&P data (1997–2013), researchers found that board gender diversity "aligns a firm's risk exposure closer to risk-neutral shareholders' preferences" by being cautious with reputation risk exposure and bold with financial risk when a great deal is within reach.[37]

Uncovering Value in Values-Based Procurement

Just as different lenses can lead to better decision-making, they can also uncover value elsewhere, such as in procurement (what a company buys and from whom). Purchasing is both economically important and an area where a company can show its true values since some of the biggest impacts a company can have are outside of its "four walls." For most companies, the majority of their environmental impacts come from what they buy (e.g., how ingredients are grown, how parts are manufactured). It's not just environmental either; normally their suppliers employ several times more people than they do, shaping their social impact. (One company I worked with employed under one hundred thousand people directly, while its supply chain employed over a million.)

Because of supply chains' importance, many companies have policies preferential to suppliers with better environmental records, or that prohibit buying from firms who fall short in terms of combating forced labor in their own vendors, or on providing safe working conditions for their own staff. Such policies not only help realize a company's values, but they actually create value. One company I worked with, with over one hundred thousand vendors, instituted a policy of grading those suppliers on their environmental performance, and giving preference to those who did better. In so doing, it discovered that the more environmentally sound suppliers also had better performance (e.g., quality, speed) over time.

Because poor quality and shipping delays have costs, this led to financial gains as well. As a result, even on those occasions when a less-sustainable vendor offered a lower price, it was often still financially beneficial to buy from the more sustainable ones after quality and delay costs were factored in. But buying from the better environmental performer usually *didn't* cost more, at least over the medium and long term. This meant the quality, delivery, and other advantages (including environmental ones) were, in effect, free, making the net benefits even greater.

The reason those better environmental performers could also deliver higher-quality and better on-time performance for the same total cost was because their operations benefited from having put on their own values lenses. To care for the environment according to their values, they needed to look differently at operations and needed to create better systems to foster better performance. As in the case of IBM's water reduction efforts, this led to operational improvements as well.

Partnering with vendors providing better working conditions and pay was similarly profitable. Those suppliers had lower attrition, higher productivity, and more consistent quality. In addition, they were less likely to have labor disruptions, such as strikes and slowdowns (even in nonunionized facilities). The cost of increased frequency of labor disruptions, once quantified, was much higher than small differences in purchase price.

The Benefit of Balance: Sodexo

Sodexo is a global leader in food service and facilities management, serving about one hundred million people per day. With almost a half-million employees, Sodexo is also one of the biggest private employers in the world—and a leader in corporate responsibility and sustainability.

Sodexo conducted a study of gender balance and team performance from 2011 to 2014, collecting data from over fifty thousand managers at over seventy entities worldwide. The conclusion: gender balance is a significant driver of performance. When under 40 percent of management teams were women, performance suffered, and the same for men—teams that were more than 60 percent women were also not optimal. In 2015, Sodexo's CEO put it this way: "teams with a male-female ratio between 40 and 60 percent produce results that are more sustained and predictable than those of unbalanced teams."[38]

During that study, Sodexo found examples of superior performance on internal, customer, and profitability measures. For example, "between 2010 and 2012, the employee engagement rate of gender-balanced teams around the world increased by an average of four percentage points, against an average of one percentage point in the case of unbalanced teams. Similar findings show correlation between gender diversity and other business metrics, including consumer satisfaction and operating profit."[39]

After the publication of these results, however, Sodexo expanded the study further. In 2018, the company analyzed five years of data, focusing specifically on the performance of gender-balanced teams with between 40 and 60 percent women managers. Sodexo again used data from fifty thousand managers, along with examining the representation of women at different management levels.[40]

The results reaffirmed Sodexo's previous findings: "Teams managed by a balanced mix of men and women were more successful across a wide range of outcomes" compared to teams with gender-imbalanced management.[41] Specifically, teams with gender-balanced management had advantages on operating margins, employee retention, client retention,

Where to Start

Earlier, you identified your company's values: where it focuses on doing good for the world and those in it and how those values could be incorporated into products and services. Now, it's time to see what's behind the products—operations—through the lens of values.

One company realized that 40 percent of its employees were female but that 44 percent of decision-making groups did not include women,[42] which dramatically increased the chances of making suboptimal decisions.

Taking action to address the underrepresentation of women, minorities, and those without college degrees (or whose degrees aren't from the usual set of schools) is the right thing to do, and it's also a values-based action that helps combat groupthink. It also makes the remaining steps that much more effective.

Next, ask those involved to rethink how the process can do *less* of what you *don't* want rather than just more of what you do want—such as lowering waste and material use. In addition to operationalizing values, you may find resources or time savings you didn't expect as a result of changing the lenses through which you see your operation.

Then switch it up: look for opportunities that result in what you *do* want rather than what you don't. In the restaurant example, the start-up made its training program result in a greater number of skilled employees and even a new revenue stream.

Reexamine procurement as well. If your company wants to help reduce poverty or increase the economic development of a locale, can it buy from producers that pay a living wage or that operate in an area short on jobs?

Can your firm seek out suppliers owned by women or minorities or help small businesses scale up so they can sell more to you as well as to others?

Can you prioritize buying from environmentally and socially responsible suppliers, creating relationships that lead to improved operational performance as well? If you do these things, it's highly likely that, over the long term, doing so won't cost more—instead, it will end up being more profitable.

In sum, learn to see what you buy, what you produce, how your decisions are made, and how you operate through the lens of values. That lens will reveal hidden opportunities to create value as well.

safety, and employee engagement. And these benefits included not just static outperformance but superior growth and improvement rates as well. Take operating margins as an example: the number of entities significantly increasing their operating margins over a two-year period was 8 percentage points higher for teams with gender-balanced management. The same was true of safety: workplace accident rates were 12 points better among gender-balanced teams.[43]

When you put the picture together, you see acting on values leading to more efficiency, innovation, and better decision-making. And that leads to better business performance.

IV   CORE Risk

Since the year 2000, there have been numerous pandemics, such as swine flu, bird flu, SARS, and MERS, and many of these disrupted companies' operations, especially in Asia. Starting in 2018, one of the largest insurance companies in the world offered a pandemic insurance policy to protect against the financial implications of these disruptions. How many customers bought it? One.[1]

This part covers the growing threats, increasing vulnerabilities, and higher-magnitude consequences that businesses face today, along with how values help firms see these challenges sooner and deal with them better.

Cross-Cutting Risk

Risk cuts across all CORE business functions: from the risk of losing customers who adopt new purchasing criteria to operational risk from overloaded electrical grids to employee risk stemming from difficulty attracting and keeping key employees. It's also a bigger part of business today than before:

- More customers are changing what matters to them while, at the same time, competitors are closing previous gaps around quality, price, and availability.
- More infrastructure is getting stretched thin, from electrical grids to major shipping ports.
- More employees have a choice in who they work for as remote work becomes increasingly common.

- More issues are approaching thresholds where their severity rises significantly—such as when temperatures become high enough that it's physically hard for people to work or when flooding becomes common enough that fewer insurance companies offer flood insurance at all.

Since risk has its own special characteristics and is growing ever more important, it merits its own section in the CORE framework. In fact, because of the nature of risk—especially risks related to the environment and society—it needs not only its own section within CORE but also some additional, risk-specific frameworks.

The TVM (Threat, Vulnerability, and Magnitude) Model

The risk model I suggest is different from the traditional one in two ways: first, it includes submerged risk and, second, it explicitly breaks out vulnerability. Submerged risks, like submerged value, matter a lot. Because they're usually missed, they have more potential to create problems since a risk going unseen almost always leads to an organization being unprepared. They are therefore critical to identify, and as a bonus, once you raise submerged risks to the surface, a new set of previously hidden opportunities appears.

In terms of vulnerability, the risk model Valutus uses is adapted from one used in IT.[2] That's because, like IT risks such as malware (e.g., viruses), a number of environmental and social threats effectively have a 100 percent chance of occurring—which makes a traditional likelihood and magnitude model not quite right. To address these risks properly, you need a model that includes vulnerability as well, which is what the TVM model does. I'll say more about the TVM model in just a minute, but I'll first provide a very brief sketch of the traditional model.

The Typical Model

Typically, people consider the seriousness of risks by exploring what could happen and then, for each item, how likely it is to happen (likelihood) and what the consequences would be if it did (magnitude). The model typically used is to multiply likelihood and magnitude together. For example, say there's a 5 percent chance of something happening. If it does happen, it would cost $1,000 to recover from, which means the value at risk is 5 percent (likelihood) times $1,000 (magnitude), or $50. As risk models go, this one is very popular because it's not too complicated and it's a big improvement over not thinking rigorously about risk. But it's still not quite right.

Weaknesses of the Traditional Model

The traditional model doesn't quite match up with some of the big types of risks that matter in today's world. For one thing, there are risks that are 100 percent likely: they *are* going to happen. For instance, if you're on the Internet long enough, there is a 100 percent chance that someone will try to send you a computer virus, a Trojan horse, or some other kind of malware. Similarly, there is a 100 percent chance that the next few years will see a continued warming trend in global temperatures because the physics are already baked in based on the level of greenhouse gasses (GHGs) already in the atmosphere.

If the likelihood of an event is 100 percent, then the only factor left in the traditional model is magnitude, how bad it is when the event happens. But there's something else that intuitively matters, so we call it out explicitly in our model: vulnerability.

Threat, Vulnerability, and Magnitude

A threat is something external that might happen (including the likelihood that it will happen). Vulnerability is internal, capturing how vulnerable you are to that particular type of threat. And magnitude is how bad the outcome would be if your vulnerability is high enough that you suffer consequences from an event.

In the TVM model, threats (such as the possibility of being sent a computer virus) are separated from vulnerability (such as how well you've protected your computer against viruses). Separating these two makes it easier to think rigorously about them. Consider the following simple example:

- External threat level: 100 percent. There's a 100 percent likelihood that someone will attempt to compromise your computer or phone.
- Initial vulnerability level: 5 percent. This is the chance that someone succeeds in compromising your device.
- Magnitude: $1,000. This represents the cost to repair the damage/recover from a compromised device.

The value at risk in this case would be 100% × 5% × 1,000 = $50. But what we're really looking for is a mismatch: if there is a mismatch between the external threat and the internal vulnerability, then you could find yourself paying a significant cost. On the other hand, a high external threat with low internal vulnerability—likely because you have taken real actions to reduce your vulnerability—offers much less risk.

To put it simply, threat is like the weather forecaster telling you the probability it will rain. Vulnerability speaks to whether you'll get wet or not. Maybe you'll stay inside, or perhaps you have a raincoat and umbrella. These precautions limit your vulnerability. Magnitude is the consequence of getting wet. Perhaps you'll have to pay to dry clean your clothes, or you'll miss the beginning of a social outing. Or maybe you won't get the job you were applying for because you were drenched when you arrived for the interview.

All these aspects are involved when thinking about risks and their consequences. The consequences are based in part on how much it rains and how windy it is. Another part is how protected you are from the rain (such as having a good set of rain gear), and the rest centers on what you were going to do (being late to meet friends is a much lower magnitude of consequence than losing a job offer).

I'll use the TVM framework to organize the three chapters in this part, one on threats, one on vulnerability, and the final one on magnitude. Note, however, that you don't have to adopt the TVM model to understand or benefit from this section or from the chapters in it.

A Note on Foreseeability

There's an addition that some people have made to the traditional model, which is how foreseeable a given risk is. Intuitively, this makes sense: if it's easier to foresee a risk, then it's easier to prepare for it and either avoid it altogether or at least mitigate its damage. This is a good point and completely valid.

However, people being who they are, sometimes a risk is completely foreseeable, but preparations still don't get made. Consider the case of some governments knowing that COVID-19 was a risk, yet they didn't do everything they should have to prepare for it. It's clear that foreseeability is a potential advantage, but whether foreseeability reduces harm depends on what happens next. That's why the Valutus model includes foreseeability but only as an element of vulnerability.

9 Threats

As discussed earlier, people increasingly see their purchase decisions as reflecting their values, which increases the threat if you are not aligned with those values. That is, they are internalizing the idea of "voting with their dollars" to a greater extent than used to be the case. They're not looking only at what a purchase can do for them but also at what it *says about them*.

Of course, they care about the product itself: how well it works and the benefits they get from it matter tremendously. But the fact that people increasingly see their decisions as saying something about themselves is a threat to companies—especially those without values alignment with their customers. A company producing a perfectly good product (at a perfectly good price) may suddenly realize that competitors have a potential weapon to steal market share away: better alignment with customers' values.

This has been the case for quite some time—companies have marketed products as a reflection of their customers for generations. They have made sales by implying that a particular automobile shows you have class or that a gift of jewelry shows how much you care. For example, during the early 2000s dot-com era, start-ups bought Aeron chairs (which retailed for over $1,000 each) in part because of what it said about them. As an article in *New York Magazine* put it, they "became shorthand for the countless companies that didn't have a clue how to make money on the Internet, but, man, did they have the know-how to set up a cool office."[1]

Clearly, buying products based on what it says about you isn't new. But there are several ways in which the current situation, and the resulting risk level, is very different.

A New Dimension of Competition

First, the emphasis on values has the potential to upend the existing order in the marketplace because it brings to the forefront a new dimension of competition. Even a company that has done an excellent job at traditional marketing now has to consider how to orient its brand with respect to values. It's fine to have a reputation as the product that people who have "made it" use, or the accessory that fashion-forward kids prefer, or even the gear that technological sophisticates use. But what if alignment with the customer's values closes in on that level of importance? Now, there's a new dimension on which companies must be positioned. A focus on values means that someone new could threaten the leader or someone completely new could upend the marketplace.

As an example of how this works that is not related to values, consider Dyson vacuums. The first time I came across a Dyson, I was visiting the Museum of Innovation in London. There was a display about this vacuum company I'd never heard of and how it had adapted a commercial technology designed for very large installations for use in the household market. One very distinctive thing about this technology was that it didn't require vacuum bags, so there was no loss of suction and no bag to be emptied.

But that wasn't what caught my eye. Dyson, I noticed, saw that vacuum cleaners had not, to that point, considered an entire dimension of customer choice: design. I remember someone describing the existing selection of vacuum cleaners as machines made by people with no passion for vacuums. It would be as if every car were designed to be completely utilitarian, by someone who had no interest in making it look interesting or sexy or different. But Dyson vacuums weren't going to be like that. They were going to be thoughtfully designed and aesthetically pleasing.

When I came back from that trip, the US vacuum market was still mostly dominated by big brands that had been around for years, such as Hoover and Electrolux. But a few short years after that, Dyson vacuum cleaners had taken over much of the American market, just as they had in the United Kingdom.

Introducing a new dimension of competition—design—was a real part of Dyson's success. It wasn't just that the vacuum was bagless, as remarkable as that was. Dyson "introduced a revolutionary design that made the vacuum nothing short of a cool and even 'sexy' purchase," Raina Kelley wrote in *Newsweek*.[2] A vacuum industry expert told the BBC, "They changed the nature of the product into an aesthetic lifestyle product, a status symbol."[3]

The speed of Dyson's success was extraordinary. From the time the first model launched in the United Kingdom, it took a mere eighteen months to become the best seller[4]—in spite of the fact that Hoover was such an entrenched brand that vacuuming was often called "Hoovering."[5]

This is why any new dimension of competition—such as values— can be either a threat or an opportunity. As people become more likely to see that their purchasing decisions reflect their values, a company that connects to those values can redefine the competitive set. If the results are anything like the introduction of Dyson vacuums, values have the potential to be transformative.

The Values Differentiator

Like design, values are not the primary determinant of purchasing for most people. Yet strengthening values *as a differentiator* matters because so many key factors that people use to make decisions cut across different brands. To put it plainly, values matter more when factors such as price, quality, and convenience are fairly similar. When products are seen as commodities, values can become a much bigger differentiator than when they're viewed as dramatically different.

One company I worked with surveyed thousands of customers and learned that being active in society and doing things for the environment were not at the top of customers' list of key decision-making factors. At the top were performance and price, followed by aspects such as service, quality, convenience, and style. Environmental and social actions were much further down the list. They seemed not that important—until we looked at their effect on purchase preferences. In the abstract, quite a few attributes were more important than environmental or social ones. But when you gave people the choice of buying from two different companies, one that was doing more to live its values and one that was doing less, the shift in preference grew dramatically. That's because products were close to evenly matched on price, performance, and style but not on values. Those were differentiators.

Values didn't matter as much in the past because there were bigger differences when it came to attributes such as price, performance, quality, and durability—and those were more important to the customer. But in today's marketplace, we constantly hear that products and categories are becoming ever more commodified. This means that the risk of falling behind on values becomes greater since there's less differentiation available on other dimensions to protect your brand.

Values in Communication

Values encompass both your products and how you get your message out, including whether you support channels that don't reflect customers' values. Communications firm Porter Novelli asked American consumers about this topic and found that "76% say if they see a company advertising on a platform that perpetuates hate speech and fake news, they will be more likely to boycott that brand."[6] (Note that this survey was conducted before the violent insurrection at the US Capitol on January 6, 2021, which brought even more attention to the problems of fake news and speech meant to incite.)

While people are more likely to boycott a company, it doesn't mean they definitely will, but it does increase the amount of risk. What the Porter Novelli result shows is that customers may turn away from you not just because of what you do or what you say but also because of *where* you say it.

Values are an available avenue of differentiation that is significantly underused for both individual consumers and B2B buyers. Although the other traditional factors are ranked by buyers as more important in decision-making, I've found that values, environmental impact, and social action really matter to people when they make buying decisions.

A Force for Good? Or Evil?

As an example of a company-facing values-related issues, consider Facebook (or Meta, to refer to it by its new name). Facebook makes an enormous amount of money on advertising, and it has sales reps, customer reps, and an enormous messaging apparatus and reach. But a small group of committed people, joined by other organizations, created Stop Hate for Profit and started pressuring advertisers to cut back their spending on Facebook's and others' platforms because of well-documented problems with extremism and hate groups. For example, as *Wired* notes, "Facebook's own research revealed that 64% of the time a person joins an extremist Facebook Group, they do so because the platform recommended it."[7] This effort didn't bring Facebook down. But quite a few large companies cut back on their Facebook ad spending even though Facebook reaches so many people.

Cutbacks cost Facebook money and market capitalization. On June 26, 2020, Unilever announced it would stop all advertising on Facebook, Instagram (owned by Facebook), and Twitter for the rest of the year because "continuing to advertise on these platforms at this time would not add value to people and society."[8] In a statement on its website, the company specifically cited its responsibility framework in explaining the decision. Facebook lost about $20 million in ad revenue that day and about 7 percent of its market capitalization.[9]

Of course, Facebook is a giant company. The $20 million in lost revenue is a fraction of what it makes per year. And, after a while, the company's stock went back up. (Although it then went down again, losing more than half of its market value in a span of under two years.[10])

But values also contributed to the company's woes. Recalling the revelations from whistleblower Frances Haugen, a reporter for the financial network CNBC wrote that "the main takeaway from the Haugen saga, which preceded [Facebook's] name change to Meta, was that Facebook knew of many of the harms its products caused kids and was unwilling or unable to do anything about them. Some US senators compared the company to Big Tobacco." Furthermore, the article continued, this values disconnect continues to dog the company. As a branding expert quoted in the same article put it, "I think the company still suffers from a lot of criticism and skepticism about whether they are a force for good or evil."[11]

The pattern is clear: your customers, whether they're individuals or giant corporations such as Unilever, are more likely than before to vote with their dollars. Tying customers' dollars to companies' values is a big and growing trend. You therefore face more risk if you lack values that include society, the environment, and other elements—or if you have them but don't discuss or act on them. The risks grow if you wait. Although stocks go up and down, beyond any specific company or incident, there's no need to wonder if this kind of customer behavior will spread—it will. The confluence of events, awareness, population changes, and other factors will make sure of that.

Customer Downside Risk

Years ago, I started helping companies think about the potential upside, that is, the benefits of aligning with their customers' values. (These are the benefits that were detailed in the section on customers, part II.) As my thinking has evolved over the years, however, I've added more risk emphasis to my approach. In addition to looking at the value (including the submerged value) of aligning with customers' values, I also started looking at the risks (including submerged risks) of not aligning with them.

For example, for one client Valutus talked to B2B customers and surveyed tens of thousands of individual consumers to see how much it mattered if one company was less aligned with their social or environmental values than another. The result? A lack of alignment on values can reduce sales by as much as 30 percent once buyers become aware of the alignment differences between companies.

At the extreme end, consider the case of companies that vocally supported an attack on democracy. The CEO of My Pillow, Mike Lindell, repeatedly pushed false claims that the 2020 election was stolen from Donald Trump and went to the White House to discuss declaring martial law.[12] Consumers who didn't appreciate this attack on democracy started to hold his company to account. One way they made their voices heard was to add reviews to the My Pillow pages of various online merchants. The *Washington Post* reported that one review on Amazon said, "It is okay not soft! But Mike Lindell wants to declare martial law in America, he won't be getting my business! Stick to pillows pal," while another said, "Horrible product, just like it's [*sic*] CEO."[13]

The repercussions went beyond bad reviews posted to online retailers. Companies that didn't want to be associated with undemocratic actions stopped carrying My Pillow. Bed Bath & Beyond, Kohl's, H-E-B Stores, the Canadian Shopping Channel, Wayfair, and others dropped these products.[14] Between consumers that care about democracy and the rule of law, and retailers who share those beliefs (or don't want to get caught on the wrong side of consumers who do), Lindell's company lost access to multiple retailers that he himself had called "good partners."[15]

It wasn't just My Pillow. Less visible companies also were held to account for their role in the January 6, 2021, attack on the US Capitol. A *Washington Post* article reported the following: "It can happen to businesses large and small alike. Suzi Tinsley, the owner of the Sugar Shack, a Menlo Park, Calif., candy shop, learned as much when a photo of her at President Trump's Jan. 6 rally was posted on Twitter, according to the *San Francisco Chronicle*. In response, her shop's Yelp page flooded with bad reviews, one of which read, 'If you support what happened in dc [*sic*] yesterday, patronize this establishment. If you don't support what happened, don't patronize this shop.' Her shop now has a rating of 1.5 stars out of five."[16]

(Notice that the article doesn't say Sugar Shack went out of its way to advertise Tinsley's support for the events of January 6, so it's not the case that she was trying to use it to drive business. Nonetheless, consumers who found out about it were very vocal, in keeping with the earlier discussion of vocality.)

Consumer Response to Laggards versus Leaders

Obviously, supporting a violent insurrection against the government of the United States is a bit of an outlier. But other, less over-the-top, actions also evoke a response from customers. For example, research I conducted showed that both consumers and B2B customers were less likely to buy from a company that was a laggard on environmental or social issues. In other words, not only would they support buying from a social or environmental leader, but they would also *avoid* buying from companies that were below average on those issues.

This risk cuts two ways. First, if your brand comes to be seen as below average, you can lose sales and customers. If your competitors start trumpeting their values, or your industry comes up with new standards for social or environmental performance, you may lose ground. Or if investors begin saying you're behind the curve, or if nongovernmental organizations publish a report to that effect, then you can lose customers.

The second risk is that the expectations, standards, and other organizations are not standing still. What is acceptable today in terms of acting on values may not be acceptable tomorrow and probably won't be. In our research, Valutus has found that opinions differ (even within the same company) about how motivated customers currently are by environmental and social issues. The one thing both sides agree on, however, is that the importance of those issues to purchase decisions is growing.

This is not to say that there is no downside at all to talking to prospects and customers about your values. In fact, Valutus conducted research, involving tens of thousands of individuals, that showed that things such as climate leadership can help you with some customers and hurt you with others. For example, we compared equal quality, equally priced products from two different companies, one a climate leader and one not. We found that many people showed an increased preference for the climate leader's product, but some showed the reverse—they were *less* likely to buy from the climate leader.

This doesn't mean that companies shouldn't talk to customers (and others) about their values—they should! There are three reasons for this:

- The *net* change in preference (which is what I've been using in the examples in this book) was still positive, meaning that, on net, climate leaders saw customers' preference for them increase.

- In other research, Valutus discovered that changing the words used affected how communications about values changed preference. In one case, a negative statement ("we oppose . . .") decreased preference by a bit under 10 percent, while expressing a very similar sentiment positively ("we support . . .") did not have that effect.

- This balance between those customers attracted by social or environmental values is, as discussed above, already positive. But it's not static: customers are making this more and more important to their decisions, which is making these kinds of values ever more important.

Giving a New Competitor a Try

It's clear that some investors will punish you and some of your customers will desert you if you go against their values. But it isn't just about the company itself; it's also about the competition. That was the discovery of a national household brand that makes cleaning supplies, household goods, and similar products.

Many of the company's products have competitors that command a bigger share of the market. For example, a competitor's laundry detergent has a much larger share than the company's detergent. A few years ago, company management decided to try a new approach in their advertising. They bought ads to inform consumers about their core values as a business and specific values-related actions they were taking, and they produced TV ads and ran print advertisements in big, prestigious publications. These ads generated a 30-percent-plus increase in their brand awareness, and they also increased the willingness of competitors' customers to consider switching. The increase in consideration was more than 8 percent,[17] from a single ad campaign that lasted less than a month—a very strong result.

As in many mature markets, detergent sales growth is modest. In the United States, sales of the liquid laundry detergent category in general increased 0.9 percent in 2020, while unit sales rose by 0.7 percent.[18] This means that even a small percentage of competitors' customers switching to the company's product could wipe out several years' worth of sales growth for the competition.

B2B Customers

If you have B2B customers who act as distributors, selling to other customers, you'll see a back and forth between the values of distributors and their end customers. Distributors may choose what to carry based on their own values, and they may be influenced by their customers' values. Many natural foods stores have had higher product standards in place for decades, and they've begun spreading to other types of businesses as well.

When Walmart began to establish sustainability standards over a decade ago,[19] it marked a major advance for the effort to mainstream the use of values-based standards in purchase and stocking decisions. Since then, Walmart and The Sustainability Consortium have continued to add new product categories, creating key performance indicators that cover more than one hundred categories.[20]

Along with tracking progress, this data is used to set baselines and benchmark suppliers. Imagine if one of your biggest customers started comparing your performance on values-related issues to those of your competitors, with those issues affecting what they buy and how they stock and display it (which significantly affects in-store sales). Would you be ready?

For large outdoor brands, REI's unveiling of its updated supplier sustainability standards in 2018 shook the market. The *Seattle Times* described its impact this way: "Suppliers that can't or won't meet REI requirements in areas such as manufacturing, labor safety and fairness, chemical usage, environmental impact, and animal welfare won't be considered for its store shelves."[21]

While it's not the size of Walmart, REI is a multibillion-dollar business and the largest customer for many outdoor brands, which brings into stark relief the consequences of losing access to its shelves. REI didn't cut off suppliers immediately; the standards were announced in 2018 but didn't have to be fully met right away. By late 2020, however, some products that were previously okay could get expelled. As the *Seattle Times* explained at the time of the announcement in 2018, "by the fall of 2020, every tent REI sells will be free of harmful flame-retardant chemicals. Sunscreens will not contain coral-reef-bleaching oxybenzone. Wool or down products will come from humanely treated sheep and geese."[22]

What would be the consequence of losing access to your largest customer? What about having only two years to reformulate key products so they no longer contain harmful chemicals, or having to change the animal-raising and production processes for everything you sell to your largest customer? That's what standards require for companies that sell to customers that are strengthening the role of values.

Now More than Ever: Falling Behind

Years ago, people would tell me that values, caring for the world, how you treat your people and suppliers—all of those factors—didn't matter and weren't going to matter in the future either. Nowadays, even when someone tells me that they are skeptical about how much values matter to their customers today, they typically add something like, "but I think in a few years it will matter more." Everyone can feel that social and environmental issues are growing in importance and that they'll be a bigger part of purchasing decisions in the near future—three to five years.

The risk is clear: if you're not moving forward, you're falling behind. When you consider customers' rising expectations that brands must articulate values and live up to them and then look at the increasing commoditization of products and services, you see that both these pressures push in the same direction, toward greater social and environmental performance expectations for brands.

As an illustration, consider the case of a multibillion-dollar US company that sells primarily to high-tech and science-focused companies. The year before working with Valutus, the firm had set an emissions reduction goal; at the time, the company's commitments put them in the top 25 percent of its industry. A year later, however, that same goal was in the *bottom* 25 percent. The company's competitors had accelerated, blowing right past the commitment made just a year before.

If customers' expectations are increasing (as are competitors' actions) and you're not moving forward to improve your own performance, you're falling behind. In fact, you're falling behind faster and faster on a competitive dimension that's quickly growing in importance. Add to this the fact that it's getting harder to win customers by having a product that's head and shoulders above the others or a service that's clearly differentiated. When it's harder to differentiate on the core attributes, values increase in importance. Falling behind on values is a huge risk to take.

Now More than Ever: Changes in the World

We are in a world of major changes, where disruptions happen more often. At Valutus, we refer to the period from 2020 to 2030 as "the decade of disruption" because disruptions will happen so regularly. This amplifies the riskiness of not performing well in social or environmental terms because many of the megatrends shaping this and future decades are related to the environment and society.

As mentioned in chapter 3, research Valutus conducted showed that climate change was the number one megatrend for this decade, with other values-related topics also among the top issues. As a result of the kinds of disruptions we're seeing, future success is not just about meeting customers where they are today, though they're placing more emphasis on values than they used to. It's also about anticipating where your customers are going tomorrow, and it's clear that they're headed for an even greater values emphasis.

Getting caught flat-footed by these changes represents a significant risk. If almost half (45 percent, according to Accenture[23]) of customers start to shop more sustainably and you're not ready for that—or are less prepared than your competitors—you could lose significant revenue very quickly. And if events this year and the next (and later in the decade) continue to reinforce and accelerate these shifts toward values, companies lagging on values will fall farther and farther behind.

Being ready means seeing these shifts coming, which requires engaging with your customers and markets around values. It also means doing more to emphasize acting on your own values, getting underway before a new set of upheavals rocks your market. Becoming more environmentally sustainable takes time since doing it well requires examining your supply chain, how your products are used, your production processes, and many other factors.

It also takes time to improve your effect on society and your own employees. This entails changing how people are evaluated and promoted, hiring differently, reworking "how things are done around here," and changing systems and processes. These things are quite worthwhile, but they aren't fast. It can take several years to make a big improvement, even in an area where techniques are well-known and tested, such as reducing GHG emissions. But changing how products are designed takes even longer, and it's slower still to make changes in things like gender balance in the workforce.

This is why you can't wait to begin changing your social and environmental performance or placing more emphasis on living your values. If you do, you'll just be getting started when others are realizing significant results. Couple that with consumers' and B2B customers' increased attention to values, and you risk playing catch-up while your competitors pull ahead. And it's far more difficult to get customers back than it would have been to keep them in the first place.

Now More than Ever: External Changes Drive Internal Ones

Here's another way changes in the world are increasing the risk that results from low environmental and social performance. People rarely change their views on what's important and how to make decisions—except when they see big important events in the world or in their lives. People's unchanging views are usually a recipe for stability, but the catch is that today's world changes more often and more significantly than in times past.

Expect more occasions when something in the outside world triggers your customers to reevaluate their priorities, as happened during the COVID-19 pandemic. Many people came to realize that their own priorities had become clearer, and some fundamental ones were amplified, such as the importance of family, the need to spend time outside, and the primacy of health. But here's the kicker: as the BBC reported, many people reacted to COVID-19 by elevating their values when it came to purchasing decisions: "with Covid-19 and the resulting lockdowns increasing work and financial insecurities for many of us, you might think that we have had to quietly drop our ethical and environmental concerns when shopping. However, numerous reports and studies have in fact shown that the opposite is true, and that coronavirus has focused our minds on helping to create a better, healthier world."[24]

Marketing data company Kantar, which boasts one hundred million survey respondents in ninety markets, found that the number of "eco actives" (environmentally conscious consumers) grew by 4 percent during the pandemic, while the number of consumers who dismiss ecological concerns ("eco dismissers") shrank by 8 percent.[25] In other words, COVID made people who are environmentally aware even more so, as it reduced the number of people who didn't care about ecological concerns.

Similarly, consulting company Accenture discovered major changes in consumer attitudes and behavior. It surveyed over three thousand people in fifteen countries on five continents and concluded that "the COVID-19 pandemic is likely to alter consumer behaviors permanently and cause lasting structural changes to the consumer goods and retail industries."[26]Changing behaviors were seen early on, as people adjusted to the pandemic and the new reality, for example, by ordering groceries online for the first time. People shifted their purchasing patterns rapidly—and permanently—creating additional risks for companies that don't follow suit.

Accenture's survey found that "45% of consumers said they're making more sustainable choices when shopping and will likely continue to do so,"[27] a similar amount to the percentage of people (50 percent) who shifted their consumption in a health-conscious direction. These results show that this reorientation wasn't strictly about their own health, even during a pandemic. It also included prioritizing their own values more highly when making purchasing choices. Accenture's global practice director for consumer goods summed the changes up this way: "the pandemic is likely to produce a more sustainable, healthier era of consumption over the next 10 years, making consumers think more about balancing what they buy and how they spend their time with global issues of sustainability—suggesting a healthier human habitation of the planet."[28]

This is a key insight: when there are major changes in the world, many people react by returning to their core values and reprioritizing, giving more emphasis to those values.

Now More than Ever: Demographics

The increasing focus of millennials and Gen Z individuals on values, society, and the environment is well-known yet still underestimated by many. Even in the middle of the worst of COVID, GlobeScan and

BBMG surveyed twenty thousand young people in twenty-seven countries and found that 60 percent of them wanted the post-COVID recovery to "prioritize restructuring our economy to deal with inequality and climate change rather than just getting back to normal as soon as possible."[29] Since, as ESG employee engagement technology provider WeSpire[30] notes, Gen Z will be 30 percent of the workforce soon,[31] it strongly indicates that their priorities—values—now animate a large fraction of that workforce.

Values are even more salient for the retail sales force since in 2020 over half of all US retail workers were between sixteen and thirty-four years old [32] and almost a quarter (twenty-three percent) were between sixteen and twenty-four years of age.[33]

Given that, among members of Gen Z, "75% believe that work should have a greater meaning than just bringing home the bacon," and that they "need to see [a] connection between what they are doing and broader social impact,"[34] would it be any surprise that they are more likely to identify with, purchase from, and recommend to buyers a company that shares their values? Or, conversely, that not showing your values risks having them buy from and endorse a competitor?

As millennials and Gen Z become bigger slices of the economy—in 2020, Gen Z comprised about 40 percent of US consumers—their beliefs about companies and values become more economically important as well. And this presents risks for those companies that fall behind on values. A 2018 report found that "40% [of Gen Z] have stopped purchasing or boycotted a brand or company because they stood for something or behaved in a way that didn't align with their values. Another 49% haven't done this yet but would consider doing it in the future."[35]

In other words, millions of consumers come from a generation that believes strongly enough in expressing values through their purchasing that four out of ten of them have already stopped purchasing or boycotted a brand because of values—maybe not every time, and maybe not even often, but this is still a major change. And the vast majority of those who haven't yet stopped purchasing or boycotted a brand would consider doing so in the future.

Now More than Ever: Vocality and Speed

Another factor is the increased vocality of people around issues of values. A large number of consumers want to avoid supporting companies whose values don't align with theirs. What's more, values issues make them more likely to be vocal about it. Increased vocality about values means that more people will find out that others feel your company has a values issue. That's why such issues garner more word of mouth than standard business concerns.

Compounding the effects of increased attention to values issues is the fact that Gen Z and millennials are already more likely to be vocal online than other generations. So, if you don't show your values related to the environment and society, you're out of step with individuals who are more vocal than most, about a specific issue that they're more vocal about. You face greater risk that other customers will hear from those who are unsatisfied with how you put values into action.

And there's an additional factor to consider: the speed of information. You've got more vocal people and issues about which they are more vocal. Now add the fact that communication around these issues moves quickly, another accelerant that could cause what looks like a smoldering risk to catch fire quickly.

An example of how quickly things can happen is that Loews Hotels was hosting a fundraiser for Josh Hawley, a US senator, in January 2021. Shortly after the violent attack on the capital, carried out by people to whom Josh Hawley gave a fist pump salute, a number of individuals and groups who value democracy started to call on Loews to decline to host the fundraiser. It took less than twenty-four hours for the pressure to build sufficiently for Loews to tell Josh Hawley that the company would no longer host a fundraiser for him—even though he was a US senator.

This speed of action stems partly from social media and the news cycle and partly from so many people who care about values. As a result, a message can find a more receptive audience than it would have in the past and spread more quickly. Many news stories that bring values to the forefront are big news stories in their own right, so they pour fuel on the fire. Put this all together, and you get a story like this: the CEO of a Canadian casino tried to skip to the front of the line for a COVID-19 vaccine and was fired for it within days.[36]

The speed is also driven by many organized groups that keep an eye out for behaviors that cross the line on their values. Organizations get more traction faster in today's media environment by putting pressure on others to make sure that key information, as they see it, gets spread faster. Of course, sometimes these organizations work at cross-purposes with each other. For example, a news release put out by a climate action group may be challenged by a climate disinformation organization, such as the Heartland Institute,[37] and then the original storyline is reinforced by something like a letter from BlackRock CEO Larry Fink. Each organization tries to shape the message and control the speed of its spread.

Each plays a predictable role. The climate action group wants to make people take the climate crisis more seriously, while the Heartland Institute attempts to sow doubts and confusion about changes to the climate and Larry Fink links climate and related risk to company financial performance and thus investment performance. Meanwhile, some government figures may try to stop companies from shifting away from fossil fuels, while others spread misinformation and denial.

Denial is very harmful as it delays acting on important issues in a time of great urgency. But even strenuous denials end up not being able to stop change entirely. And that brings us back to where we started, with a convergence of customer-related trends that increase the risk of being cut short and losing revenue, market share, margin, distribution, or market value.

10 Vulnerability

Vulnerability is separate from magnitude and threat. It often doesn't get as much attention as it deserves, but it's a big part of understanding what's at risk. In fact, in daily life, it consumes a lot of our actions. For example, people buy antivirus protection for their computers to reduce their vulnerability to cyberattacks. Businesses buy insurance to reduce the chance they'll be ruined if there's a fire, they get sued, or their computer systems get hacked. And drivers leave a little bit early so that if there's more traffic than usual, it doesn't cause them to be late.

Giving vulnerability the attention it deserves matters for several reasons:

- People underestimate vulnerability because much of it is submerged.
- Sometimes events reinforce themselves, amplifying threats and greatly increasing vulnerability—and this is happening more often now.
- A lot of baseline factors have changed—for example, intense storms becoming more common—and threat levels have increased, which makes vulnerability more important.

Vulnerability Is Its Own Factor

Vulnerability deserves to be discussed on its own terms. When talking about risk, it often gets lumped in with threat levels or the likelihood of something going wrong, but it isn't either of those things. Interestingly, this is mostly a problem of intuition when it comes to business;

it's much clearer in day-to-day lives that it's different, with a lot of the things that people do on a regular basis being oriented around reducing vulnerability.

Take people's thinking about the risk of getting the flu (or COVID, or measles), for example. Of course, part of the thinking should be "how widespread is the flu right now?" (or even just "is it flu season?"). When the incidence of the flu is low, that's a low threat level. But when people decide to get a flu vaccine, that's something different—that's a reduction in their vulnerability. The vaccine makes them less vulnerable whether it's flu season or not.

Here you can clearly see the difference between threat and vulnerability. Threat is how prevalent the flu is, while vulnerability is how likely you are to get it if you are exposed to someone who is sick. (Magnitude would be how bad it would be for you if you got sick, such as being less bad if you are young and healthy versus worse if you are older and immunocompromised. Magnitude will be the subject of the next chapter.)

Vulnerability Matters More When the Threat Level Is High

Although threat levels and vulnerability are different, they are connected in a very important way: how vulnerable you are matters a lot more when the threat level is high. To continue the flu example, reducing your vulnerability by 50 percent matters a lot more to you when the chance of coming in contact with somebody who has the flu is 50 percent than it does when it's 5 percent. This is analogous to why vulnerability matters more now, which is that baseline threat levels are elevated—and increasing.

Changing weather patterns are causing more heat and lower water levels in rivers and lakes. What happens when the water level in the Rhine River in Germany is low enough that it's close to affecting the ability of ships to get through? Not only is that more likely now than before, but it has already happened. In August 2022, Bloomberg wrote that "the Rhine—a pillar of the German, Dutch and Swiss economies for centuries—is set to become virtually impassable at a key waypoint later this week, stymieing vast flows of diesel and coal. The Danube, which snakes its way 1,800 miles through central Europe to the Black Sea, is gummed up too, hampering grain and other trade."[1]

In this new reality, random events, such as a shipping accident, are harder to deal with because vulnerability is already higher. The possibility of major supply chain disruptions from a shipping accident was made clear when the container ship Ever Given blocked the Suez Canal in March 2021, causing a series of cascading issues. As reporter Hanna Ziady wrote for CNN Business, hundreds of other vessels were affected, with effects felt far and wide: "The blockage exacerbated container shortages, port congestion and capacity constraints that have made it much more expensive to move goods around the world and caused shortages of everything from exercise bikes to cheese at a time of unprecedented demand."[2]

This was the case even though, when the Ever Given was cleared, shipping was able to resume at regular speed. If low water levels slow baseline shipping speed (through the Rhine or the Danube or somewhere else), then supply chains are that much more vulnerable to random disruption and especially to severe disruption. It's like when you're driving: if there's an accident during a light traffic time, you are less likely to be made very late (i.e., your arrival time is less vulnerable to an accident on the route) than if that same accident happens during rush hour, when traffic is already heavy and slow. Lowered water levels because of changes in the climate have an effect similar to heavier, slower traffic: they increase how vulnerable your logistics and supply chain are to disruptions.

Climate, social, and other values-related issues are piling on top of other vulnerability-increasing factors, such as infrastructure operating near the peak of its capacity. A port that is already very busy is that much more vulnerable when a disruption strikes, which is exactly what happened in Vancouver, Canada. Kat Eschner of *Fortune* wrote that "in mid-November [2021], Vancouver's port was already piled high when record-setting rains resulted in flooding and mudslides that destroyed roads, bridges, and train tracks, effectively cutting off North America's third-largest trade hub from the rest of the continent."[3]

It's not just about shipping or environmental risks, however. Apple was hit by production problems because of political conflict between the US and China as well as China's stringent COVID lockdown policies. After Apple announced the iPhone 14, the combination of these two factors made it much more difficult for the company to produce enough phones to meet demand during the holiday shopping season. As one observer said, "Apple is discovering that geopolitics drive business models—not the other way around . . . This whole collection of supply chain risks are creating a real liability for them."[4]

From emphasizing security and ideological concerns to implementing a "zero COVID" policy for much longer than expected, as the *New York Times* reported, "China's leader, Xi Jinping, has forced business leaders to reconsider long-held assumptions about operating in the country."[5] But that same sort of rethinking is beginning to happen much more broadly as well. Ideologically driven actions aren't limited to the Chinese government, and the increasing likelihood of new diseases and new governmental conflicts are making the act of reassessing assumptions something companies around the world need to do.

This is especially true since vulnerability doesn't just come from the production side of the business. Whether it's COVID lockdowns in China or floods in Pakistan or conflicts leading to higher food and fuel prices, there are also lots of forces that can affect your customers. When they do, they can drive demand below what you anticipated as customers' disposable incomes or priorities change.

Amplified Disruptions

The vulnerability effects are even greater when the changes interact with, and amplify, each other. The Vancouver area suffered because of just such a cascade of events: drought caused vegetation to dry out, wildfires then scorched more of the area, and later heavy rains arrived and brought flooding. Had there been less of a drought, the wildfire season wouldn't have been as bad, and had there been more vegetation, more of the rain might have been absorbed. But instead, each factor amplified what followed. This eventually led to evacuations, train derailments, a pipeline getting shut down,[6] constriction of highway traffic, and a pileup of goods at the Port of Vancouver—Canada's largest port and the third largest in North America.[7] The result was months of problems and delays at a facility that usually processes over half a billion dollars of goods per day.

While the magnitude of the problem was increased by chance events (e.g., lightning strikes that can start wildfires), the combination of higher baseline vulnerability and more common amplifying events (e.g., drought) increased the danger. As the *New York Times* reported, "Experts said that events in this sequence—heat, fire, drought, flood— could produce so-called compound effects. . . . A drought can dry out vegetation, which in turn can fuel and intensify fires. Fire itself can weaken or kill plants and make the soil less permeable, meaning that rain is more likely to run off rather than soak in, causing flash floods and landslides."[8] It may seem unlikely for events to happen in this sequence, amplifying each other, but it will only get more common in the future. A *Forbes* headline stated it plainly: "Backlog at the Port of Vancouver Is a Sign of Supply-Chain Disruption to Come."[9]

Raised Baseline Risk

The reason that amplifying events will become more common is that the overall baseline of risk factors is changing. This is most obvious in terms of the climate, with average weather being hotter and drier and therefore producing more droughts—which, as Vancouver experienced, set the stage for more damaging floods as well. But it's not just heat and drought; changes in the climate mean rain will frequently be more intense. Because warmer air holds more moisture, on the occasions where there is rain, the total amount can be greater. In 2021, New York City experienced its first ever flash flood emergency, with intense rainfall reaching three to five inches (7.6–12.7 cm) per hour. Although it was the first time in the city's history that such a flash flood warning had been issued, it was the second time that the New York weather service had ever had to issue one. The first time was one hour earlier, when it issued one for New Jersey.[10]

The baseline for supply risk has also increased as companies have made their supply chains more complex and more global. This means they are more exposed to events that happen elsewhere in the world, especially if they are sourcing key inputs from only one place or only a handful of suppliers. Consider how chip shortages affected automakers after demand for cars returned following the easing of COVID: "by the end of March 2021, chip shortages forced Ford to reduce production significantly at six plants in North America and to cut it even further in June. Earlier in the year, the company said it expected to lose 50% of its vehicle production in the second quarter of 2021; in September, it said it would again cut truck production due to chip shortages."[11]

Even when there isn't a problem with sourcing parts and inputs, there is still a higher baseline risk for global supply chains due to the need for shipping. Here's what happened when demand began to return after the initial shock from COVID:

> As Western countries swung back to higher levels of economic activity, ports could not process the increased shipping volumes. . . . The result was long delays, with ships anchored for weeks outside major ports—and a consequent shortage of maritime containers that were stuck on waiting vessels and could not be reloaded and shipped. . . . Shipping costs skyrocketed: The cost to ship a container from Asia to the United States' East Coast climbed from around $1,400 per container to around $20,000.[12]

But it's not just a case of the climate baseline changing or even of physical risks changing. As mentioned in the section on customers, part II, the baseline of competitiveness is changing too. There is less differentiation between competitors and more commodified markets, meaning that the impact of sharing customers' values is greater—as discussed in part II—and so is the downside of being out of step with their values.

The musician Ye, who started his career as Kanye West, found this out after publicly making antisemitic comments, including posting on

Twitter that he was "going death con 3 on Jewish people." While he had risen to billionaire status because of his music and commercial successes, this statement made it clear that he didn't share the values that the customers of his company, Yeezy, wanted to be associated with. As a result, he was dropped by JPMorgan, Gap, Balenciaga, Creative Artists Agency, and others.

Adidas, which had a partnership with Ye's company Yeezy worth over $1 billion, severed its ties also. The company released a statement saying that it "does not tolerate antisemitism and any other sort of hate speech. Ye's recent comments and actions have been unacceptable, hateful and dangerous, and they violate the company's values of diversity and inclusion, mutual respect and fairness."[13]

According to estimates by *Forbes*, his antisemitic comments cost Ye hundreds of millions of dollars, dropping him out of the ranks of billionaires.[14] All of this happened fast—within three weeks from the time he posted his "death con 3" tweet.

Combining Amplifying Factors and an Increased Baseline Threat Level

Sometimes, the baseline level of risk rises because of the amplifying dynamics discussed earlier. In fact, it turns out that hate speech—a threat to social cohesion and peace—is an example of something that is currently headed toward a higher baseline because of other accentuating factors.

A trio of researchers discovered this when they used AI to assess about four billion tweets from Twitter users in the US and compare them to a United Nations definition of hate speech. The researchers found that "the prevalence of hate tweets was lowest at moderate temperatures (12 to 21°C) and marked increases in the number of hate tweets were observed at hotter and colder temperatures," with the increase at hotter temperatures almost double that resulting from lower temperatures (22 to 12.5 percent). They also found that the relationship between temperature and hate speech held across all climate zones and socioeconomic groups they examined.[15]

The effect of temperature on people's moods isn't limited to the US. An examination of over four hundred million social media posts by over forty million individuals in China similarly found that extreme weather made people more negative. The researchers also found that there was a noticeable effect of air pollution on mood. Although temperature was the factor that had the highest effect on the emotional content of people's posts, air pollution had a much stronger effect than many other factors they examined, such as precipitation.[16]

As the climate warms, it will increase the baseline frequency of periods of hate-speech-inducing temperatures. Recall that the study of US Twitter users found hot weather had about twice the effect on hate tweets as cold weather; in addition, when it came to users of Chinese social media, the temperature effect happened with both cold and hot weather, but heating mitigated the effects during periods of extreme cold, while air-conditioning had no such effect during periods of extreme heat. This suggests that as climate changes raise the baseline temperature, extremist postings, with all their negative effects on society (including physical violence[17]), cannot be mitigated simply by access to air-conditioning.[18]

An added element of the situation is that authoritarianism is growing around the world, and research suggests that people become more receptive to authoritarianism in the context of crises such as COVID and climate disruptions. Adding this to the increase in hate speech and violence creates an even more toxic stew, one that gets worse from the interaction of climate, heat, and authoritarianism.[19] Since many authoritarian governments lag on climate action, this has the potential to make the cycle a reinforcing one and therefore that much worse.

Luckily, a self-reinforcing cycle doesn't always take hold. However, even when it doesn't, new baselines can still increase the risk and frequency of amplified disruptions.

Vulnerability Factors: The V Model

Over two decades ago, I was working to identify—and remember— which factors led a company to need to hold inventory. Holding inventory lowers the risk of problems such as factories running out of parts, fulfillment not being able to meet a sudden increase in demand, or spikes in the prices of key inputs, so when circumstances make those events more likely, companies need more.

Years later, while thinking about vulnerability to events such as external shocks to a company's supply chain, customers, home countries, and distribution partners, I realized the model I'd created all those years ago was, at its core, about *risk*. Specifically, it was about key factors that affect *vulnerability*, such as:

- visibility
- variability
- velocity
- volume
- variety
- vitality

The "V Model," as I call it, isn't specific to values, so this chapter won't cover all its elements in detail. But it does illuminate many places where values help reduce vulnerability, and the focus of this chapter will be on those areas.

Visibility

Values can bring issues into focus faster (or, conversely, not using values lenses can lead to not seeing something important). In 2019 and 2020, surveys demonstrated that one of people's top two environmental concerns—along with climate—was plastic pollution.[20] While the issue of plastics had been pointed out before, how many people up to that time really thought it such a grave environmental concern?

More importantly, how many businesses that rely heavily on plastic, such as bottling and packaging firms just to name two, had contingency plans in place in case plastic pollution suddenly became a major issue? Few things render a company more vulnerable than being surprised by a big issue, particularly because, as mentioned above, the adjustments can take longer than the time you have to make them.

Before your changes are complete, the issue begins eating into your business.

Not having your vision expanded by values, and therefore having less advance notice of some of the key changes in the world, increases your vulnerability. As a quintet of McKinsey partners put it when writing about the benefits of companies having a sense of purpose across ESG priorities, "purpose can make you more aware of shifting external expectations, policy directions, and industry standards—thereby helping you identify risks you might otherwise miss."[21]

Such risks include changes in expectations and regulations. A year earlier, two (different) McKinsey partners had called this out in an article they wrote with Witold Henisz, a professor at the Wharton School at the University of Pennsylvania. "Bans or limitations on such things as single-use plastics or diesel-fueled cars in city centers will introduce new constraints on multiple businesses, many of which could find themselves having to catch up," they wrote[22]—and, not long afterward, plastic bag bans (as the State of New Jersey implemented in 2022) and the removal of diesel vehicles from cities (as Paris, Madrid, Mexico City, Athens, and Rome have committed to do by 2025)[23] were established features of the business landscape.

It's worth emphasizing that even when these trends are not encoded into regulations and bans, they still make a difference. If enough large companies go the route of hospitality giant Accor, for example, and commit to eliminating all single-use plastic,[24] it will have a large effect—even if other countries do not follow the lead of France and consider legislation mandating refill systems and restricting single-use plastics.[25] (Incidentally, Accor committed to achieving its plastic goals even while hosting 120 million guests and serving 200 million meals annually, making it hard for others to claim that taking action is just too difficult. And three years later, the company had met the goal at over 80% of its properties, over 4,000 total).[26]

As another illustration, consider what happened with fur. With no regulation in place, clothing manufacturers who use fur in their garments can no longer sell them at retailers such as Walmart, Macy's, Bloomingdale's,[27] or Nordstrom.[28]

Visibility and Validity

Visibility is best seen as a two-way street: it's important to see what's happening in the world and to enable people to see what you believe. If you don't make your values visible, your company can be seen as not sharing your customers' values even when it does. This increases your vulnerability to shifts in your customers' buying patterns and values because it's much easier for them to see you as misaligned with their new criteria.

Validity—whether or not the information you or others have is based on flawed assumptions, bad data, or misinformation—is another part of this dynamic. There is a lot of accidental misinformation out there along with quite a bit of intentional disinformation. This is true when it comes to disinformation purveyors trying to prevent you from seeing the realities of the world—such as climate deniers spreading disinformation about the reality and effects of climate change—and also when people are actively telling lies about your company.

For example, after Elon Musk bought Twitter, for a time he made it so anyone could have a blue checkmark—which had previously signified an account that was who it said it was—simply by paying $8 a month. Within days, some users started impersonating celebrities, major corporations, and public figures. One account pretending to be the pharmaceutical company Eli Lilly cost the company billions of dollars in market value.[29]

Companies can choose to adapt in a way that leads to even greater success in the future—perhaps by changing before competitors do and therefore gaining a better position to win in the new competitive environment. In contrast, brands that aren't seen as sharing their customers' values become increasingly vulnerable.

Variability

Demand can vary greatly and so can physical conditions, customer expectations, regulations, and many other factors. The more variation there is in key factors—such as temperature, supply, or demand—the more vulnerable you're likely to be and the harder it is to mitigate these vulnerabilities.

Over the years, I've done a good bit of work with companies in the apparel sector and having the right amount of the right garments at the right time has always been a challenge. For example, you don't want to run out of the hits in your spring line and miss sales, but you also don't want unsold spring inventory left when the season is over since it then (best case) has to be sold at a heavy discount. This has been a longstanding problem, with discounted or discarded clothing running into the billions of dollars. When you add increased external variability, things change further.

Sometimes areas of variability interact, such as seasonal and demand variability. Not long ago, I was talking with an executive at an apparel company, and she said that supply chain issues are making seasonal challenges worse since it's harder to get garments where they need to be on time. Compounding this is the effect of changes in the climate on seasonality—if fall comes later or is hotter (or spring comes earlier but is drier), that changes when people are looking to buy. This again makes it harder to get the right garments on the shelf at the right time, resulting in lost sales, unsold inventory, and increased discounting—or all of these.

Variability and Domino Effects

Although hospitality, travel, tourism, trade shows, and indoor shows were obvious casualties of COVID, plenty of other sectors were affected—often without having realized they were at risk. As we now know, a majority of small businesses were utterly unprepared, and a huge number were forced to shutter their shops. At one point, in the depths of the first wave, credit card processor data showed that 30 percent were shut down[30] while others experienced severe declines in revenue.

Almost a year into the pandemic, the situation remained dire, with fewer small businesses open in the United States in January 2021 than the same month a year earlier.[31] Overall small business revenue was also down more than 30 percent.[32] Many small businesses—even ones where the effects of a pandemic weren't obvious up front, such as advertising agencies—were vulnerable to risks they hadn't anticipated. Companies that were highly dependent on such businesses for their revenue, such as software and service companies that cater to small businesses, discovered very serious vulnerabilities in places they hadn't considered before. While techniques exist to illuminate potential issues—from scenario planning to identifying which key factors are normally distributed and which have "fat tails"—that's not the same thing as having them actually *used*.

By the way, this discussion about variability is a bit different from the earlier point about visibility. It wasn't just that businesses, large and small, didn't see COVID coming (although they mostly didn't); they also underestimated how *vulnerable* they were to a major shock like a pandemic. Many people couldn't imagine the US being brought to its knees because of a pandemic, and they therefore didn't take sufficient precautions.

Variability at a Bedrock Level

The underestimation of vulnerability goes far beyond specific risks such as pandemics. Importantly, there is a consistent blind spot when it comes to fundamental changes in the bedrock on which businesses and the economy are built.

There is a difference between changes in the areas that people are used to seeing shift over time—such as customer preferences, the level of competition, and regulations—and changes in areas that were previously thought to be constant. These seemingly immutable areas are "bedrock" elements, which have very little thought or said about them precisely because they are (or seem) so permanent.

After all, it seems to go without saying that when you're planning your distribution strategy for the next few years, you'll be able to ship things on the same rivers where they've been shipped for hundreds of years and use the same roads, bridges, and railways that have served for the last fifty. And in Western capitalist democracies, it goes without saying that you'll be free to make basic business decisions without the government telling you to use their friends' businesses and that if one competitor is clearly inferior, it won't win the business no matter how politically connected it is. These are bedrock truths on which you can confidently build your business and your plans, until they're not.

Does it go without saying you'll be able to ship via rivers that have been in use for hundreds of years? Not anymore. As mentioned earlier, the Rhine and the Danube were both affected by low water levels.[33]

Does it go without saying that you'll be able to use the roads, bridges, and railways that have served for decades? Not anymore. The flooding and mudslides that "destroyed roads, bridges, and train tracks" around Vancouver[34] saw to that as did the results when the UK experienced temperatures of over 40°C (104°F) for the first time ever. The heat got so great that it exposed vulnerabilities in the rail system, with some tracks buckling or overheating, overhead wires failing, and some routes having to be closed entirely.[35]

Does the freedom to make your own business decisions, such as where to advertise, go without saying? It's less certain than it used to be. For example, after Elon Musk bought Twitter, several companies paused advertising on the platform, with GM explaining its choice this way: "We are engaging with Twitter to understand the direction of the platform under their new ownership. As is normal course of business with a significant change in a media platform, we have temporarily paused our paid advertising."[36] Whatever you think of the decision to pause advertising, a bedrock assumption of Western capitalism is that a business such as GM gets to make it. But that wasn't the reaction some powerful people had.

A US senator, Republican Ted Cruz, responded to a tweet from Musk that ad revenue had dropped by saying that "the Fortune 100 have become the economic enforcers for the radical left" and were in bed with those "trying to silence Americans,"[37] and fellow Senator Tom Cotton said something similar. But Josh Holmes, an influential political advisor (and the former chief of staff and campaign manager for the Republican leader of the US Senate) went further. He made it clear that the companies that paused Twitter advertising might face political blowback over that decision, including being required to testify before Congress to justify their decisions.[38]

These statements clearly represent a challenge to a fundamental assumption of the relationship between businesses and politicians; previously, companies have been free to spend their money as they see fit (even to the point of being able to buy ads on networks that criticize the party in power or spread misinformation) without official retribution. But as the example of Josh Holmes makes clear, that can no longer be taken for granted.

When officials see a specific business as their ally—a writer for the influential conservative magazine *National Review* tweeted that he had expected Musk's purchase of Twitter to deliver robust Republican majorities in Congress[39]—reducing your support for that company could get you seen as an enemy. This isn't just the usual disagreement over tax rates, regulation, or other subjects that have long been understood to be subject to change depending on who is in power. This is something new and represents a threat to the fundamental order of business.

That's why it's important to distinguish between different classes of change. When bedrock aspects of politics, society, and nature are under pressure, businesses are much more vulnerable than they realize. If you're looking through the lens of values, you're much likelier to see that vulnerability.

Visibility, Blind Spots, and Blunders

Before COVID-19, it appeared that big hotel operators were well capitalized and nicely positioned to continue to grow and perform in the future. Similarly, coworking spaces such as those operated by WeWork and Regus had been on the rise for years, doubling between 2015 and 2018 to almost nineteen thousand, while the number of members per space tripled.[40]

High growth rates for some of these companies, such as WeWork, had already caused financial troubles. The pandemic added a swift decline in demand on top of tremendous competition on the supply side. Now these companies have to compete with the reality that employees can work from home rather than from a dedicated workspace in an office building. While it's likely that there are real benefits to teams working in physical proximity, that's not necessarily the conclusion companies or employees took away from the pandemic growth in remote working.

A few industries that seemed poised for success turned out to be vulnerable to events that shook the foundation of society and the economy in ways for which they were not prepared. An example of this lack of preparation is that before its planned IPO, WeWork listed potential risks in its S-1, enumerating dozens of items in its "risk factors" section. These risk factors ranged from big, fairly conventional items—from its ability to manage growth, weather economic downturns, and develop properties—to much smaller risks such as whether employees or visitors would misbehave and whether competitors would attempt to use social media handles and domain names similar to its own.[41]

But the possibility of a pandemic wasn't mentioned. In fact, there wasn't a serious discussion of any condition that would cause people to practice social distancing or even that would dramatically increase the proportion of people working from home! These factors were omitted even though there had been examples of outbreaks such as SARS in the recent past—and even though Bill Gates had warned, two years earlier, about the potential for harm posed by the next global pandemic: "The threat of the unknown pathogen—highly contagious, lethal, fast-moving—is real. It could be a mutated flu strain or something else entirely."[42]

This kind of occurrence—missing major risks because of blind spots—has become so frequent that I've given it a name. Inspired by the term GIGO (short for "garbage in, garbage out" and used as a reminder that bad data leads to bad conclusions), the term I use is BIBO: blindness in, blunders out.

Visibility and BIBO on a Global Scale

Such blindness wasn't limited to WeWork, however. It's very clear that before COVID, vanishingly few organizations were prepared for the possibility of a pandemic—even though they could have been. Since, as mentioned at the beginning of this part, pandemics like swine flu, bird flu, SARS, MERS, Ebola, and others had already come and gone, businesses, especially multinationals, had seen pandemic-related disruptions before.

Yet, as mentioned earlier, only a single company bought the pandemic insurance policy before COVID. Despite a clear and recent history of pandemics—all those listed above happened post-2000—across the world, only a single company purchased the pandemic insurance coverage.

What made Bill Gates so prescient about the possibility of a global pandemic? Perhaps it was because he was thinking about what problems and risks the less fortunate around the world were exposed to. By looking at risks to more vulnerable populations (such as those in developing nations), you'll often get early warning of something that could affect you too—as Bill Gates (and others) did.

One organization that did prepare for a pandemic was SimpliPhi, a battery start-up. Why was this small company prepared when much larger companies, with entire departments dedicated to risk management, were not? A big reason was that board member Hunter Lovins helped the company prepare during a scenario-planning exercise with the company's leadership in December 2019.

Now, scenario planning is not that unusual. Many organizations talk about it, and a good number actually perform some. However, this case was different. A Bloomberg article stated that "[Lovins] suggested a global pandemic might torpedo the economy. SimpliPhi CEO Catherine Von Burg remembers rolling her eyes at the suggestion. 'I couldn't imagine, certainly not the US, being brought to its knees because of the pandemic,' she says."[43]

Why did Lovins suggest such a scenario? It could've been that she had great foresight, like Bill Gates, specifically about global pandemics. (Just two years before COVID-19's appearance, Gates had said that a pandemic was his number one fear for the future.) Maybe it was not just intelligence and foresight, however: as a long-time sustainability thought leader, Lovins was also looking through lenses that revealed social and environmental risks—and therefore saw things differently and sooner.

What were the results of this foresight? In the depths of the pandemic, August 2020, Bloomberg wrote that "[SimpliPhi] weathered the economic slowdown so well that sales of its power storage systems are up roughly 30% over last year, and the company hasn't cut salaries; in fact, it had to hire eight more employees. . . . Von Burg credits scenario planning for the company's resilience. The process 'forces you to think about these very unlikely scenarios. You don't have to believe them. You just have to figure out a way to survive or thrive in them,' she says."[44]

"Chance favors the prepared mind" as the saying goes. The SimpliPhi example reveals that a better early warning system, one that includes looking through values lenses, can help.

Velocity

Another consideration is how vulnerable you are to competitors and entrants who clearly live their values. In my conversations with buyers for a billion-dollar company, I learned they would be more likely to give a new entrant a chance if it were more sustainable than existing players or created more social benefit.

This recalls the old joke about two people being pursued by a lion: one bends over to put on running shoes and the other says, "what are you doing? There's no way you can outrun a lion!" Whereupon the first one replies, "I don't have to outrun the lion . . . I just have to outrun you."[45]

You can't outrun climate change. You can't outrun changes in what people care about. The question is, can you outrun your competitors— the ones you have today and those you'll have tomorrow? Can you run fast enough that, even when changes bring them down, you're still standing? That's why velocity is a critical component of vulnerability.

Of course, if you don't see the lion coming in time, you can't outrun your competitors and you'll be eaten. But just seeing the threat isn't enough; do you have the internal capacity to understand when values change and to react, and do you have the capabilities to do something different? Or, to put it in terms of the story, do you have running shoes? And do you recognize when you need to put them on?

The Velocity of a Pack of Lions

Of course, there's usually more than one "lion." Sometimes you do face very specific, individual threats but, as *Sloan Management Review's* Paul Michelman said in December 2020, today's world has many: "Consider the conditions that will greet us on New Year's Day 2021. We will be shepherding ourselves into a world still battling a pandemic, though perhaps one in its later stages. There will still be dangerously yawning social and political divides, with spiraling global economic inequality further threatened by fast-advancing technology. There will be eroding trust in every institution you can name. And, oh, we'll have less than a decade to save the planet" from becoming uninhabitable.[46]

This is not a world with a single lion stalking your business but rather a world where many threats and challenges are present. In such a world, succeeding is less like a "marathon" or a "sprint" than it is like a survival race where you run through obstacles and over muddy, harsh terrain. This risk is compounded if your organization isn't nimble and you lack the solid foundation needed to underpin values-based changes. Put more plainly, if you have a deadline of two years to make changes and that's not enough time to complete them, you're in trouble. Valutus conducted research on how long it actually took to make certain kinds of environmental and other changes, across hundreds of companies in dozens of industries, and we found that many changes weren't completed within two years.

In fact, most companies hadn't even set the goal of overhauling or eliminating harmful practices—such as changing animal treatment practices or halting the use of problematic flame retardants—within two or three years. Instead, most of the goals we examined were things like "reduce waste by 30% within three years" or "cut our GHG emissions by 50% within five years."

Years ago, improvement expert Art Schneiderman discovered that types of improvement processes had consistent "half-lives." That is, it takes the same amount of time to get halfway to a new goal as what's needed to get halfway from there to the final goal.[47] To make this concrete, if it takes two years to get 50 percent of the way to a goal, as might be the case for a complex problem, after four years expect to be 75 percent of the way to the finish line. If it takes only one year to get to the halfway point, there will still be 25 percent of the distance remaining two years later.[48]

The first implication of this is that waiting is higher risk than it appears (another way of putting this is that there's submerged risk involved with being slow to act). The more complex a change is, especially if it's organizationally complex, the longer it takes to complete. If that's longer than you have, you suffer the consequences.

The Velocity of Changing Demands and Regulations

It isn't just individuals and companies shifting their behavior; in many cases, regulators are too. From specific requirements (e.g., certifying that your supply chain is free of conflict minerals) to more general, information-related requirements (e.g., requiring additional disclosure around climate), regulatory requirements have been changing—and will continue to do so. As Deloitte wrote in 2021, "across jurisdictions, regulators are finalizing new rules that will require companies to disclose information on their ESG footprint in their annual reports and mainstream regulatory filings. Unlike some regulatory changes, the introduction of ESG data into financial reports will likely make a lasting impact on how business gets done because these signals from regulators respond to a deeper truth about what matters to the world today."[49]

Such regulatory changes are unlikely to stop happening because governments bear much of the cost of things like natural disasters, public health emergencies (payments for COVID-related economic support alone topped $20 trillion[50]), and social problems, so it is only logical they would consider new regulations to limit their exposure. In addition, governments may respond to changes in the values and beliefs of their citizens; this combination of changing values and changing circumstances further increases the likelihood of changing regulations and rules.

One potential effect of regulatory change is a shift in the economics of the business or at least in the way it's currently conducted. As McKinsey notes, "regulatory responses to emissions will likely affect energy costs and could especially affect balance sheets in carbon-intense industries. And bans or limitations . . . will introduce new constraints on multiple businesses, many of which could find themselves having to catch up."[51]

Catch-Up Speed

Note what McKinsey says about the potential need to catch up. As discussed, a stronger set of values increases the likelihood of being prepared for, and able to respond to, change. Values help increase employee engagement and innovation as well as the speed with which your company can decide and act—all of which help you be less vulnerable as the velocity of regulatory change increases.

I worked with a company that eliminated one of the most potent GHGs (many times worse than CO_2) from its production process. The company knew it was a significant problem for their environmental performance, and that it was probably going to be regulated at some point, and therefore embarked on a multiyear effort to eliminate its use.

Not too long after the effort began, the GHG did indeed become the subject of regulation. A new European directive meant that the company would no longer be allowed to use it in its products. Further, if it couldn't be removed, one of the company's most lucrative product lines would lose access to the EU market.

However, the regulation didn't take effect for a few years, and since the company had already begun the work to eliminate it, it appeared to be sitting pretty. As the project went on, however, the team discovered how difficult it was to make the changes in technology necessary to produce the same product without the gas, and this took some time. The compliance deadline approached and with it the potential loss of access to a huge market.

Fortunately, the firm's values-enhanced foresight paid off. It made the deadline but only because the effort to replace the gas had started in advance of the requirement even being announced. Had the company waited until the regulation was publicly announced, it would have meant significant economic losses. (As it turned out, there was a submerged benefit to making this change, beyond continued access to the European market. It also turned out, as it often does, that the required change led to innovation, not only eliminating the now-regulated gas but also enabling the company to make better, more sophisticated products that created revenue growth.)

Even if your organization is well capitalized and good at making changes to products, technology, or practices, things can still take longer than you think—and, more importantly, longer than you *have*.

The Velocity of Change

Another form of risk is lacking the capability to make changes because sooner or later customers or distributors or regulators—or someone—will come to you for a values-based change. If you can't accommodate them in a timely fashion, you'll be subject to the consequences.

If you lack the organizational capability to view your products and production processes through the filter of values, or if you're lacking the ability to take the results of that vision and put it into practice, you'll sacrifice the advanced warning others have, and making necessary changes will take longer. That in itself is a risk. It exposes you to the consequences of not meeting your customers' expectations.

This dynamic goes beyond scorecards and sustainability, however. Take the example of Walmart, which not only has a sustainability scorecard but has many other policies as well, such as requiring suppliers to treat pigs humanely, only purchasing 100 percent cage-free eggs by 2025, requiring suppliers to deal with potential conflict minerals in their supply chains,[52] and selling no products containing animal fur.

These policies are not specifically about the environmental impact, although Walmart has plenty of policies about that. These are about what the company is, and is not, willing to sell. The world's largest retailer is already changing its purchasing decisions based on values, and that trend will only expand: the threat of losing customers by not aligning with their values is growing.

Variety

The most obvious effect of variety is that the greater the variety of products you make, and the more inputs you require, the more failure points arise, meaning you're more vulnerable to disruptions. Businesses are realizing that their complex supply chains are also sources of risk—again, the more complex the chain, the more failure points. Indeed, it seems as if there's a disruption, somewhere—a labor issue in Europe, flooding in Asia, or backed-up ports in North America—almost all the time. Wherever there are crucial inputs and operations, there is potential risk.

The pressures for increasing variety are growing. Whether it's different regulations in Europe, unique tastes in Latin America, or distinct use cases in Asia, there are many forces pushing you toward greater variety. Of course, that brings with it both the opportunity to perform better by tailoring what you offer to local characteristics and an increase in vulnerability.

Values don't necessarily change the variety of products you make or inputs you need. But they can help you contain this source of potential vulnerability. On the demand side, as more customers include their values in their purchasing, you will likely have demands for a greater variety of products (e.g., a version of your face cream that is not tested on animals or more energy-efficient versions of your electronics).

Building in values can help you respond to these demands without an explosion in the variety of your products. To the extent you build in values to all of your products (e.g., not testing any of your products on animals, or making all of your electronics as energy efficient as possible), you contain the increase in variety that would otherwise result from these new demands.

In addition, as discussed earlier, the visibility benefits of values help you see and understand potential disruptions sooner. This helps mitigate the risk that comes from increased variety.

Highest Common Denominator

The highest common denominator approach is already used in many cases—for example, remember when you needed different power supplies for European and North American electronics because of voltage differences? Now, cellphones, computers, electric razors, and numerous other types of electronics ship with power supplies that work with any voltage from 110 to 240 (although you may need a plug adapter, you don't need a voltage converter). This reduces complexity on the manufacturer's side and allows for greater economies of scale.

Volume

The greater the volume of resources you need, the higher your vulnerability. In a lot of cases, this is obvious. For example, if you need more fossil fuels, you are more vulnerable to oil price increases; if you need more raw materials, you are more vulnerable to fluctuations in availability. This is one reason why efficiency improvements driven by environmental concerns can have such a beneficial impact.

One company I worked with developed technology to take back used products, break them down into raw materials, and reuse them as inputs for new production. When I started working with the firm, the economics of this process were about the same as the economics of buying new materials. However, as the company pointed out, the ability to recycle used products back into new production meant needing a smaller volume of virgin inputs, which reduced vulnerability to increases in the prices of those inputs.

There was another vulnerability reduction as well, one that can be a big deal in some cases: the ability to use recycled material lessened the company's dependence on suppliers. It wasn't a big issue for the company, but this can matter should a supplier decide to try to use its market power to extract additional payments or concessions. Plus, even if that never happens, reduced dependence on suppliers also has the beneficial effect of reducing the disruption caused by a raw material supplier having production, quality, or distribution issues.

Another example is the case of one of the top ten wine producers in the United States, which set out to reduce the water intensity of its operations. The company changed how wine barrels were washed, monitored the soil to prevent overwatering, and made a number of other adjustments. A few years in, the winery had reduced average water intensity per gallon of wine to well below the industry average—other wineries used two to three times as much water per gallon.[53] Suddenly, this producer was much less vulnerable to droughts, water rationing, and other water-related problems. It also shrank the magnitude of any future water problems that might occur because if the price of water rises, the increased cost will be dramatically lower than for the company's competitors.

How much more expensive can water or energy become? Quite a lot. Some electricity bills were seventy times higher during the Texas blackout of February 2021.[54] And in major cities such as Mumbai, private companies trucking water in charge fifty times more than piped public water.[55] Such shortages will continue to become more common as water stress grows and climate change adds stress to electrical grids.[56] This makes action to reduce the volume of resources you use all the more valuable.

Vitality

Vitality is important because it addresses one cause of the difference between theory and what actually happens: sometimes people know what to do, but they can't do it—or simply won't. This is the business version of the fact that people know that they should eat less and exercise more and yet most don't do that.

Sometimes this is a matter of capacity, of whether your business's financial position isn't strong enough to enable you to respond to a threat. But sometimes it's more of a matter of engagement or will—when change is hard and requires real effort, it's less likely to happen. Luckily, acting on values can help. In fact, values decrease vitality-related vulnerability in multiple ways, from improving capacity to engaging employees and increasing persistence.

When it comes to capacity, the extent to which you have improved efficiency to reduce your negative environmental impact helps to keep your business capital and finances in a better position. (As we saw earlier, such investments often have ROIs well above the hurdle rate—and the true ROI, including submerged value, is typically far greater.)

In addition, acting on values engages people's full capabilities much more. Since people not only work harder but also persist longer when a task is related to their values, your company is far more likely to find a way around the obstacles and reach its destination if values are involved. This is another way values help mitigate vulnerability.

Now More than Ever: Megatrends

As mentioned earlier, climate rose to the top in Valutus research on the most powerful megatrends—yet, incredibly, most organizations *still* don't include it as a central part of their planning. Global professional services firm EY found that while many companies had included the fact that climate posed risks to their business in some of their reports, their disclosures were underwhelming. After studying 970 companies in thirty-four nations, EY found that while about half those companies (54 percent) had made some disclosure about potential climate risk, the average disclosure quality score was low, only 27 percent.[57]

In addition, EY noted that even at a time when "companies face increased scrutiny and pressure on their actions to mitigate climate change," progress has not been strong. As the firm said in its report, "companies have made limited progress in addressing the quality and coverage of climate-related financial disclosures." Further, when we look for more sophisticated ways of thinking about climate, we find performance even weaker. For example, EY stated that "the elaboration and use of climate scenarios, or lack thereof, continues to be a major gap in companies' reporting. Less than 10% of the assessed companies disclosed the use of climate scenarios (similar to 2018 findings)."[58]

In both 2018 and 2019, strategic impact was one of the weakest aspects of climate-related disclosures according to EY. As the company reported in 2020, "disclosures relating to 'strategy' and 'risk management' [remained] the least developed."[59] The weakness of strategy and risk management activity related to the top global megatrend is shocking.

Having strong values helps with this as it makes companies more likely to consider climate and other issues when creating strategy since strong values will inform such strategic discussions. A values lens brings the consequences of the climate crisis into sharper focus because thinking about caring for the world makes it more apparent just how much changes to the climate matter.

The Future Is Here; It's Just Not Reliably Powered

You may be tempted to think that these supply and cost risks are problems for the future—but the future is upon us. As mentioned earlier, in a six-year period, the world saw all six of the hottest years ever recorded to that point[60] and, in an eight-year period, the eight hottest.[61]

More "one-hundred-year" (or one-hundred-thousand-year) events just make the situation worse. Greater heat and power demand is headed straight for a US electricity grid where, according to Teri Viswanath, lead economist for power, energy, and water at CoBank ACB, "about 70% of [the US] grid is nearing end of life."[62]

Beyond Hotter and Drier

It's not just that the world is generally hotter and drier. That's difficult enough; now add unpredictability and rapid change. More droughts and more floods. More heat waves and more raging storms. And, maybe, more sudden changes too.[63]

When you live your values and care for the world and those who live in it, that increases the visibility of these risks, thus improving your foresight. As you've seen in this chapter, it also decreases your vulnerability and reduces the magnitude of negative consequences from those risks. In other words, it's a kind of insurance against social, environmental, and commercial risks that are growing in importance.

As with insurance, you can "save" money by not investing in values-related initiatives, which leaves more money to spend on other things.

However, this approach isn't actually "saving" anything—it's ignoring the monetary value of coverage against these risks. Once you see that acting on your values provides insurance-like benefits (by doing things such as improving your vision and response speed), it's easier to recognize its financial value. Insurance is clearly not free, but it's certainly worth having. Acting on values is similar. It's not free, but it can save your firm from ruin.

That's another reason investors should pay attention. Acting on the kind of values in this book reflects a proactive attitude toward risk. It shows a sophistication that leads to a greater ability to reduce both vulnerability and magnitude. And it also provides greater transparency, giving investors information they need to make better decisions.

Unfortunately, real sophistication about the risks posed by issues such as climate is rare, as EY found that "among this small group of companies, only a small number (8% of this sample—being the leading companies) made a connection between the financial repercussion[s] of climate risks and a climate scenario. Other companies (27 percent) provided a quantitative and detailed description of the methodology used to estimate the financial impacts. However, the majority (65 percent) provided limited quantitative information and only a vague explanation regarding the methodology used to assess the financial impact."[64]

For this reason, among many others, investors care and are asking the companies they invest in to include values in their planning and include climate in their risk assessments. But vulnerability isn't just about climate, and it isn't important just because investors are asking about it. Vulnerability is a fundamental part of your company's risk exposure, today and tomorrow. In addition, dealing with vulnerability is not just going to be a part of your success tomorrow; it's going to be a *bigger* part.

Now More than Ever: Resilience

In 2020, workplace rating organization Great Place To Work (GPTW) studied publicly traded firms just before, during, and after the great recession of 2007 to 2009. "The data," the organization wrote, "shows that the experience of certain groups of employees—including historically disadvantaged groups—predicted whether organizations flatlined, merely survived, or thrived during the last major downturn."[65]

GPTW found that programs designed to improve the experiences of these groups—"women, people of color, front-line workers, hourly male workers and long-tenured employees"[66]—also built organizational resilience. "In effect," the company wrote, "an inclusive culture enabled organizations to soar over the recession chasm—the deep decline most companies experienced during the recession."[67] Efforts to create an inclusive culture and to improve the welfare of employees are ways that leading companies act on values. In fact, many frameworks used to assess companies on their social and environmental performance[68] include such activities when they look at employee-related performance.

The same is true for providing opportunities for diverse talent to grow and thrive. As BCG noted, such organizational diversity helps improve the company's ability to respond to disruption: "Long-lived systems display six characteristics, one of which is diversity. Diversity is crucial for organizations for two reasons. First, diversity builds resilience. An effective way to bring down a system is to narrow how it responds to change. . . . Second, diversity is the basis of adaptiveness. Diversity of problem-solving heuristics and behavior permits a system to evolve and learn from experience."[69]

In a world of disruption, reducing vulnerability is more important than ever. Values help you do that, providing protection and insurance against the growing threats your company will continue to encounter.

11 Magnitude

In addition to reducing vulnerability, values also help reduce the magnitude of problems if they do occur. As mentioned earlier, one way is helping companies respond more quickly to changes once they hit: "If a crisis does strike, preexisting alignment on the organization's core reason for being will enable a coordinated, values-driven response that is authentic to your people and compelling to stakeholders."[1] A faster, more coordinated response helps contain the direct harm and repair any collateral damage. Moving quickly to deal with direct impact is crucial, as often such damage continues to worsen over time.

Fixing a Flood

Problems can be like a flooded basement—it's bad enough when it happens, but if you don't drain the water and dry out the fixtures quickly, you run the risk of mold, a far thornier issue, setting in. In a customer setting, if there's a mistake or a time when you don't live up to your values and it's immediately identified, owned up to, and rectified, that's like speed drying the basement: it prevents far worse ongoing damage.

But if customer-related problems happen and they *aren't* rectified immediately, rot can set in. The damage will spread with time, pushing away more and more customers who see that you've come up short once, and then again by not owning up and fixing it—increasing the magnitude of the damage.

The Cost of a Crisis

Acknowledging and fixing problems is key to limiting their effects, but there are also other ways to reduce their magnitude. A faster, more coherent response helps as does building trust before an incident occurs. In both cases, values have a big part to play.

Dr. Deborah Pretty has studied risk, response, and the effect on a company's reputation premium, defined as "a firm's earning power that's not captured in either the brand or net assets." This premium is of real importance to leading companies; for companies in the study such as Apple and Coca-Cola, it exceeded both their assets and their brand value. As Pretty and global advisory firm Aon stated in the company's 2022 report, "The valuation of the world's top brands greatly depends on their reputation premium."[2]

The study, a collaboration between Pretty and Aon, quantified the effect of 125 reputation events (such as cyberattacks and technology failures) on the market value of the companies involved, finding an average value loss of 5 percent in the ensuing year. For a company with a market value of $150 billion (about equal to the number-ten brand included in the study), that's a $7.5 billion loss.

It's intuitive that a faster, higher-quality response matters when it comes to limiting the damage. Not surprisingly, Pretty's study found that this was true: crisis communications have to be "instant and global." In fact, she found that it was possible to predict the one-year impact of a negative event after just five days.[3] A good response is very important since it not only addresses the immediate issue but also shows investors the quality of the company's management.

Pretty emphasized this when she said that "at times of crisis, the market receives substantially more information about a company and, in particular, about its management than would be received in usual circumstances. Investors use this additional information to reassess their expectations of future cash flow. The result of this reestimation process is a dramatic divergence in the consensus view that is reflected in the market price. Some management teams impress. . . . Others disappoint."[4]

This divergence in how a company's response is perceived has significant economic effects. Although the average company lost 5 percent of its market value, there was a marked difference between those companies that suffered over the long term because of the crisis and those who came out of the event stronger than before. The former saw market value decline by almost 30 percent, while the latter saw their market value *increase* by an average of 20 percent.

Values, Rebound, and Resilience

Values not only help facilitate a compelling crisis response, but they also build up a reserve of trust and goodwill before a crisis even strikes, helping the company rebound faster. In the McKinsey report on corporate purpose mentioned earlier, the authors analyzed how purpose changes recovery speed. They observed that trusted brands come back more quickly, which reduces the magnitude of a crisis's negative effects: "'Trusted' brands bounce back faster after product mishaps and economic shocks, particularly when they respond effectively. This remains as powerful a truth as it was in 1982, when Johnson & Johnson recalled and repackaged Tylenol following a tampering tragedy."[5] Note that while this is separate from reacting effectively in the moment, it's even better if a company both builds up trust beforehand and reacts well when there is a problem. And values help with both.

Separate from the overall resilience of the company and its brand, what about the resilience of its people? It turns out there are measures, albeit imperfect ones, for how resilient your organization is and they, too, show the benefits of values. For example, Aon offers an assessment companies can use to assess the resilience of their workforce;[6] five of the top ten factors contributing to resilience are:

- encouraging health-positive behaviors,
- protecting physical health,

A Tale of Two Crises

To illustrate a company that weathered a crisis well, Pretty points to Samsung's problems with its Galaxy Note 7 phones catching fire due to battery issues. In 2016, one month after the product debuted, Samsung issued a recall of the Note 7 devices and issued a final recall and stopped manufacturing the devices entirely just over a month later.[7]

While some observers faulted the company's initial response, it's clear why Pretty uses it as an example of an eventual success. A May 2017 survey showed that 89 percent of customers were willing to consider another Samsung phone, and YouGov brand data showed the company's favorability rebounding.[8] In fact, Galaxy S8 preorders were up 30 percent from S7 levels,[9] and the company added almost $50 billion in market value in the year after the issue, an increase of over 20 percent in the company's valuation.[10]

Contrast this with the case of Volkswagen (VW), which both Pretty and others[11] use for comparison with Samsung. VW's scandal, which resulted from modifying its engine software to cheat on emissions tests, hit much harder over its first twelve months. Fallout from the scheme, which became public in September 2015, cost the company over $20 billion in market value in the following year, approximately a quarter of the company's precrisis value.[12]

In addition, US sales had still not returned to their previous level two years later,[13] and observers said the episode was a factor in the bankruptcy of large VW dealerships in Germany up to five years later. Casualties included the largest chain of dealerships in the German city of Hamburg, which boasted 1,400 employees.[14]

The reason for this was that the scandal caused a drop in the value of used VW diesel vehicles, which meant those returned after their leases expired had to be sold for less. This led to unanticipated losses for dealerships, which added to their preexisting financial pressures.

Although it is obvious, it bears emphasizing that the VW scandal was about intentional deception—fraud—and making it happen required bad behavior by multiple people at different levels of the company. Stronger values would've made it less likely that everyone who had to go along with the deception did so, which would have saved the company tens of billions of dollars. (It would have benefited quite a few individuals as well: in addition to the VW executives who were sued and agreed to pay hundreds of millions of dollars to the company for their roles in the wrongdoing,[15] several others went to prison[16]).

- delivering clarity and purpose,
- operating with compassion and engaging community, and
- embracing inclusivity.

If these sound to you like things a company with strong values would naturally do, you're right. As noted earlier, many frameworks used to assess companies on their social and environmental performance include categories that line up with these initiatives. For example, the employee category, nearly universal in such frameworks, covers the first two initiative areas (encouraging health-positive behaviors and protecting physical health) as well as the last (inclusivity). The community engagement category covers the fourth (operating with compassion and engaging community) and the category of corporate purpose covers the third (delivering clarity and purpose).

But beyond being good things to do in their own right, Aon notes that these behaviors help contribute to having a resilient workforce, one that can better handle the ups, downs, and events of the world while continuing to do good work: "Forward-thinking businesses are seeing real value on investment from their health and wellbeing initiatives; making them better placed to retain talent, adapt to change and have a happier, healthier and more productive workforce."[17] In other words, workforce resilience—which lowers the magnitude of problems by enabling faster recovery—is part of the benefit that comes about when companies live up to their values.

Even though Pretty's research didn't focus on the workforce effects, it came to a similar conclusion about the importance of values-related actions as part of limiting the harm done by a reputation event. As Randy L. Nornes, enterprise client leader for Aon, says, it is one of the top three factors influencing the impact of an event. He writes,

> Research shows that the impact [of an event] on value is greatly influenced by three factors:
>
> - The ability to produce instant and global crisis communications
> - Perceptions of honesty and transparency
> - A program of active social responsibility.[18]

Strategy and Speed

Sometimes you have no choice but to change—the market has been irrevocably altered or regulations prohibit continuing to do things the same way as before. These are difficult challenges, but, again, values can create an advantage.

A company with expertise in making electric cars, for instance, gains advantage from regulatory changes limiting internal combustion engines, say in a given city or between certain hours. Electric vehicle makers also gain advantage when government agencies pivot away from buying gas-powered vehicles.

Similarly, a carbon price-setting regulation is much less of a problem for companies that have already adapted to producing low-carbon products. And businesses that have already learned to operate without reliance on rock-bottom labor costs adapt more quickly and easily to a higher-wage environment.

It's not essential that these changes come by official fiat. A shift in government, private purchasing patterns, or simple economic shifts can make it impossible to continue old ways of doing business.

Of course, not all of these changes are related to the climate, equality, or other values-related topics. But a lot of them are. Companies that have already started using their values to see more clearly, and to direct their investments and activities, have a head start. This means a lower magnitude for negative consequences of change and also more opportunities to benefit. As Hermann Scheer, the architect of Germany's renewable energy law, said in 2006, "We should not wait for international treaties. . . . The common rule is: be faster than others, because the speediest will have [the] most opportunities."[19]

Unintentionally Self-Insuring

Some threats, such as loss of customers, are uninsurable. Even many threats that can be insured against in theory are, in practice, hard to buy insurance for. For these and other reasons (especially underestimating the need), few companies have insurance policies that protect them against social or environmental threats. This means that, fundamentally, almost all companies are self-insuring (mostly without realizing it) against some of the most powerful megatrends that are reshaping the world. And although its cost is sometimes unseen—as it very often is in the case of environmental and social risks—of course self-insurance isn't actually free.

When a company is aware that it's self-insuring, it takes steps to lower its exposure. For example, when I worked for a company that had hundreds of thousands of employees, the company chose to self-insure rather than purchase supplemental liability insurance from rental car companies. At the same time, the firm took steps to limit the magnitude of its risk exposure (e.g., with policies prohibiting renting expensive luxury or sports cars).

However, very few companies are spending enough on values-based initiatives to really lower their exposure to environmental and social threats. How many companies are, for example, modifying their real estate portfolios in the New York-New Jersey-Connecticut area of the US because, even as early as 2017, the area had already seen a $6.7 billion effect from sea-level rise?[20] How many have done so to limit their exposure in the Miami area, which is barely above sea level? Those that haven't are self-insuring against potential real estate losses, whether they know it or not.

Similarly, how many companies have taken steps to lower their exposure as portions of their supply chain become hot enough to be dangerous for workers[21] or more prone to droughts affecting the crops their suppliers depend on? Without taking steps in these areas, companies are effectively accepting the full magnitude of any potential problems, without doing anything to lessen it. While *consciously* self-insuring can be a rational choice, unconsciously self-insuring by default—through a lack of awareness or action—leaves you expensively exposed.

Regulatory Impacts

Reducing your exposure to risks generated by the biggest megatrends has real value. And the same is true for reducing your exposure to values-related threats. Sometimes the exposure is limited to a part of the supply chain, though it can have cascading effects from there. As one illustration, in June of 2022 a new US law went into effect, the Uyghur Forced Labor Prevention Act,[22] because, as Robert Silvers, Under Secretary for Strategy, Policy, and Plans at the US Department of Homeland Security, put it, the use of or purchase of forced labor goods anywhere "offends our values."[23]

The law was designed to prevent imports into the US of goods made with forced labor in the Xinjiang Uyghur Autonomous Region of China. To this end, the law prevents the import of goods from that region unless a business can provide clear and convincing evidence that it wasn't made with forced labor. This means that goods sourced from that region would be, in the best case, delayed while companies proved they weren't made with forced labor. If that couldn't be proven, the goods would simply not be allowed entry into the US (in fact, because of trade agreements between the US, Canada, and Mexico, this applies to the North American market more broadly). As a result, a company whose supply chain included goods from the area would experience either delays or shortages compared to what they had been expecting to receive.

According to Silvers, the new law prevented the import of over $400 million worth of goods within the first six months of enforcement.[24] This number is one way to look at the magnitude of the law's effects, but there's another aspect that makes the magnitude that much larger—the restriction on goods that even have components from the Xinjiang region.

Many companies don't have good visibility into all the components used by their suppliers, which means they may not know if one of their suppliers uses a subcomponent from the Xinjiang region. As Koray Köse of Gartner's supply chain operations team noted, when it comes to geopolitical risks and other supply chain issues, a small component can have a big effect—or, as he put it, $40,000 of inventory could be held up by a component costing $0.10.[25] This means it's not the price of the component that matters but what gets affected in the end, which can greatly magnify the financial magnitude.

Finance-Related Impacts

There are also finance-related impacts from environmental and social issues, both systemic impacts and company-specific ones. At the systemic level, costly disasters and other disruptions have the potential to create larger issues. As a report of the US Commodity Futures Trading Commission noted, "risks [from changes to the climate] include disorderly price adjustments in various asset classes, with possible spillovers into different parts of the financial system, as well as potential disruption of the proper functioning of financial markets."[26]

This kind of disruption makes sense given that Swiss reinsurance giant Swiss Re found that the world economy is set to lose up to 18 percent of global gross domestic product (GDP) if no climate action is taken.[27] If China were to lose 24 percent of its GDP, as Swiss Re warns is possible, that would, of course, upend growth plans and supply chains—but even smaller losses could tip countries or regions into recession, affecting the economic circumstances of companies around the world.

On an individual company scale, there are finance-related impacts as well. When Lazard researchers, working with other experts, examined the GHG emissions and stock prices of over sixteen thousand companies (as mentioned in the operations section, part III), they were able to quantify the magnitude of the relationship between a company's GHG emissions and its P/E ratio. On the low end, for a large US company with $5 billion in earnings and a P/E ratio of twenty, its market value would be almost $4 billion less if it had 10 percent higher GHG emissions than if it didn't. If the company happened to be a large European industrial (for which the magnitude of the emissions penalty is greater), however, 10 percent greater emissions would instead change the company's market value by over $8 billion.

This type of effect hasn't always been the case. As recently as the 1990s, stock analysts often issued more pessimistic recommendations for companies engaging in socially and environmentally responsible activities—but the effect reversed by the 2010s.[28] Since then, the change has accelerated. As the former CEO of Etihad Airways put it, in terms of sustainability there was more change in the five years from 2017 to 2022 than in his previous twenty-five years in the industry combined.[29]

Customer Loss

Supply chain and regulatory issues are far from the biggest determinant of magnitude, however. Both of those can drive customer loss, of course—if you can't get your goods to market because your supply chain is broken or because your products are blocked at the border, your customers are likely to go elsewhere—but you can also lose out as a result of being out of step with your customers' values. While this was covered to some extent in the section on customers, here's a bit of an illustration of the risk of customer loss:

- You and your competitors both offer similar products, such as high-quality apparel, luxury skin cream, or leading-edge computer equipment.
- Customers care more about price, quality, style, and availability than they do about values-related issues such as your company's environmental and social activities.
- However, they do care at least a little about values-related issues.
- If you're lagging on values, you're more likely to lose when other factors are approximately equal.

This is a very realistic starting point. The idea that your products and those of your competitors are similar is, as discussed before, a reality faced by most companies these days. In fact, companies typically tell us that between 50 and 70 percent of their sales are in product categories where the products are seen by their customers as very similar (i.e., they've become commoditized).

It's also quite realistic to believe customers care at least a little about your company's values-related actions, although those concerns are not as important to them as core attributes such as price, quality, and style. Valutus projects have typically found that over half of a customer's buying decision is driven by the combination of price and quality (in fact, sometimes these can be as much as 80 to 90 percent of the decision). In contrast, values-related attributes tend to be between 4 and 15 percent of the buying decision—although, of course, the exact amount varies by industry, geography, and customer characteristics.

Calculating Potential Revenue Loss

The companies that Valutus works with often ask us to create quantitative models for calculating the potential gain, or loss, based on how customers believe they're doing on values-related dimensions. While the exact calculations and results vary, a few key factors are the following:

- Customer priorities, as some companies are in industries—such as natural food and many types of outdoor equipment—where customers place a higher priority on environmental and social factors.
- The company's current performance on social and environmental issues relative to the competition.
- The momentum behind specific issues (which can be measured quantitatively), especially those where the company's relative performance is average or below average compared to competitors.
- The industry's relative maturity on environmental and social issues, such as whether most of the industry is just beginning to engage with these kinds of issues or is already putting a lot of effort into addressing them.
- The performance variation among the companies in the industry— that is, if most companies are similar or if some are far ahead and others far behind.
- The speed of change within the industry—that is, if most companies are standing still (or even moving backward, though that's unusual) or if they are improving their social and environmental performance.

Using these and other factors, it's possible to quantify the revenue at risk for a company. (Interestingly, the revenue at risk is not just the inverse of potential revenue that could be gained through improved performance; the statistics and market dynamics differ and so does the result.)

For the business-to-consumer (B2C) division of a fast-growing $600 million agricultural company, Valutus found that values-based attributes were about 4 percent of the buying decision (which is not particularly high since that meant everything else was twenty-four times as important to the final purchase). The company was somewhat ahead of the competition in terms of social and environmental performance, which meant that the revenue at risk depended on how far its performance fell relative to the competition's.

Even though values-based attributes carried only 4 percent weight in the buying decision, if the firm fell back to an average level of performance, the marginal reduction in revenue would be a bit over 4 percent; actually falling behind the competition would risk about a 7 percent penalty. Since the B2C division was both growing rapidly and was a high-margin business, this would be an especially painful loss.

Falling Behind Your Industry

After examining the environmental and social performance of more than twenty agricultural companies over the previous five years, it became apparent that the magnitude of the potential loss was growing. The average performance of those companies had increased, while the spread between the best and worst performers had tightened (because the laggards had increased their performance more than average). If this held true for the company's competitors over the next few years—and there was every reason to believe this trend would accelerate—it would make it easier to fall behind.

In addition, something that came through both when reviewing existing research and when conducting original research with over 3,800 consumers was that the division's customers were placing growing weight on environmental and social factors. If this trend continued, it wouldn't be long before the revenue risk was 9 percent, and growth rates were likely to suffer.

The amount at risk can also be greater for companies that primarily sell to other businesses. While people often mistakenly think that

B2C companies have to be more worried about conforming to their customers' values, that is not the case. Business customers normally have specialized procurement personnel responsible for researching and choosing suppliers, which means that they are less likely to be unaware of your company's performance on environmental and social issues. And since most businesses now have their own environmental and social goals—and recognize that a big part of their ability to meet those goals depends on their suppliers—they are more likely to consider such issues when deciding on a supplier.

This doesn't necessarily mean that they are willing to pay more to buy from a company that has better values-related performance; while some are, many companies are not. However, recall that in most industries 50 to 70 percent of products are minimally differentiated on attributes such as price and quality. In those instances, as the agricultural company discovered, a small difference in environmental or social performance can tip the decision to one supplier or another—meaning that underperformance risks losing significant amounts of revenue.

Now More than Ever: Increasing Magnitude of Disruptions

It's one thing to look at the *current* magnitude of potential risks, which is a lot greater than most people think. Even so, however, that understates their true magnitude. Because of the combination of the increasing impact of environmental and social issues and the attention being paid to them (much of which was covered in previous sections), their potential consequences continue to grow. To take one straightforward example, as environmental changes lead to more destructive natural disasters, the magnitudes involved go up. As the *New York Times* reported, changes in the climate have made hurricanes stronger,[30] and the international scientific group the Intergovernmental Panel on Climate Change has said storms will continue to get stronger with each one degree rise in temperature:[31] "[in 2020] all 94 major natural catastrophes—severe storms, droughts, wildfires and floods, along with earthquakes—caused insured losses of $74 billion in the United States.

Over the next three decades, climate change could raise the annual losses in the country from hurricanes alone by one-fifth, according to a new analysis by AIR Worldwide, a catastrophe modeling firm."[32]

Social disruptions will likely also increase in frequency and magnitude. This is partly because of the connection to environmental changes—for example, rising temperatures will increase the number of refugees and individuals displaced from their homes, and it will also increase the number of places where extreme temperatures make it harder to live and more expensive to stay healthy. But it's also because of economic changes (such as changing expectations due to hundreds of millions of people joining the middle class), social changes (such as increasing tolerance in some societies and increasing fundamentalism in others[33]), and political changes (such as the rise in support for authoritarianism around the world[34]).

And both climate and other changes will continue to increase the pressure on countries and regions. The National Intelligence Council of the United States warned that "shared *global challenges*—including climate change, disease, financial crises, and technology disruptions—are likely to manifest more frequently and intensely in almost every region and country. These challenges—which often lack a direct human agent or perpetrator—will produce wide-spread strains on states and societies as well as shocks that could be catastrophic"[35] (emphasis in original).

Now More than Ever: Increasing Expectations

As a result of these facts, companies—especially leaders on environmental and social issues—will continue to ask more of their suppliers and business partners, increasing the penalty for being a laggard. For example, in 2021, over two hundred large companies that spend over $5.5 trillion with their suppliers convinced over twenty-three thousand of their suppliers to disclose their emissions.[36] And governments will continue to ask more of companies as well. For example, in 2022 the EU agreed on a new law that would restrict the importation of many products unless they can show a due diligence statement that their products are not linked to deforestation.[37]

Customers will also continue to ramp up their expectations of companies. As mentioned, the agricultural company's customers were increasing the importance they placed on social and environmental issues, and Valutus has found the same across industries and buyer types, from B2B buyers in the IT and outdoor equipment industries to consumers in the food and personal care segments. This raises the magnitude of the penalty for not measuring up.

Increasing importance is leading to increasing competitive intensity as well, further raising the magnitude of potential losses. In addition to the twenty-plus agricultural companies that Valutus found had increased their average environmental and social performance, the same was true of one hundred personal care companies and fifty cosmetics ones. There's every reason to believe this pattern holds across the majority of industries (I haven't yet found one where it doesn't), with some, such as IT and electronics, accelerating even faster. Because losses increase with how far you fall, the fact that your competitors are raising their performance—which makes it easier to fall farther and faster—increases the amount you stand to lose.

Previous chapters have discussed the increase in the frequency of disruptions, but that's not the end of the story. The National Intelligence Council report referenced earlier predicts that global challenges will manifest more intensely, which means more costly disruptions when they happen, which will be more frequently. Putting the two together means greater exposure from more frequent and more costly events. Add in increasing vulnerability (e.g., due to expanded supply chains or evolving cyber threats), and you are looking at the potential for more frequent, costly events that you're less protected against.

This brings us back full circle to where we started this part: with threats, vulnerability, and magnitude all on the rise, risk is growing increasingly important. You can't outrun the changes in the world, but values can help you see them better, lower your vulnerability to them, and recover better when disruptions hit.

V CORE Employees

I was talking to an experienced, respected CSR leader for a sixty-thousand-person hospitality and entertainment company, and she mentioned that the company's involvement in social and community issues helped it attract and retain employees. That's common, I said. Had she thought about how much the resulting financial benefit was?

She said she estimated it was worth $3 million per year. But, she added, her executives would estimate its value at only $300,000, ten times less. However, when we ran the numbers, using two dozen different inputs, the resulting estimate was $30 million per year—ten times what she had thought and *one hundred times* the executive estimate.

This part covers how values help you attract a better workforce, connect more powerfully with them, and reap the business rewards of doing so.

12   Magnetic Values

Good values are like a magnet—they attract good people.
—John Wooden[1]

Companies often assert that employees are their most important asset. Their actions don't always reflect this, certainly, but there's a reason this view is so common: there's a lot of truth in it. In any venture more complex than a sole proprietorship, a staff is necessary to make business processes work. Without people to run the machines, do the research, innovate, and grow sales, not much could get done.

This is, I realize, glaringly obvious. It's like pointing out that cars can't drive without a power source, but that's the point: employees are taken for granted precisely because they're so obviously essential. But not all fuels are the same grade and have the same power. That's why the talent-related effects of values matter so much. A values-based approach makes it easier to recruit, and hold onto, top people—including many who share those values. This helps power your company more effectively.

Speed of Attraction

First, being able to attract talent quickly is an underrated source of value. Obviously, if it costs you more to fill a position than the value you get from having it filled, you wouldn't bother hiring. Therefore, if you're hiring, by definition, you need that position filled to make the business better. An unavoidable consequence of this logic—one that is overlooked way too often—is that *you are losing value every day that position isn't filled.*

Clearly, there's a direct financial benefit to being able to fill positions—with the right people, as I'll explain shortly—more quickly, and this is a key area of submerged benefit from acting on values: faster hiring and the resulting reduction in lost value.

Here's a quick, numerical example. Say you're hiring for a sales rep with a quota of $1.1 million in sales per year, and the salary is $225,000. Accounting for benefits, tech, and other costs, the number rounds up to $300,000 annually. Gross margin on the product is 40 percent, well within the normal range,[2] so sales of $1.1 million generates a gross margin of $440,000. This is significantly more than the cost of employing the salesperson.[3]

Taking longer to make the hire costs money: at quota, the rep will generate $140,000 annually in net benefit, which means that if the position isn't filled for three months, there's a loss of $35,000 in potential income during that period. A fast hire reduces this drag on projected income as long as it doesn't lower the quality of the hire.

Luckily, values not only don't reduce the quality of hires; they actually increase it. Being more attractive to candidates can offer a better quality of hire, and, wouldn't you know it, values ramp this up even further.

Better Hires

To start with the basics, modern workers see their jobs more as an extension of themselves than was usual in the past. Not only do many work long hours, but they are likely to socialize with colleagues, and they tend to feel that the work they do should reflect *who they are*, not just what they do. As such, "what do you do?" and "where do you work?" have become weightier questions. This makes sense given the years of preparation required for many jobs today. But that preparation has led

---

A Sought-After Hire

Valutus once had the opportunity to interview an executive at a large, well-respected company who, before her current job, had headed one of the groups campaigning to reverse North Carolina's anti-LGBTQ+ "bathroom bill" in 2016, a campaign that ultimately succeeded.

With this executive's high-profile background and skills, she could have had her pick of employers. Why, we asked, had she chosen to work for this particular firm? It was easy, she said. The firm's public stand on equality—so well aligned with her own—had drawn her to apply, and continued action on similar issues had kept her there.

---

to more choice of sector and workplace. Modern workers can be at least as selective in this regard as potential employers.

Today, Gen Z is about a third of the US workforce, and a large segment of Gen Z respondents discuss the importance of finding "workplaces with values like their own."[4] They also "read mission statements and expect cultures built on social purpose and consistent application of values."[5] At the same time, though, they expect your company's culture to be consistent in reflecting its own values, and they also want to work at a place whose values align with their own.

The same is true for young professionals, such as MBA graduates from top programs. Employers are finding that values and action on things such as sustainability matter to job seekers like these.

In 2013, researchers experimentally designed sixteen job offers, changing variables such as salary and promotion opportunities along with different aspects of corporate reputation—including social reputation such as CSR. While they found that MBA students gave strong weight to traditional factors (such as salary), social reputation had a definite impact. The effect was a bit larger than an additional $5,000 in salary,[6] and it's likely even larger now as social and environmental issues continue growing in importance among younger generations.

In the real world, of course, companies that want the best talent will have to offer both a competitive salary and an emphasis on values if they want to maximize their attractiveness to this type of talent. Those that can will have a real advantage. Luk Van Wassenhove, director of the Humanitarian Research Group at INSEAD, reiterates this when he says that "companies are interested in attracting and retaining talent but this is difficult. . . . They will use whatever helps them achieve this goal, including sustainability."[7]

When competing against top companies for top talent, every little edge can help. Making an impact on the world is fast becoming a trait that top students look for in an employer. As Derek Walker, director of careers at Oxford University's Saïd Business School, put it, "a career which includes creating positive social impact is definitely becoming a mainstream choice for MBA students internationally."[8]

How mainstream? In a study of more than one thousand millennials—the largest generation in the US workforce[9]—from one hundred countries, researchers asked respondents to imagine their careers ten years hence and to list three criteria to judge how successful they'd been. About half said that work that has a positive impact on society was one of the three. Meanwhile, less than 14 percent listed a high salary, while only one in thirty, 3 percent, listed having power over others.[10]

Clearly, companies have an advantage when they recognize the importance of values and impact to top MBA grads—*if* they can demonstrate that making a positive impact is part of their company culture: "As companies, from Unilever to Phillips and from PepsiCo to Procter & Gamble, warm to the green economy they are able to attract and retain employees more easily, and in particular hire younger executives, who increasingly want to make a social impact."[11]

The Economist made a similar point, saying that maximizing long-term value requires "firms to adapt to society's changing preferences. If consumers want fair-trade coffee, they should get it. If university graduates shun unethical companies, employers will have to shape up."[12] If St. Gallen Symposium and GfK Verein are correct about the belief that for millennials "values are more important than a company car or fringe benefits,"[13] then the pressure on employers to "shape up" is real.

And the pressure on employers isn't just coming from millennials. Large fractions of older workers also care about the meaningfulness of their work—even in times of turmoil. According to a January 2021 survey of global consumers by IBM's Institute for Business Value, "the need for greater flexibility (32 percent) was the top reason workers changed jobs in 2020—followed closely by the desire to find more purposeful, meaningful work (27 percent). One in four said they were looking for work that better fit their values—the same portion who said they were looking for a salary increase or promotion."[14]

Similarly, an outright majority (51 percent) of people polled for the Edelman Trust Barometer in 2022 said they were more likely to work for a pro-LGBTQ company. That was more than four and a half times as many as said they were less likely to do so (11 percent).[15]

Expressing Values through Benefits

LinkedIn founder Reid Hoffman points out that fringe benefits and values need not be separate—benefits can be an expression of values. He says that "the founder of one particular small, money-losing retailer decided that his first priority was to provide health insurance and stock options to his blue-collar, part-time workers. That founder was Howard Schultz, and that small, money-losing company is Starbucks."[16]

Starbucks has made its share of controversial decisions over the years, including actions opposing unions (which were enjoying about 70 percent approval at the time[17]), but its commitment to providing health insurance to part-time workers is often cited as one of its best. It provided security for thousands of people, and as a business proposition, it worked. It reset the way employees related to the company. Hoffman continues that Starbucks's actions led to "higher staff retention, happier 'partners' and ultimately happier customers and greater profits."[18]

Starbucks took this strategy one step further when they expanded into China. The company was having difficulty retaining employees in the country, which caused problems with customer retention. (This dynamic is common, where better employee retention means better customer performance.) Recognizing the influence of parents on career choices, they offered health insurance not only to all employees but also to their parents. This resulted in employee retention skyrocketing and store performance improving markedly.[19]

Gaining Employee Trust

Of course, there are other paths to attracting and retaining staff than benefits alone. EY found, when surveying thousands of employees about trust, that while elements such as pay, benefits, and following through on promises topped the list of trust factors, a majority of respondents (57 percent) said both "equal opportunity for pay and promotion for all people regardless of differences" and "operates ethically"[20] were key factors as well.

In addition, almost two-fifths of respondents (38 percent) said a "very important" determinant of trust is working for a company that has a "diverse environment," meaning it strives to recruit, retain, and promote diverse people—including diversity of gender, country of origin, and thinking style.[21] When EY got more specific and asked what supported trust in their *current* employers, a significant number mentioned doing something good in the world. Indeed, more than a quarter of respondents (27 percent) said providing "opportunities to do community service on behalf of the company" was a "very important" trust factor.[22]

Lorenzo Zambrano, the late CEO of Mexican cement giant CEMEX, helped turn the company into the largest producer of ready-mix concrete in the world, a global company with operations in fifty countries. But the company wasn't just known for its financial success; it was also known for its social and community initiatives, which got it named the most responsible company in Mexico multiple times.[23]

Discussing the challenges of running a global company, Zambrano pointed out that competition for top talent is always fierce, saying "even in areas of the world where unemployment is high, unemployment for very talented individuals does not exist."[24] That made the talent benefits of CEMEX's reputation that much more valuable. Zambrano said "at first, we thought of our reputation conceptually, as something that we needed to keep improving. Now we know it affects our ability to attract the right people. After all, businesses are a network of people working toward the same end. And everyone has to be proud of what they're doing."[25]

As Harvard Business School professor Rosabeth Moss Kanter wrote in her book *SuperCorp* (in which she profiled CEMEX), "talented people with many options are increasingly attracted to companies and stay there because of compatible values."

Compatible Values

The values compatibility Kanter highlights doesn't just encourage people to join and remain with the company; it has many other benefits as well. Take the example of REI, the world's largest cooperative, with over 19 million members.

REI, which sells billions of dollars of goods every year, sees itself as a values-driven organization whose values help it succeed. As Alex Thompson, then VP of Brand Stewardship and Impact, explained in 2017,

> consider that a cooperative that was founded in 1938 has grown to become an organization with 16 million members and $2.6 billion in revenue. It's steady, sustainable growth that has outpaced others in this space, significantly. . . . It's ample evidence that when you put your values first, instead of share value, your organization can be very healthy over a long period of time. In the past three years [2015–17] we have seen 10 percent, 9 percent and 5.5 percent growth. If you know retail, those numbers are breathtaking.[26]

In the years since, REI has continued to grow; in 2019, revenue topped $3 billion.[27] That means REI gained a half billion dollars in sales in two years, a 10 percent growth rate that is unusual for retail. In contrast, competitor Dick's Sporting Goods grew approximately half as quickly, 5 percent per year, during the same period.[28]

What does REI believe about its relationships with employees? Here's how Thompson expresses it: "Consider the role of the company today with its employees: We provide health benefits. We help people spend time with their family, outdoors. We, as an employer, are actively engaged in any number of things that, in generations past, might be perceived as the role of government. And we're also expected to live up to and advocate for our values."[29]

One of REI's key values, one of the foundations of the organization, is connection with the outdoors. Note that this is something Alex specifically mentions in terms of REI's relationship with employees: helping "people spend time with their family, outdoors." That's because REI intuitively understands the match between the organization's values and those of employees.

This values match has a powerful effect on the relationship between organizations and their employees. Professors Jeffrey Edwards and Daniel Cable write about the importance of this fit between organizational and individual values: "A substantial volume of research has underscored the importance of congruence between the values of employees and organizations . . . This research suggests that when employees hold values that match the values of their employing organization, they are satisfied with their jobs, identify with the organization, and seek to maintain the employment relationship."[30]

This is true even in industries that are inherently more values oriented, such as healthcare. Ting Ren of the HSBC School of Business found that even when restricting the study to nursing homes, values congruence had important effects: "The results show that value congruence between employees and the organization complements delegation of decision-making, substitutes for monitoring, and further improves organizational performance . . . These findings suggest that value congruence can serve as a source of intrinsic motivation for employee effort and mitigate agency problems in the workplace."[31]

Something to notice is the last part of Ren's conclusion, which is that value congruence can mitigate agency problems in the workplace.

Agency theory "suggests that employees may value self-interests more than those of the organization they work for [and therefore are motivated] to avoid work responsibilities when opportunities exist,"[32] which is an academic way of saying that people don't normally put their all into their jobs. But values congruence reduces this problem as well.

The Satisfaction of Doing Good

When employees feel that the company does something good for the world, and they're contributing to it, their job satisfaction goes up. Studies show that taking part in official company-sponsored volunteer activities causes higher job satisfaction. Bea Boccalandro, author of *Do Good at Work*, worked with voluntarism network Voluntare and corporate partners in three different countries to study the effects.

Boccalandro designed a study made up only of people who hadn't engaged in any corporate volunteer activities in the past year, thereby ensuring the volunteer and nonvolunteer groups started out alike in their level of engagement. Then the subjects were randomly divided in two: a control group and an experimental group. Both groups were surveyed on job satisfaction and engagement, after which only the experimental group volunteered for either a half day or two-and-a-half days.

Then both groups were surveyed again and then, twelve weeks later, both groups were given a third survey to determine if satisfaction changes persisted.[33] The employees who volunteered saw their job satisfaction increase by an average of 13 percent, while the control group saw no increase at all. And satisfaction levels for the volunteers remained 13 percent higher even twelve weeks later.[34]

As the experiment demonstrated, being part of something larger, something that makes the world better, increases people's satisfaction with the organization that orchestrates this effort. Because almost everyone has values, participating in a group where those values are expressed in action is a powerful experience and, in the workplace, binds employees to the company that brought the group together.

Authenticity and Inclusion

In addition to the benefits of job satisfaction, there are real benefits to having an inclusive organization that makes people feel welcome and lets them be who they really are. In other words, there are benefits to having employees who can be authentic at work. This may not come as a surprise. It makes sense that people who feel they belong and can be their full selves at work would bring more of their full capabilities to the job. Organizations that place a strong value on being inclusive and making people feel like they belong are better able to acclimate new hires, which means new employees do more and do better in the organization.

As research out of London Business School found,[35] when employees feel welcome to express their authentic selves at work, they exhibit higher levels of organizational commitment, individual performance, and a propensity to help others.[36] A separate meta-analysis of fifty-one studies covering over 36,500 observations found that authenticity was related to employee engagement and to employees' well-being, which, researcher Anna Sutton notes, is consistent with other studies about the benefits of authenticity in a range of contexts.[37]

As Sutton says, authenticity's benefits are both real and important: "This meta-analysis unambiguously concludes that authenticity, or the feeling of being true to oneself, is key to both well-being and employee engagement. As both of these outcomes become increasingly important for measures of economic and societal success, creating the space and encouragement for diverse authentic expressions of self is therefore likely to have wide reaching positive impacts at work and in wider society."[38]

Better Work from a Better Workplace

A company with values out front—that helps people feel they belong—enjoys higher satisfaction and happiness among its staff. But there are many positive results beyond that, and here's one that isn't well-known.

The Work of Inclusion

Creating a feeling of inclusion takes more than a simple policy or a poster on the wall or an "add diversity and stir" approach with no real effort behind it. It requires work.

Someone who identifies as gay told me the following story: at an event for LGBTQ+ businesspeople, one individual asked those in the room how many of their companies were rated high performers on LGBTQ+ issues. Nearly everyone in the room raised their hands. Then the same person asked how many felt like they could fully be their true, authentic self at work. This time, almost no one's hand went up.

It takes real work to build an organization where people can be who they authentically are. Policies are a start, but research—such as consulting firm Bain's list of ten actions that work[39]—shows that policies are not enough.

Making the effort is worth it, however. What company wouldn't want higher individual performance and a greater willingness to help others? Or greater engagement and well-being? Companies hire people with all kinds of differences—and smart ones make them feel like they belong and can be their authentic selves.

For one, people doing work that has real meaning actually *do better work*. Meaning is so critical to us; it has an effect even when the job is temporary and the employee knows it.[40]

When people are paid by quantity, by how much work they do (not how well they do it), meaningfulness doesn't change how much they produce. However, it does affect the quality of their work. When the task is more meaningful, such as when employees are told the images they're scanning will contribute to cancer treatments, work quality goes up *without diminishing the quantity* of work they produce. Conversely, when the work is made less meaningful—for example, by telling people their work will be discarded after completion—quantity remains steady but quality goes down.[41]

Research reveals that across cultures, nations, industries, and employee demographics, those who see their work as more meaningful are more engaged and less likely to leave. For example, a Stanford team identified six characteristics that marked a positive workplace, one of which is "emphasizing the meaningfulness of the work." They also found that positive workplaces are more productive with reduced absenteeism, fewer accidents, lower attrition, and fewer errors.[42]

In the same vein, MIT's John Sterman observed that "people are hungry for the opportunity to work professionally in a way that is consistent with building a sustainable world instead of one that undermines it. The idea that 'I'm going to work in a corporation that may have the impact of further degrading the capacity of the planet to support life and then in my spare time I'm going to use the money that I've made to do good deeds'—that just doesn't cut it for people anymore. You can't have that kind of dissonance."[43]

Indeed, meaningful work inspires better performance by employees, and the results of that work are more attractive to customers. The work may be about fair-trade goods, or getting suppliers to raise their labor standards, or something else. Those are meaningful tasks and reflect a desire to help people around the world live better lives. As a result, it activates the values and motivations of values-aligned employees.

Now More than Ever: The Best People, Giving Their Best Effort

Unemployment rises and falls, but as CEMEX CEO Lorenzo Zambrano said, competition for the *best* talent doesn't go away.[44] When you combine the changes in the world with the changes in the workforce, it's no surprise that companies are increasingly using their environmental and social activities as part of how they attract and retain employees. As a 2015 article in *Business Because*, a publication of the Graduate Management Admission Council, which is an association of leading business schools, put it, "in the war for talent companies are increasingly deploying a new weapon—sustainability."[45] This is still true today—except that this is no longer a *new* weapon.

A few years later, many companies from Morning Consult[46] to McKinsey[47] were writing about corporate purpose—described as "a clear

---

How Much of Themselves People Bring to Work

For several years, I included the following exercise in talks I gave to a group of high-performing young professionals. I started by asking them how much of their full, true capability they brought to work on a daily basis. First, I would ask people to raise their hands if they brought an average of at least 30 percent of their true capabilities to work every day. Normally, all or almost all of the hands in the room went up.

"How about 40 percent?" I then asked. At this point, a few hands fell. Now we were typically looking at two-thirds to three-quarters of the audience still having their hands raised. The shift from 50 percent to 60 percent typically started a significant decline in the number of hands that were raised, leaving a minority of hands still raised.

At 75 percent, almost all the remaining hands fell. Very few people would say they brought as much as three-quarters of their real capabilities to work. And not one of the high-potential individuals in the audience claimed to bring as much as 80 percent of their true capacity to work.

---

purpose beyond turning profit," a "core reason for being," and having "unique, positive impact on society"—and its (positive) effect on talent. And as events continue to push environmental and social issues into the spotlight, their prominence in the minds of employees will continue to increase—not just as a way to attract the best talent, but also as a way to increase their level of engagement. In fact, in one study the talent and career professionals at global staffing leader Manpower found it was the #1 driver for boosting engagement.[48] Companies that want the best talent to give their best effort and help others in the organization need to show those individuals their values, especially if they want to keep them around.

13   The Clean Energy of Purpose

One of the biggest reasons for underestimating the benefits of values and purpose is that although people understand that these effects are real, they don't know how to quantify them and value them financially. When something is known to have value but it's not clear exactly how much, the most common response is to not include it in ROI calculations. Since it's not possible for someone doing a calculation to enter "I don't know" into a spreadsheet and get a good result, most of the time it's simply left out.

The problem is, as MIT Sloan professor John Sterman taught me years ago, if you *know* something has value but don't measure it, you're giving it the only value *it can't possibly have*: zero. And yet, that's the norm; employee longevity, employee engagement, and employee attraction obviously have value. But since their value hasn't been determined, it gets left out of the calculations. This, in effect, assigns it a value of zero—even though everyone knows that's not really true!

Talent Value for a Fortune 500 Company: A Case Study

One firm, which I'll call Fternal, provides a clear example of the value of values when it comes to employees. The company has annual revenues of about $25 billion, annual growth of about 2 percent, and about sixty thousand employees, about 25 percent working in developed economies with the remainder in the developing world.

Fternal also has an employee attrition rate of about 15 percent (this is the voluntary attrition rate, not including those who are laid off or fired). This means the company must hire just over ten thousand people each year to maintain its current size and employee growth rate. Other important stats for this case are that the overall average salary per employee is $49,000, and the average time it takes to hire someone is two months.

Quantifying Employee Engagement Value

Next, let's add in numbers that reflect employee engagement. We've established that employees engage more fully when aligned with their employer's values. And we know that most companies don't know how to quantify the value of that engagement, so they don't. But engagement can, in fact, be quantified.

To start quantifying, you need a baseline figure for engagement, without any effects from shared values. Fternal, like most big companies, had employee engagement data from its internal surveys; these surveys pegged it at 90 percent. Although this is an exceptionally high number—Gallup typically finds engagement levels between 30 and 40 percent[1]—to be conservative while quantifying the benefits of values, we decided to use that number in the analysis. (Using 90 percent engagement is conservative because the higher the baseline engagement level, the less "headroom" there is for improvement. This means shared values have less ability to increase engagement and thus are less able to improve financial performance.)

The next step is where many attempts to quantify engagement value break down: assessing the increase in engagement stemming from shared values. Doing this precisely requires tracking engagement over time and using carefully constructed experiments; unfortunately, our work with Fternal hasn't yet run long enough to do that. However, we did create estimates of the benefits, ones that were accepted by the business and high-level executives. I'll use those estimates in this example.

As discussed earlier, there's a lot of research showing that values increase engagement, such as Bea Boccalandro's findings that volunteering raised engagement by 16 percent.[2] Among companies I've worked with, a 9 percent gain is considered reasonable—though this likely understates the true benefit given what we saw when we conducted tests at company stores (including using a control group of stores for comparison). For Fternal, we used a conservative estimate for the engagement gain: 7 percent of the available "headroom" for improvement. We did this both to acknowledge the high engagement Fternal already had and to account for the fact that some people were not fully aware of the company's efforts.

Since engagement was already at 90 percent, and over 100 percent engagement isn't possible, that makes the headroom for potential improvement 10 percent and potential gain 0.7 percent, which leads to a new engagement level of 90.7 percent. (That was the default, but we also ran scenarios to see what would happen if the number were higher or lower.) Note that this is a very conservative estimate, as is our habit at Valutus. Some people would have used 7 percent of the *current* engagement level, which would mean a gain of 6.3 percentage points (90 percent times 7 percent). However, as mentioned earlier, it's better to be extra conservative with estimates because if you can show the value with conservative numbers, everything else is a bonus.

Productivity

How does an increase in engagement translate into an increase in productivity? Intuitively, it's clear that as more employees use more of their full capabilities at work—because their values and the company's values are aligned—productivity goes up. Studies back up this intuition; according to a US Department of Defense report, "organizations may think of the relationship between commitment, effort, and performance as conforming to a '10:6:2' rule. For every 10% improvement in employee commitment, employees will realize a 6% improvement in discretionary effort, which in turn results in a two percentile point improvement in performance."[3]

In other words, a 10 percent increase in engagement yields about a 2 percent increase in productivity. Similarly, a 2012 Gallup study also reported a link, finding that highly engaged teams were 21 percent more productive[4] than less engaged ones, and a 2017 study found business units in the top quartile for engagement were 17 percent more productive than those on the bottom.[5]

As is the case with engagement, measuring productivity gains requires controlled experiments and time, so with Fternal we again had to use estimates. In this case, a 0.7 point increase in engagement translates to about a 0.14 percent increase in productivity. If this doesn't seem like a lot, that's because in percentage terms it isn't—we were very conservative with our calculations and that shows. However, even this gain does add up in dollar terms.

Examining the company's financials, we found that the gross margin per employee is about $180,000 (sales per employee was higher). That means a 0.7 percent increase in productivity is worth about $15 million in increased margin annually—even using very conservative numbers for both current engagement and the engagement gain from values. (If Fternal's engagement had been at the high end of Gallup's normal range, 40 percent, instead of 90 percent, the annual margin gain would have been $90 million.)

The Value of Improved Retention

I rarely find someone who doesn't agree that showing employees that you share their values can improve retention—this idea both makes intuitive sense and is backed up by significant data. However, it's also rare to find an organization that has quantified the value of this benefit. For Fternal, we set out to do so.

Working with company management, we pulled together numbers for the company's average salary ($49,000), attrition rate (15 percent), and estimated attrition reduction from shared values (10 percent, making the new attrition rate 13.5 percent). We were also able to get information on recruiting and training costs for new hires (10 percent of salary) and to find reasonable numbers for other costs such as IT and real estate (5 percent of salary).

Since the company had to hire more than ten thousand people each year to maintain its growth rate, a 10 percent reduction in attrition meant a reduction of hiring and training expenses for over one thousand people a year, a savings totaling just under $8.5 million. Because the firm took an average of two months to hire a new employee, and the average margin per employee was $180,000 per year, the two-month vacancy period before a replacement could be hired caused a hit of $30,000 ($180,000 ÷ 6) in forgone margin for each employee who left. Across one thousand employees, this is a benefit of just over $30 million annually.

Putting this all together, the benefit of higher retention (again, conservatively estimated) was a bit over $39 million per year.

Submerged Subtotal

Since we've examined a series of talent-related benefits and calculated their costs, you might be wondering what the net result is. Even using the highly conservative figures above, the answer is that employee benefits from values were, per year:

- $15 million in productivity gains from improved engagement,
- $8.5 million in hiring and training savings from increased retention, and
- $30.6 million in vacancy loss reduction from lower attrition.

In total, this is over $54 million per year in value for the company.

To reiterate, this captures the benefit (very conservatively estimated) of certain aspects of how acting on your values affects employees. This calculation covers engagement and attrition but not the cost of mistakes or the effects on customer service. Nor does it include the improvement in teamwork from shared values or the growth in innovation.

Customer Service

For a variety of reasons, airlines are almost universally unpopular. They are monolithic and are often impenetrable when answers are needed.

The Cost of Acting

The costs to act on values depends on what you do, of course, but it's typically much less than the benefits. I've already discussed the ROI of investments in operational efficiency and the customer benefits of acting on values. But even limiting the discussion to employee-related initiatives, such as hiring and HR policies, the costs are low compared to the benefits. For example, recruiting at different schools or changing job descriptions to grow your pipeline of minorities, women, and first-generation college students requires effort, but the cost involved is not high.

Even actions that do impose some costs, such as family leave policies, aren't very expensive on average. For example, ten years after California passed a family leave law that covered thirteen million workers, it reported that benefits paid out the previous year amounted to $554 million, or about $42 per covered employee.[6] When Google expanded paid family leave from twelve to eighteen weeks, here's what it found, according to Laszlo Bock, senior VP of Google's people operations: "When we eventually did the math, it turned out this program cost nothing. The cost of having a mom out of the office for an extra couple of months was more than offset by the value of retaining her expertise and avoiding the cost of finding and training a new hire."[7]

When Bock said the program "cost nothing," he didn't mean that it was free; he meant that the cost was offset fully by the effect on attrition.[8] Therefore, if I were to apply this cost to the Fternal case, I wouldn't use a cost number of zero. At the California figure of $42 per employee, the cost for sixty thousand employees would be about $2.5 million. To be conservative, however, say that the cost of family leave and other HR-related initiatives was $100 per employee, which means a total cost of $6 million per year. Fternal's initiatives have a talent-related value of $54 million annually, nine times this $6 million in cost. That's quite an ROI.

Yet a 2018 study of 1,800 people found that when an airline had a timely response to their needs and questions, they were willing to pay about $9 more for a future ticket. Wireless carriers, too, have few real fans. Even so, the comparable figure for good service by wireless providers was $8 a month, just under $100 a year.[9] That is a huge jump, about 20 percent.[10]

Responsive and productive customer service really, *really* matters to customers. Even so, everyone has a long litany of service horror stories built up over a lifetime of neglectful, arrogant, useless, thoughtless, unempowered, or, worst of all, apathetic service experiences. Consider the lost revenues engendered by bad service, or those gained by strong service performance, based on the examples above.

But what if companies suffused with values inspired their staff to provide better customer service? One Drexel University study looked at frontline employees at a financial services company to determine whether CSR programs affected job performance. As you might expect by now, the study found that CSR programs changed employee relationships with their companies and leaders, "often boosting employee engagement and customer-service levels."[11]

One thing that's very clear in the work I've done is that talking about values with customers creates a new commonality that improves the relationship between the company representative and the customer. This is true for both B2B and B2C relationships. In one company I worked with, it became clear that the salespeople who talked about environmental efforts had better, stronger, and more extensive networks within the companies they supplied. Deeper interpersonal relationships with buyers are a real advantage, especially in a competitive market, and strong, palpable values increase this advantage.

Indeed, the Drexel research came to a similar conclusion, with lead researcher Daniel Korschun writing that "CSR can be an icebreaker in conversations with customers."[12] Furthermore, "employees told us that . . . once they find out that a customer shares a passion for social or environmental causes, it creates a bond that is highly motivating. . . . As a result they are more motivated to serve those customers because they see that both of them care about the same sorts of things."[13]

Human Capital

Human capital is the knowledge and skill in an individual person's mind, such as their familiarity with a computer, knowledge of the company's products, or skill with manufacturing machinery. Acquiring human capital takes time, and accumulating a lot of it requires individual effort. For example, are you likely to put a lot of time into learning how to use a company's machinery really well, or its custom software, if you don't expect to remain with the company for long? Probably not.

Some benefits of human capital accrue to the individual, such as their education or generalized skills like proficiency with technology. But other kinds of benefits accrue more to the company. For example, the ability to use the company's custom software or machinery helps the worker be more efficient and therefore benefits the company. But if the worker leaves, those individual skills are much less likely to be valuable somewhere else.

A third kind of human capital benefits both the company and the employee, for example, when an employee earns a bachelor's or advanced degree while at the company. This learning helps the employee in their current job, and it's valuable to them even if they leave the company and go somewhere else.

All the different sources, and all the different benefits of human capital, make human capital acquisition a bit of a "dance" between employees and employers. When the employee makes the effort to learn something that benefits the employer, it makes sense for the employer to help. On the other hand, if the employer doesn't believe that the employee will stay at the company very long, it may not want to help the employee acquire skills—since the employer would bear the cost but not reap the benefit of the resulting skills.

For example, for decades fast food chains did not have programs to help their employees get their college degrees. With high turnover at fast food restaurants, it may not have seemed like a good investment. However, Starbucks decided to do something different. It decided to make it easier for employees to get their college degrees, even paying for them to do so. In 2020, sixteen thousand Starbucks employees were taking advantage of the program. Given that employees don't have to pay for these classes at all, this investment is a significant one for Starbucks. Add to that the fact that most employees don't spend their whole careers at Starbucks (there's no requirement they stay at the company after graduating). That may be why other companies weren't doing this when Starbucks started its program.

But what if we looked at the situation differently? Looking at human capital makes us consider two things: first, employees know that Starbucks is investing in their human capital, which may have little to do with their duties at the company. (Students can choose from more than seventy-five courses of study, including subjects such as animation and film.) Second, Starbucks benefits from doing this—regardless of how applicable the classes are to employee's jobs—because of the effect it has on the company's relationship with its workforce.

If you realized that a company is investing in you, even knowing that you can leave and take the benefits of that investment with you, wouldn't you feel more valued and trusted? And wouldn't you want to work for a company that made you feel that way? Maybe this is why, five years into the program, nearly a fifth of all job applicants cited it as one of their main reasons for wanting to join Starbucks.[14]

What's more, participants in the program stay at Starbucks 50 percent longer and are promoted at three times the rate of US retail employees who are not in the program. In other words, offering a degree program creates loyalty to Starbucks. Not only do employees improve their Starbucks-specific human capital, which benefits the company, but they also improve their general human capital by taking college courses and even getting a degree—which also benefits Starbucks.

This isn't a Starbucks-specific story, however. In some cases, values show up in the form of benefits, while in other cases it's through bringing purpose up with employees and making it a regular part of the discussion. One of the world's largest professional service firms, KPMG, found that talking more about its purpose and creating a greater appreciation of the company's role in the world had a huge effect on its highly educated, high-performing workforce:

> Among employees who told us their leaders discuss higher purpose, 94% said KPMG is a great place to work, and 94% said they are proud to work for KPMG. But among those whose leaders don't discuss purpose, the

corresponding results dropped to 66% and 68%. This group also reported they are three times more likely to think about looking for another job than those whose leaders do talk about purpose. Not surprisingly, year-to-date *actual* turnover of these two groups is dramatically different, 9.1% vs 5.6% respectively. What's more, employees whose leaders communicated about purpose were far more motivated to strive for continuous improvement and high performance than colleagues whose leaders failed to discuss this important topic.

Was it only younger employees who cared? No. KPMG continues:

> These big differences show up across generations of employees, regardless of whether someone is a Millennial or Baby Boomer. Moreover, relative to their representation in our workforce, older employees (those over 40) had proportionately somewhat higher participation in our 10,000 Stories Challenge than younger employees—suggesting that with all we hear about the difference in career attitudes among Millennials, Gen Xers and Baby Boomers, desire to recognize and express the higher purpose in one's work, seems to cut across generational boundaries.[15]

Job Happiness Score

The effect of a company's values on how employees feel about it is further reinforced by what the mega job-hunting site Indeed does. The site calculates a "Work well-being" score based on surveys completed by employees at the company—an overall score, based on fifteen measured elements such as happiness, support, learning, and compensation.

But all fifteen dimensions don't show by default when you look at the employers' snapshot. Instead, Indeed chooses four dimensions to highlight: happiness (how enjoyable people find their day-to-day lives at work), stress-free (how manageable people find their work stress), satisfaction (how content people feel with the way things are at work), and purpose (how meaningful people find their work).[16] This is worth emphasizing: purpose matters enough to be one of the top four areas highlighted. (Although it's possible that Indeed doesn't highlight salary because people will ask about it on their own, without any prompting from the site).

Why highlight work well-being and purpose within that? The simple answer is that Indeed has the business model of a two-sided market, so it has two types of customers to serve: the employers who advertise jobs on it and the job seekers who use it to apply for a job. The attraction for job seekers of learning about work well-being is obvious: it helps them choose where to work. Since Indeed offers that information, applicants are more likely to use the site, which expands the pool of potential job seekers.

The other side of the coin is that companies pay Indeed to list their job openings, so Indeed has to deliver the candidates hiring companies want. By offering a bigger pool of potential employees—and demonstrating that potential employees care about the company's purpose—Indeed's job listings entice individuals to apply while convincing them that Indeed should be their default job search home.

Indeed's inclusion of purpose (and other happiness measures) provides another kind of resource for companies. Well-run companies want employees to be happy because happy employees are better strategically, organizationally, and financially. This is one reason companies conduct employee surveys, to see how well they're doing and improve their performance in the eyes of employees. But Indeed offers an external window on employee happiness, one that's not potentially clouded by employees who think their answers are not anonymous or that they should answer questions a certain way.

Happy Teams

A better understanding of whether employees feel the company has a purpose, and that it truly lives up to it, is beneficial because it makes employees happier to work for a company with a purpose, and happier employees have many organizational benefits. A 2019 systematic review of how happy workers affect team performance concluded that team well-being is related to performance, creativity, customer satisfaction, and financial performance.[17]

Do you notice the difference when you work with a company whose employees are more engaged and bring more of themselves to work?

Most people do. The company C Space uses surveys to calculate what it calls the customer quotient (CQ), which is designed to measure the strength of the customer-company relationship. A high CQ score indicates a more human, stronger customer-company relationship, and higher CQ scores are associated with greater rates of growth, recommendations, and repeat purchases.[18]

According to C Space, "customers want their relationships with companies to have the same qualities they value in their personal relationships—qualities like trust, respect, empathy, openness, and reciprocity." And who are the top performers on this metric? One you have already seen is REI, which clearly sees the value of values. Another is L.L. Bean, which received top scores on trust, authenticity, and shared values.[19]

Now More than Ever: Expanding Expectations

When expectations of companies are higher, and people see more threats to the fundamental fabric of democracy and the world—from disinformation to voting restrictions to social and economic upheavals caused by changes in climate—companies find it harder and harder to stay quiet, both commercially and morally.

As Richard Levick, who hosted the Corporate Counsel Business Journal's In House Warrior podcast, wrote in *Chief Executive* magazine, "Companies may not want to be pulled into politics because it's not a winning proposition—but they also cannot avoid it . . . In 2010, after *Citizens United*, we wrote that the unintended consequences of the Supreme Court's split decision to find First Amendment rights in corporations also meant that companies would have First Amendment *responsibilities*."[20]

Voters, citizens, and employees are giving more consideration to companies' responsibilities as well as their rights. Corporations, more and more seen as having power and influence, are increasingly expected to recognize that with that power comes the responsibility to use it for good. And corporations *have* used their influence for good (and not so good) in the past. Some, like IBM, made clear their position on segregation decades ago. Just a few years ago, corporate reactions to a new antitransgender law in North Carolina resulted in billions of dollars in lost business in the state, and more recently, some companies have spoken out about LGBTQ-related bills,[21] voting rights,[22] and abortion restrictions.[23]

Employees are not seeking a one-way relationship—from the company to the employees. They want to shape what kind of company their firm is so that it better matches the kind of company that employees want to work for, one that reflects their values. When they push companies to act with values, employees are a huge force.

As Amy Walter of *Cook Political Report* noted in 2021, a 2016 survey taken of major corporations by the Public Affairs Council found that 60 percent experienced rising stakeholder pressure to get engaged in social issues such as discrimination, sustainability, human rights, and education. The two groups pushing them most in this direction were senior management (78 percent) and employees (70 percent).[24]

Events and employees both continue to change in ways that raise the pressure on companies to take stands that align with values. This is partly because big companies' employees are more concentrated in metropolitan areas[25] and partly because the new employees companies want to recruit are younger—largely millennials and Gen Z. Therefore, new employees are more apt to see their work and employer as reflections of what they value.

This is a big deal. A 2019 Edelman survey asked respondents about purpose-related aspects of companies, including whether an aspect related to purpose would have to be a fit with what they wanted. If it wasn't a fit, what would the consequence be, if any? What Edelman found was striking.

When it comes to the question of whether the employer was described by the phrase, "my employer has a greater purpose, and my job has a meaningful societal impact," 42 percent of respondents said this was a "strong expectation" and that "you would have to pay me a lot more to work for an organization that does not offer this." Another 25 percent of respondents went further, saying it was a "dealbreaker" and that they would "never work for an organization that does not offer this."[26] The takeaway is that an organization without a greater purpose, one that's not creating meaningful social impact, might not be considered by a quarter of jobseekers. An additional 40 percent plus would need to be paid a lot more to join such an organization.[27]

Of course, the company still has to offer a competitive package—a good career path, chances to move up, and so forth. But even when it comes to the personal autonomy and opportunity in a job, one aspect of "personal empowerment" is a culture that's "values-driven and inclusive." Some 43 percent of respondents said personal empowerment was a strong expectation, while 31 percent said its absence would be a dealbreaker.[28]

Now More than Ever: Civic Responsibilities

As an example of what many employees (and others) now expect of companies, consider voting rights. In 2021, Republicans in the legislature of the State of Georgia proposed a bill to make changes to the handling of elections in a way that seemed targeted at reducing the number of votes for Democrats, including by making it harder for Black voters to vote.

Many Black churchgoers vote on the Sunday before Election Day, and the draft law proposed to end the ability to do that. (Unlike the other provisions below, this one didn't make it into the final law.) The bill also banned the provision of food and water for people waiting in line to vote, which has a greater effect on Black voters because minorities typically wait much longer to vote. It also reduced the number of drop boxes where voters could drop off their ballots, with the biggest impact being in the more populated counties (which tend to support Democrats and where one-third of the state's Black voters live), where initial estimates were that the number of boxes would shrink by three-quarters.[29]

Despite the law's clear intent to slash the votes of the Black community, few large Georgia employers spoke up . . . at first. Soon, however, the pressure for corporations to stand up for voting rights began to snowball. First, Delta Airlines, the state's largest employer, faced a backlash over its noncommittal statement about the law. Then the CEO of Coca-Cola spoke out against the bill, saying that voting is a fundamental right and should not be made more difficult. Major League Baseball even pulled its All-Star game from Atlanta, moving it to Colorado.

Finally, more than one hundred companies[30] signed a joint statement opposing laws that make it more difficult to vote, especially if they selectively targeted certain people, as was the case in Georgia, Texas, and other states. A number of these were large, influential corporations in the states that considered passing such laws, such as American Airlines and Dell, both headquartered in Texas. In Michigan, thirty of the state's largest companies put out a joint statement of opposition against proposed voting restrictions.[31]

Other companies that signed on to statements supporting voting rights were large, influential enterprises on a national scale, such as Amazon, Google, Netflix, and Starbucks.[32] Former American Express CEO Kenneth Chennault, who helped organize the largest joint statement, said, "It should be clear that there is overwhelming support in corporate America for the principle of voting rights."[33]

Now More than Ever: Tracking and Transparency

The social and political actions of businesses are tracked and reported on to a far greater extent than they used to be. For example, organizations that track political donations now take note when a company donates to a lawmaker who refused to accept the results of the 2020 US election, and this monitoring continues, long after the event itself. That doesn't mean a company won't donate to those lawmakers (a little under a year and a half after the attack on the US Capitol, more than half of companies that had at one point ceased donating to election objectors had resumed their donations[34]), but it does mean that it won't slip beneath the radar.

Other organizations track public responses to governmental actions, such as banning Muslims from entering the United States. Still others track how well employees are treated, how accepting companies are of LGBTQ+ employees, and a thousand other issues. This increased visibility is not going away. In fact, it's growing.

As Elizabeth Doty of the University of Michigan put it, "Increasing company political activity, combined with the problem of internal siloes and the outsourcing of advocacy to third-party trade associations, political nonprofits and lobbying firms exposes companies to severe reputational risks with their employees, customers, investors and the communities where they do business. This risk is even higher with younger generations—who no longer ask, but expect, companies to use their political influence to address the systemic threats facing us as a society."[35] And as Richard Levick put it, "There's no longer that neutral middle. Like it or not, corporations are thrust into the public policy arena."[36]

Companies' commitment levels may wax and wane, and some may choose to tack according to the prevailing political winds (or try, with decreasing success, to "keep their heads down"). But although the leaders who hold the reins of political power may shift—as may the specific issues that top the societal agenda—these trends in the attitudes of citizens will continue to gain strength. Companies have seen this happen before, on issues from segregation to rights for same-sex couples, and they should expect the pattern to continue.

The Shift in Same-Sex Benefits

Looking back, it is hard to believe but at the beginning of this century none of the Big Three automakers offered employee benefits for same-sex partners—not GM, not Ford, not Chrysler. What caused a change? Employees. As the *New York Times* wrote in 2001, "Relations between the industry and many gay people warmed considerably last year when the Detroit automakers began offering employee benefits to same-sex partners, under a joint agreement with the United Automobile Workers.

The change came after Big Three employees jointly petitioned the companies, and the union, on the issue."[37]

Employees who make their voices heard about what matters to them is part of this new dynamic. The other part is customers, stakeholders, and others looking at how a company treats its employees. For example, in 1995 only one car company advertised in gay media: Subaru.[38] But after LGBTQ customers helped Subaru return to growth after its troubles in the early 1990s, other companies also began to see LGBTQ customers as valuable, so other automakers started marketing to them also.

Here, LGBTQ employees helped companies to avoid mistakes marketing to them. As one member of a Ford gay employee group said, "we also told Ford not to try and consider direct marketing to gay and lesbian consumers until they had their internal policies in place. You run the risk of being seen as, 'You just want to take our money but you don't care about your gay employees.'"[39]

That was good advice. In 2019, Edelman surveyed tens of thousands of individuals in twenty-seven separate markets, finding that the way a company treats its employees has an effect on what customers think about it. When asked whether they agreed or disagreed with the statement "How a company treats its employees is one of the best indicators of its level of trustworthiness," 78 percent agreed.[40] In other words, people believe that how you treat your employees reflects what kind of company you are.

Employees also pay close attention to what kind of company you are and what kind of company they want to be associated with. For example, in 2020 Edelman asked questions about how employees specifically expect their company to reflect values. The responses were very instructive:

- More than nine in ten employees—92 percent—say that they expect their employer's CEO to speak up on one or more issues ranging from income inequality to diversity and training for jobs of the future.
- About three out of four employees—73 percent—expect a prospective employer to offer the opportunity to shape the future of society in a positive way.[41]

This plays out in employees' desire to stay with their current employer. WeSpire's 2023 report on engagement and impact found that employees who agree their employer is "making a positive impact on the world" are 2.2 times more likely to be retention secure (unlikely to leave), while employees who agree that the "mission or purpose of my company makes me feel my job is important" are 2.5 times more likely to be retention secure.[42]

Now More than Ever: A Culture of Values

If it's common knowledge that purpose and values are growing in importance to today's workforce—and tomorrow's—how can you stand out? The answer is actions.

It's clear that officially espousing values (having a values statement or putting up posters) is not the same as actually *having* them. How do employees (and prospective employees) tell the difference? They look for who is acting on them. Who is disseminating them? Who is infusing their staff, their processes and practices, and their products and projects with them? Who is holding management accountable for them and using them to make decisions?

Actions like these are differentiators because research shows that in almost all companies, employees don't universally share the companies' official values—if they're even aware of them. It's not possible to have a values-based operation unless workers are clear about what the values are and have bought into them.

Consulting firm Eagle Hill found that nearly nine out of ten (89 percent) employees who said they were clear about their companies' core values also said that their decisions and behavior at work were driven by them. That sounds great until you learn that only 53 percent of respondents were in that category. The rest—almost half—had no idea. When that happens, said Eagle Hill CEO Melissa Jezior, "that's a warning signal that an organization can't effectively execute on its business strategies, has a workforce morale issue, or is vulnerable to ethical lapses."[43]

Okay, it's critical to ensure the staff knows a business's values, but is that enough? It is not. There must be constant physical reminders, such as statements embedded into internal documents and regular discussion and chatter within the firm (e.g., natural foods giant Whole Foods Market puts the company's values on the wall of every store). Salience—how top of mind something is—affects decision-making, meaning decisions can change when what is most salient changes.

Of course, putting values on the wall is not enough; they have to be part of how the business operates. When values are part of everyday actions, discussions, documents, and projects at the firm, they are salient in the minds and hearts of the staff. Salience makes it more likely those values will be put into action across the company.

Where to Start

Step one is to enable employees to see the company's values more clearly. This means talking about them more internally (as KPMG did with purpose and its role in the world) and talking more about them externally as well, especially to prospective employees (such as including them in interviews and recruiting).

Step two is to see whether your values are reflected in your actions around employees, consciously or not. Are your company's values reflected in the choices it makes around where to recruit, who to recruit, and the company's expectations for employees?

For example, if your company values fairness and equal opportunity, do you recruit at schools that are likely to be attended by individuals with diverse backgrounds or from different socioeconomic statuses? If you believe that people can be strong contributors regardless of academic background or credentials, do you look for potential hires among the 60 percent plus of individuals who do not have a four-year college degree?

When you make hiring decisions, do you encourage people to make a first, "blind" evaluation by not looking at potentially biasing information—such as a candidate's name, picture, and college graduation year—until after they have formed an initial judgment based on the rest of the application?[44]

And if you value giving both men and women the opportunity to excel, are the company's expectations and culture compatible with that? If your company has a culture of very long hours and (perhaps without knowing it) is less likely to promote those who take accommodations (as researchers found at a global consulting firm[45]), then women are likely to be disproportionately affected. (And men lose out too, of course, often feeling that they have to sacrifice important family time.)

Step three is to take evidence-based actions to bring your values to bear more often. When it comes to dealing with people, there are no shortage of theories, ideas, and service providers willing to help—but they don't all work equally well. In fact, some don't work at all or even backfire.[46] Others work in some circumstances but not others.

But just as a company wouldn't conclude that advertising can't work just because one ad campaign flops, the fact that some values-based programs don't work doesn't mean others can't. (For example, as mentioned earlier, while many diversity training programs don't work, others do.[47])

Step four is to say more about your focus on, and actions around, values. It's valuable to be transparent about the issues you're trying to address, the challenges of addressing them, and the actions you're taking. This is especially true when it comes to framing values as ways to learn more, see different perspectives, and get better results. An inclusive learning orientation fits with the aspects of decision-making covered in the previous parts, and research suggests that having people adopt this orientation can make some initiatives (such as diversity initiatives) much more effective.[48]

Are there companies with official values that actually act in opposition to those values, in nefarious, even criminal, ways? Of course. Some companies are guilty of *values washing*, putting one face out to the world while ignoring their espoused principles in practice. But integrating values into every aspect of the company makes values washing harder. One company with tens of thousands of employees realized values should be included in recruiting—since that appeals to the people the company wants and reduces mistakes that come from hiring people who don't share its values. Added to those benefits, though, is another one: the more people who join the organization in part due to its values, the less likely it is that the company will succumb to the temptation to values wash—and the less likely it is employees won't call the company on it.

Putting values into practice doesn't happen on its own. It takes enormous, ongoing commitment to accomplish. Companies that genuinely go after values are much more likely to stick it out—and are therefore much more likely to reap the benefits.

VI Leadership

I know about myself that I could not follow a leader if we did not have shared values and if I did not believe that that person was authentic to the values that we have in common.

—LeVar Burton[1]

In this part, I'll cover a key *individual* benefit of values: they make people more willing to follow you and make you a more effective leader.

14 Why Follow You?

It's natural to wonder, "If values matter to customers, if they motivate employees, wouldn't they also have an effect on those who follow a leader? Wouldn't a leader benefit from making it clear that they base their thoughts, actions, and words on values? And they share those values with the individuals they are trying to lead?"

You want to be the kind of person that others want to follow. Although it's possible to fool people, at least some of the time, what you really want is to be the kind of person that individuals truly want to follow. When you're clear about your values and you act on them, it becomes a force shaping who you are.

Dr. Sunnie Giles asked 195 leaders in fifteen countries and over thirty global organizations to rank seventy-four leadership competencies. "Has high ethical and moral standards" was number one.[1] This makes sense; ask yourself, are you more likely to follow someone who you believe has real character? Of course. And, as Dr. Giles says, values are the key: high ethical and moral standards are "all about behaving in a way that is consistent with your values."

Interestingly, this is true even when it comes to "following" yourself. You are more likely to follow yourself—to commit, follow through, and put real energy and creativity behind your decisions—when you recognize them as driven by your values. It's also the case when you recognize yourself as someone who has true character. Focusing your thoughts on values, and on the things that truly matter, shapes your actions, habits, and character in a way that shapes your destiny.

The idea of "following yourself" may seem strange. But there's fascinating evidence that we can "see" ourselves from the outside, and it changes our decisions and behaviors. For example, thinking of your future self, years into the future, actually changes what you decide in the present.[2] One explanation for this change is that it pulls you away from immediate pressures and temptations, focusing your mind on the long term and on who you really are.

Dr. Giles describes her preferred technique this way: "If you find yourself making decisions that feel at odds with your principles or justifying actions in spite of a nagging sense of discomfort, you probably need to reconnect with your core values. . . . Envision your funeral and what people say about you in a eulogy. Is it what you want to hear?"

Values that emphasize doing good for the world bring an additional benefit: they push people to focus less on themselves, which improves leadership potential. Analyzing data from the U.S. military, research found that individuals who are less self-centered are better set up to be leaders.[3]

Trust and Leading by Example

In addition to helping you be a better person, values help you connect better with others and make others more likely to follow you. Have you ever met a person who struck you as really values driven, someone who you can see has the integrity to take the harder path because it aligns with their values? Maybe you've admired someone like that even when you disagreed with them. Maybe you have noticed the strength they have and found value in it even when you believe they were wrong about something. That's a second way in which values help you lead: they're visible to others, and they make you stand out. Values can draw others toward you or can prevent them from pushing you away as strongly.

What happens when people at your company see you as more ethical, more trustworthy, and exhibiting higher integrity? They're more likely to trust you. Luigi Guiso, Paola Sapienza, and Luigi Zingales examined employee responses from over one thousand firms and found that when employees perceive top managers as trustworthy and ethical, the firm's performance was stronger. Specifically, high levels of perceived integrity were related to higher productivity, profitability, better industrial relations, and higher level of attractiveness to prospective job applicants.[4]

That sounds great, right? But values aren't only about what you say—they're about what you do. Guiso and his coauthors continue: "For a social norm to be enforced it must be shared by most people in a community. In particular, in a firm it must be shared and followed by who is at the top. This is really a case of 'lead by example.'"[5] Note the emphasis on leading by *example*, not by words. Guiso's team also examined what firms said characterized their cultures—their official corporate values. They found that "proclaimed values appear irrelevant."[6]

While Guiso and his coauthors looked at things in terms of overall firm performance, the dynamics they note—increased productivity and profitability—are also valuable at the team level. Whether it's a division or an office or a task force or a department or just a small working group, people are people. Being who they are, they're more likely to follow and put in effort for a leader they perceive as having strong values.

When you have strong values and are clearly a person of integrity, someone who cares about things beyond yourself, it increases the likelihood that people trust you. Trust has been covered before, but it's worth reiterating here: trust is a large part of why people believe you and follow you. As leadership pioneer Warren Bennis says, "trust is the lubrication that makes it possible for organizations to work."[7]

This is true whether it's a small department, a big office, a division, or a complete company. When people believe that you have values, when people share your values, and when they see you living your values, they're more likely to trust you. And that makes the organization work better.

Ethos

The role played by the values of a person in gaining followers has been discussed for millennia. Aristotle divided the key strategies for persuasion into three: ethos, pathos, and logos. Logos is about the logic of an argument, and pathos is about the emotions stirred by the argument, but ethos is about the individual speaking—who the speaker is as a person.

At its core, ethos means being convincing in part because of the character of the speaker. Or, to put it simply, "We tend to believe people whom we respect."[8] Part of that respect is about an individual's values or ethics—in fact, the word "ethics" is derived from the same root as "ethos."

Without values, you cannot inspire the same level of trust, which robs you of important, fertile ground for persuading people. You need to be seen as a competent, intelligent, and moral figure.[9]

Inspiration

Simon Sinek, who wrote the book *Start with Why*, also gave the third most-popular TED talk in history, "How Great Leaders Inspire Action," which has been viewed well over 60 million times. Sinek says that the secret to inspiring people is not to start with the "what," (such as "this is a great computer") or the "how," (such as, "it's beautifully designed and easy to use"), but to start with the "why" (hence the title of his book). He says, "People don't buy what you do; they buy why you do it."

That "why" starts with your beliefs. If you talk about what you believe, you will attract those who believe what you believe.[10] That's the power of values to attract people to you, to inspire them, as Sinek says. When you talk about your values, about what you believe, then you attract others—and you inspire them to join with you. As Sinek says at the conclusion of his TED talk, "It's those who start with 'why' that have the ability to inspire those around them."[11] Which raises the question: what makes *why* answers so powerful?

Morning Consult research suggests the answer, in business at least, is *purpose*. The company surveyed Americans on the question of how they judged CEOs, and they found that almost half of the top factors used to judge CEOs related to purpose. In fact, the top driver for CEO reputation was that he or she "is contributing positively to society." In third place was "has led / is leading their company to make a positive impact on the world," with "demonstrates a sense of responsibility to act in the best interest of customers and society" and "leverages their position of power to help others, give back, and/or make a difference in society" also making the top ten.[12]

People say that one way to get a higher position is to act as you would if you already had it. When you reach the C-suite, do you want to be seen as a success? If you're being judged on values and purpose, then acting with values in mind helps. Learning to act on values, and making a habit of it throughout your ascent, helps you land the job—and helps you be the best leader you can be along the way.

Values Framing

Values help in yet another way too: showing people the connection between an issue and their values changes how receptive they are to your message. In a set of experiments involving more than four thousand people, Jan Voelkela, Joseph Mernyka, and Robb Willer, all affiliated with the Stanford department of sociology, discovered that framing the same public policy in terms of different values makes a significant difference in its popularity. This was true even though the policy itself and the speaker describing the policy stayed the same.

They found that simply framing the same policies in terms of different values meant that the candidate's positions got more support from people who would otherwise be predisposed to oppose policies such as same-sex marriage or raising the US minimum wage. The research found that the effects of increasing support for the policies occurred specifically because of the way the messages resonated with people's moral framework and values.[13]

The right framing also matters for candidates themselves, more than their policy positions. In two studies involving about eight hundred participants, framing arguments in terms of the opposition's values affected conservatives' support for Donald Trump and liberals' support for Hillary Clinton. When opposition to Trump was framed in terms of loyalty instead of fairness, conservatives were less likely to support him. Conversely, when opposition to Hillary Clinton was framed in terms of fairness rather than loyalty, liberals' likelihood to vote for her dropped.[14]

Reframing

It may seem as though environmental concerns are different between people who hold different political ideologies, such as liberal and conservative. However, research has shown that differences are at least partly a result of the way that environmental issues are framed in terms of values. Reframing issues enables you to reach people with different political ideologies.

Matthew Feinberg and Robb Willer conducted an experiment to see if expressing support for environmental policies in terms of different moral foundations would reduce the gap in support between political liberals and conservatives. It did.

Feinberg and Willer found that "reframing proenvironmental rhetoric in terms of purity, a moral value resonating primarily among conservatives, largely eliminated the difference between liberals' and conservatives' environmental attitudes."[15] This finding is crucial since it shows that many values-based actions actually have broad support— when they're connected to values that appeal to different people. Actions that have been adopted by many different groups of people— the young, the old, people from different countries, cultures, and time periods—have had champions who appealed to many different kinds of values.

Caring for the natural world (whether you call it "creation care" or "environmentalism" or "cleaning up after yourself" or "preserving the purity of nature" or "passing on a beautiful world to your children") has latent support from many different kinds of people—when each sees how it connects to their values. However, framing an issue in a way that leaves out one of the supporting values can obscure its appeal. Another problem can be when a value itself resonates but not the way it's expressed. In other words, sometimes a certain value is more universal than its usual expression makes it seem. For example, "fairness" and "equality" resonate more with liberals, but "opportunity" and "freedom" resonate more with conservatives.[16] Showing how your actions create more opportunity for all (more fair, equal opportunity) can help bridge this divide.

Beyond these types of values, plenty of other types of beliefs support the kinds of values-based actions discussed in this book. For example, environmental action can be supported by those who prize innovation since technical and organizational innovation are important levers that companies can use to dramatically reduce their environmental impact. The same is true for gaining support from those who value efficiency. After all, waste is, by definition, inefficient. The more you turn your input into things you want (products), and the less it turns into things you don't want (waste), the more efficient your process is.

My Failure to Persuade

When I was getting my MBA, I took a class about how to do better in your career, along with dozens of top-performing students at one of the most famous business schools in the world. The class used a case study about decision-making, a fictional case of an auto-racing team that had to decide whether it should run its car in a race when the temperature was much colder than normal.[17] One expert (the engine mechanic) believed that cold temperatures were behind a lot of the engine problems they had been having, so they shouldn't race. Another expert (an engineer) disagreed, saying that the engine problems weren't related to the cold.

The graphs presented in the case provided important information, based on correct data, but the presentation of the data was slightly flawed (which students weren't told). The key lesson of the case is to take the data presented to you and make sure it's organized and visualized in the correct way to draw a valid conclusion—in this case, a conclusion about whether or not to race in the cold temperatures.

But that's not what I remember most vividly. As I mentioned, there were several dozen of us in the class. We got the information, analyzed it individually, and then discussed it in a group. I thought that the mechanic was right, that the cold temperature really was likely behind the engine problems that the team had experienced, so I recommended that we not run the race. A few of the people in my group agreed with me but most didn't.

The professor next moved us to one part of the room or another depending on whether we thought the team should race or not. Then we discovered that only a handful of us thought the team shouldn't race. Everyone else was ready to race.

Here's where my memories stick with me: The professor offered people in each group the chance to explain why they recommended racing or not racing—a chance to change other people's minds, drawing them to your side. A few of us took that chance, including me. I said that this situation was like the situation with the space shuttle *Challenger*, which exploded shortly after takeoff because the temperature at launch was too cold. They shouldn't have launched the *Challenger* that day, and for similar reasons, we shouldn't run the race and risk blowing the engine.

After I stated this position, someone who recommended running the race gave their reasoning. Then the students were allowed, if they wished, to change their minds and change where they stood in the room. I eagerly waited for my persuasive prowess to pay off, leading to a stampede of people from the "yes" area of the room to my small group of "no" proponents. But that's not what happened at all. Instead, one member of our already-small group walked over to the "yes" part of the room. And no one came from that group to join ours. My speech had fallen flat.

As it turned out, the case was in fact meant to be similar to the data and the situation of the space shuttle *Challenger*. The graphs were laid out in the same, slightly flawed way that some analysis was laid out before the *Challenger* decision to launch. I had correctly identified the general thrust, pointed to the crux of the case, seen the risks from running at too low a temperature, and had even mentioned the *Challenger* as part of my effort to persuade others in the class. Yet I failed to increase the size of the group agreeing with me, and I'd even failed to prevent my side from *decreasing* in size.

The Answer Is Just the Beginning

When I got the right answer but failed to persuade any classmates, I felt both proud and humbled at the same time. I was proud that I'd figured out the core of the issue and that I'd analyzed that key issue correctly. But it was humbling to see that my attempt to persuade others, to inspire them to join my group and support my conclusion, had utterly failed.

That day brought home to me that knowing the "right" answer is nowhere near the end of what you need to do to be effective and successful, to get people to follow you. I wondered later: if I'd known then what I know now about persuasion, about appealing to core values and about ethos, if I could've been more effective at presenting my case and convincing others to join me.

In this case, the data was interpreted differently by different people. In an ambiguous situation like that, it helps if people trust you and trust your judgment, and it helps if you appeal to their values. Had I embodied the right ethos in my speech, and had I appealed to my classmates' shared values, that would have helped.

In fact, on a different occasion, I experienced this dynamic when a student at a different top university was trying to decide what to think about a complicated public policy proposal, one that included social, economic, and environmental considerations. He asked if he should be in favor or opposed since he was uncertain. Then he said that my opinion would be the deciding factor in his own decision because he knew I both thought about and *cared* about the issues involved.

Would It Have Mattered?

If I had been able to build a strong reputation with my MBA classmates, would it have been enough? I don't know—there is no guarantee that enough of them were uncertain of their decision to have their minds changed. But it definitely would have helped.

In the case of my MBA class, the end result of my failure to convince anyone to join my side was nothing more than a little bit of added humility. But what about those people who'd tried to make the case that the *Challenger* shouldn't launch, failed, and then watched it explode? And what about the executives or public servants who try to convince people to take a course of action, fail, and then see the company, the community, or the nation hurt by the exact things they warned against?

In such cases, being more persuasive, more inspiring, and convincing more people to join you is not only good for you and your personal success, but it's also good for the company, the people, and the community that would otherwise be hurt. Being known as someone who has real beliefs, expresses solid convictions, starts with why, acts in a trustworthy way, and exudes the ethos of being someone worth listening to—in all of these ways, values help you make your case.

Even If You Fail to Persuade

Appealing to common values helps you even when you don't persuade people on a specific issue. For example, in 2005, Tim Kaine was running for governor in Virginia. He didn't believe in the death penalty, but his constituents did: just before the 2005 vote for governor, about 70 percent of likely voters statewide said they favored the death penalty, and 30 percent opposed it.[18]

This result was no surprise; support for capital punishment was high for that entire decade. For example, a 2001 poll found Virginia support for the death penalty at 69.5 percent, while a 2010 poll showed little change, with support at 66 percent (31 percent opposed).[19] And Kaine's opponent criticized him harshly for his position. As the *Washington Post* noted, Kaine's "personal opposition to the death penalty prompted harsh criticism from his Republican opponent Jerry W. Kilgore during the 2005 campaign."[20]

For Kaine, this meant his personal opposition to the death penalty was a political risk even though he promised to carry out the law if elected (and in spite of his personal opposition). But he reduced the risk by framing his opposition in a way that demonstrated both conviction and a shared set of values: he shared with people that his opposition stemmed from his deep religious faith.

A Catholic, he shared that he believed the death penalty was wrong based on the tenets of his faith, saying that "the church's teaching is that you ought to have a presumption toward life and toward the protection of life."[21] Referring to the portion of the New Testament where Jesus comes upon a crowd about to stone a woman to death and stops them, he said, "the real guidance is Jesus. I mean, that's the real arbiter. And the adulterous woman [was] about to be legally executed. Christ stopped the execution."[22]

Again, most of his constituents disagreed with him—even a majority of Catholics did.[23] But Kaine won the election in spite of his opponent drawing a lot of attention to an issue on which the vast majority of voters didn't share Kaine's position. (Note that this example is not about the *source* of Kaine's values, Catholicism. As mentioned early on, this book won't focus on personal or religious values. Instead, this is an illustration of the *effect* of shared values—whatever their source—to partially transcend policy differences.)

This is only one story. It's quite possible that something else enabled Tim Kaine to be elected in the face of such a large difference between his position on the death penalty and the one held by most voters. There were certainly other issues raised during this campaign and plenty of other confounding variables that might prevent us from saying for sure why he won. But Kaine's appeal to common values appeared to prevent his unpopular opposition to the death penalty from hurting him even more.

This outcome is consistent with the research about the power of values and the fact that people whose livelihood depends on persuasion—political figures—believe it works. They might be right. Furthermore, this story isn't limited to Tim Kaine; at the same time, the governor of neighboring Maryland was a Catholic death penalty opponent. As Marc Fisher wrote in the *Washington Post* in 2009, "both Kaine and O'Malley are Catholics whose personal opposition to the death penalty is rooted in their faiths. . . . even among death penalty supporters, the idea of a governor who stands up for his religious principles has some appeal."[24]

Values and Team Performance

Values also affect how potential conflicts are handled. In a negotiation, two parties often see themselves in conflict or believe that one side has to lose for the other side to win. To improve outcomes, negotiation students are taught to start with their interests, rather than fixed positions, to create space for a win-win resolution. For example, an employee might start with "I am looking for job security" rather than "I need a two-year contract."

One study compared this interest-first method with a values-first approach to see how the two differed in terms of process and results. Both techniques worked better than the control method, produced more resolutions, and fostered a better negotiating climate. But there was also a difference in the pairs' behaviors: the values-first pairs, who underwent pre-negotiation exercises to increase understanding, "were more cooperative in the discussions from their initial positions than were those in the interests-first condition."[25] They were more effective than the usual way, just as effective as the interests-first way, and more cooperative. That's pretty good.

Maybe the combination of effectiveness and collaboration, which is so important for innovation, is why former Apple CEO Steve Jobs once said that "the only thing that works is management by values. Find people who are competent and really bright, but more importantly, people who care exactly about the same thing you care about."[26]

This brings us to another aspect of the benefit of values: increasing cooperation among team members.

Values and Team Functioning

One study found that "three factors together predicted 67% of the variance in team members' trust towards leaders, namely: consulting team members when making decisions, communicating a collective vision, and sharing common values with the leader."[27] In other words, the presence of jointly held values is one of the top factors that creates trust between a leader and members of a team. And, not surprisingly, greater trust and greater effectiveness go hand in hand.[28]

Not only do shared values increase trust in you as the leader, but they also increase trust among team members. This is important because one underappreciated scarce resource is management attention. It's not like financial resources; you can't just take out a loan or issue shares to get more management attention. (Even if you hire more managers, that doesn't necessarily solve the problem in the short term because you have to spend time training, acclimating, and getting them situated.)

One of the benefits of shared values and trust is that the team requires less attention because it works better together, pulling in the same direction more. As Thomas Stewart wrote in *Fortune* magazine more than a quarter century ago, "almost all workers are making decisions, not just filling out weekly sales reports or tightening screws. They will do as they think best. If you want them to do as the company thinks best too, then you must hope that they have an inner gyroscope aligned with the corporate compass."[29]

Trust and smooth functioning are only the beginning of the benefits realized when you put values into your leadership. Broadening the scope of values increases their power.

Expanded Concern, Expanded Power

Honest, ethical leadership matters to how employees behave at work,[30] but when the values in use are expanded to include benefiting the world, the effects on behavior expand as well. This is especially true for employees who are prosocially motivated to help others.

As we saw in the employees section, part V, values matter even when someone's not going to be with the organization long term. Vanessa Burbano of Columbia Business School conducted two experiments with temporary, online gig workers and found that a socially responsible message increased the willingness of many of them to complete extra work.[31] While not all employees were affected, some of them were, which means that a message of social benefit helps motivate increased output overall even among individuals who know that their employment is temporary.

Others also have found greater commitment to the organization as a result of an organization's socially responsible activities. In 2021, Min-Jik Kim and Byung-Jik Kim found that CSR increased organizational commitment and performance and that this link was stronger for prosocially motivated employees.[32] And while prosocial motivation varies by individual, studies have found that engaging in socially responsible activities can increase it, leading to organizational benefits. For example, Inyong Shin and Won-Moo Hur found this effect when studying hotel workers.[33]

Now More than Ever: Leadership

Leadership has changed. Purpose and values matter more, to more people, than they did before. In 2021, McKinsey found the following:

- Almost two-thirds of US-based employees said that COVID-19 had caused them to reflect on their purpose in life.
- Nearly half said that they were reconsidering the kind of work they do because of the pandemic.
- And this was even more true for millennials, who were three times more likely than others to say that they were reevaluating work.[34]

First, if you want to lead a workforce like this, you'll be expected to understand this rethinking and to have thought about values and

Where to Start

In some ways, the place to start is obvious: by clarifying your own personal values. Where do you want to focus on caring for the world and those who live in it? What does that mean to you, and how does it touch you emotionally? And what role do you personally want your work to play in bringing those values to life? (One way to think about this is to ask yourself what you want said in your eulogy.)

Step two is to think about the values of those people you want to lead, including those who might be inclined to be supportive and those who might be inclined to be skeptical. Where do your values align? How can you reach the people who are skeptical or maybe even disagree with you as well as those who already agree with you? How can you build support for doing things that improve the state of the world and those who live in it at those values' intersections? Even if you can't convince some people to join you, or support you, can you at least reduce their opposition by showing how what you want to do connects to a value they share?

Step three is to exhibit your values in your behavior. Including values in how you make decisions and how you communicate is one way. Another is to be clearly prosocial—doing things that are good for the group even if they're not immediately, directly good for you. (Of course, you can't go overboard with this. But you can't do too little either and still have people see as much leadership potential in you.)

Step four is to show how your values inform what you see—and to help others see what they illuminate for you. When you demonstrate that values lenses help you see vulnerabilities, opportunities, and important forces at work in the world (whether it's climate change, inequality, privacy, health, or something else), you give others the chance to see how you think and to see what you see. That not only helps them understand you and your perspective, but it also creates the conditions for more creativity and better decision-making for you and your teams.

Step five is to listen and be willing to learn from others. When one of your values is fairness, that means judging ideas on their merits, not on who raises them. That can mean learning from those less experienced or from those with whom you may disagree. Seek shared values with others and use them to help create the conditions for both of you to learn from each other.

purpose more deeply. Second, while the effect of any individual disruption (such as COVID) may fade, disruptions as a group are becoming more and more frequent. As they do so, the focus on purpose will remain strong and perhaps even grow with time.

Also, even when immediate disruptions fade, that doesn't mean the changes they created won't persist. For example, more than two years after the beginning of COVID, remote work stabilized at about six times the level it was trending toward before the pandemic.[35] Since hybrid work arrangements weaken loyalty,[36] it will become that much more important for leaders to use other means, such as connecting on values, to increase it.

Earlier in the book, I said that *where people are, values matter*. That applies to leadership in spades; organizations are made up of people, and people have values. Working with those values, showing that you share them, and using them to guide your actions creates benefits to you as a leader—now more than ever.

VII Coda

You've seen just how powerful values can be, for your company and yourself. This part focuses on what to do to realize that power.

15 Moving Forward

The details will vary, but at its core, putting values into practice comes down to three elements: see more, do more, and say more.

See More

Much of this book enables you to see more of what values have to offer. You can see more business benefits by including submerged value, and you can see more hidden risks (and opportunities) by looking through values lenses.

You can take this new ability to see the value of values and incorporate it into your own work—and you can help others do so as well. Start noticing and challenging the assumption that acting on values "costs too much." Just this simple change—asking if it's really true rather than simply assuming it is—makes a big difference in your thinking and planning. This is especially true when you consciously include submerged value and CORE in your thinking. Because values matter to customers and employees, and values lenses matter for operations and risks, there's tremendous value to be found now that you're looking for it.

If you've experienced learning a new term or concept and then seeing it everywhere, you'll recognize the feeling. Once you know how to think about acting on values, you start to see new opportunities to create and capture value everywhere.

Do More

Doing more builds on the changes that come from seeing more. After you see opportunities to build values into products and services, engage your company's product development process and personnel to do so. Similarly, after you see opportunities for operational improvement or risk reduction, engage with the operations and risk management teams to make those possibilities into realities.

In this book, you've seen many examples of companies doing more. Whether it's creating new offerings that address environmental or social problems (as Spoiler Alert did), lowering energy consumption (as the European pharmaceutical firm did), or reducing the amount of waste sent to landfill (as Unilever and Pfizer did), these are examples of ways to do something that benefits the world and those who live in it.

The same is true for taking a stand against segregation (as IBM did), increasing gender diversity in management (as Sodexo did), and increasing supplier diversity (as the city of Montreal did). Nike took action by creating the Atsuma running shoe design and the Flyknit production technology to reduce material use, and so did the restaurant start-up when it found a way to help more people get training and jobs.

Bed Bath & Beyond, Kohl's, Wayfair, and others dropped products from companies that vocally supported an attack on American democracy. JPMorgan, Gap, Balenciaga, Creative Artists Agency, and others severed ties with Ye's company after his antisemitic tweets.

Walmart and REI did more when they went beyond their own internal operations and changed their expectations—and their requirements—of suppliers. When Accor eliminated single-use plastic from the guest experience in over 80 percent of its properties within three years, the company challenged expectations, both of itself and also of what was possible. Accor didn't just "walk the talk," it *ran* the talk.

There are many ways to do more and many models to emulate. You don't have to do everything—but you can't do nothing.

Say More

Once you're doing more, it's good for your business to say more as well. After all, you don't realize the full benefit of values-based actions until your customers, employees, or investors know you're taking them. Incorporate values into your marketing and find ways to communicate credibly with other audiences. For example, an executive at a multibillion-dollar company said that recruiters should start talking about values in the materials they gave to prospective employees and in interviews with them—and he was exactly right.

In this respect, a key equation is *differentiation × awareness = advantage*. As the senior executive recognized, you have to be different from those you're competing against, and your audience has to be *aware* of that. If you want to woo a top recruit, it helps to have an organizational commitment to employee well-being and a track record of leadership on environmental and social issues—but only if the prospective employee knows. And the same thing is true when making a sale, when customer awareness is likewise critical to getting benefit from your values-based performance. You don't want to exaggerate (e.g., "greenwash"), but you don't want to underplay your strengths either ("green hushing").

This book has also highlighted many organizations that are saying more for another reason, too: to be catalysts, helping others do more. Organizations such as McKinsey, Deloitte, and Porter Novelli, *MIT Sloan Management Review, Harvard Business Review*, and the *New York Times* have all recognized that their knowledge and reach are key levers they can use to move the world. Universities, nonprofits, and think tanks have likewise contributed greatly to awareness about what can be done—and what works.

In these pages, you've seen numerous organizations that publicize their research and experience on dozens of topics, from the effect of values on behavior to diversity on problem-solving to organizational purpose on employee commitment. You've benefited from EY sharing its work on how well companies are disclosing climate change risk, Aon discussing how inclusivity and well-being programs help companies weather crises, Bloomberg publishing articles on how changes in the natural world are affecting businesses, and you can do the same by talking about what you do and learn.

You don't have to be a consulting firm, publisher, or academic to make a difference by saying more. There's tremendous value in sharing your company's experiences, as Sodexo did when it collected and published data on the results of its internal gender balance efforts. While you're doing more, you can also say more—to customers, suppliers, and investors and to others who can learn from you.

Low-Cost Ways to Start Saying More

Starting to say more doesn't have to cost more (although you should strongly consider investing more in communication, given the likely ROI). One company I know prints little facts about its social and environmental efforts on the bottom of packing slips, which costs basically nothing at all to do.

If you use 100 percent renewable energy for a product line, why not say so on invoices or receipts for those products? If your factory has been recognized as a top performer by three environmental and social nonprofits, why not include that on shipping labels from that factory?

Similarly, you can change company email signatures to include information on your commitments and actions. This is an easy, free opportunity to get the word out with every email.

With just a little more investment, you can provide sales representatives with a quick way to see if buyers want to hear more about your values and actions—for example, give them one or two sentences they can insert into conversations to gauge buyers' interest. If the buyer isn't interested, the discussion simply returns to the previous topic, but if the buyer is interested, there's now the chance to have a different, and meaningful, conversation. As mentioned earlier, sales representatives who talk about such topics have deeper, broader, and better relationships with their customers—all of which contribute to better performance.

The Challenge of Resources

As you've heard many times now, one of the most common reasons companies don't act on their values is their belief that they can't afford to. That's one aspect of the challenge of resources. Another is that even if something is profitable, it's not necessarily easy to secure *initial* funding or investment.

The situation may seem worse for values-related projects. Why? Because while all projects are at risk of "there's no money in the budget for that," other types of projects come with backing from departments with significant existing budgets. That is, while there may be no budget set aside for an AI initiative, there's likely to be a big budget for the IT department overall.

Less often does a department with responsibility for environmental or social initiatives have a significant budget. (While I've worked with multiple companies that invested hundreds of millions of dollars in environmental and social activities, not all companies are in this situation.)

Yet values-related activities have hidden advantages to help overcome this challenge. First, there's likely to be quite a bit of low-hanging fruit because so little has been done around values compared with what's been done to optimize IT, marketing, manufacturing, or operations.

As one example, a company I worked with discovered that it could include values in its existing marketing efforts at zero additional cost— while producing a significant increase in effectiveness. Another company realized that a tiny change to operations, one that would cost a few hundred dollars at most and could be completed easily, would produce over $5 million in benefits in the next year. These kinds of results come from putting on values lenses and seeing new, submerged opportunities that were previously missed, and they generate goodwill and momentum for further changes.

Because people genuinely do want to act on their values, even when the case is not quite as immediately clear or definitive, they're often willing to sanction a pilot program to determine if any value is really

there. Managing the scope and expectations for such a pilot is important since its success will resonate throughout the company. But the
fact that values-related opportunities normally have been overlooked
means that you'll find several opportunities available to generate good
returns with a high degree of confidence.

Add the fact that people are more creative and innovative when they
look at a problem from a different perspective, and you'll find that it's
often possible to reduce or eliminate investment challenges, at least
for a pilot. The success of a pilot can be used to generate goodwill and
evidence (and often budget) for further changes.

The Challenge of Credibility

Some companies face a challenge of credibility, where a key audience or
executive is skeptical about whether a values-based change can deliver
the promised benefits. This is why, at Valutus, we start with AIM—
analyzing the key audiences and then determining what information,
metrics, and messaging they will find credible. I recommend that you
take this approach as well.

Often, we find that key audiences are more skeptical about certain
elements of benefit but are less skeptical about others. This insight is
extremely helpful. It's almost always possible to show a very substantial
return even without using every benefit element of CORE for two reasons: one, because the ROI for values-based action is so high and two,
because the fact that much of the benefit was submerged means less
has been done.

For example, one multibillion-dollar company didn't want to consider
employee value but rather focus solely on customer- and operations-
related value. Working together, we were able to identify benefits worth
hundreds of millions of dollars. Even for a large company, a benefit of
hundreds of millions of dollars is normally more than enough to gain
attention and support.

You also want to speak the language of skeptics and bring credible,
conservative numbers. In terms of language, if you say "percent" when

you mean "percentage point," that lowers your credibility with a finance expert. The need for credibility also means you need to test for causality, not just correlation, in your research and know the margin of error of your numbers. And be conservative with your estimates—skeptics aren't used to that, and it goes a long way toward raising your credibility.

Credibility especially requires "following the physics" and understanding the operational reality of the business. You don't want to be like the famous consulting firm that built a model of a leather factory only to discover later that when the price of leather went down, the model converted the leather back into cows! Such mistakes are credibility killers to be avoided at all costs.

The Challenge of ROI

But the biggest, most common challenge companies talk about with us is "We'd love to do more to put our values into practice, but we can't afford to." Sometimes this is followed up with additional detail such as, "Competition is getting fiercer, the world is becoming less predictable, and it's becoming that much more difficult to generate the growth and profits that we want. We can't get distracted by something new."

This challenge brings us back to the central theme of this book: putting to rest the myth that values are a *cost*. Values aren't a liability or a distraction, and they don't subtract from financial success—they enhance it.

Competing in a more difficult market, within a more competitive, less predictable world, means values are critical to success: to finding added value where it seemed that there wasn't any, to standing out to the world by doing good, doing the right thing, and being transparent.

The myth persists in large part because so much of values' benefits are submerged. You've now learned to surface what was submerged, to see through lenses that show you where value lies hidden and the myriad ways that acting on values truly matters: to customers, to operations, to risks, to employees, and to your own leadership journey.

Now, it's time to take action to realize the value of values for yourself.

Acknowledgments

This book was not a solo effort. Many people helped make it happen.

Dimitar Vlahov planted the seed, all those years ago, that turned into this book. Our conversation happened because KoAnn Skrzyniarz created the community and the space for it. Thank you both.

Turning this from a rough manuscript into a published book might not have happened at all without Jared Sheehan helping me get the word out and Amy Larkin connecting me with people who knew the ins and outs of the process. One of those people was Laura Yorke, who helped me refine the message and find the right home for it (and who stayed positive the whole time). I'm grateful to you all.

Andrew Winston provided invaluable support, advice, and feedback—without which this book would not have been the same. Hunter Lovins, Catherine Greener, and P. J. Simmons provided advice and a supportive community, and helped me stay sane during the depths of COVID.

Editing a book like this is a monster task, and I was fortunate to have great help from Abhi Sastry, Marc Alexis de Lacoste Lareymondie, Sean Morgan, and Dan Kempner, as well as Antonn Park, Deborah Cantor-Adams, and the MIT Press team. Any mistakes that remain are my responsibility alone.

Throughout the process, and especially when progress was slow, the encouragement I got from Holly Walker and from my parents, David and Sylvia, meant so much.

I want to add a special thank you to the many clients and colleagues who I've had the honor to work alongside.

Finally, my deepest appreciation to everyone who strives to make the world a better place. Thank you all.

Notes

Chapter 1

1. *Autobiography of Benjamin Franklin*, Project Gutenberg, accessed May 9, 2023, https://www.gutenberg.org/files/20203/20203-h/20203-h.htm.

2. IBM, "CEO Study: Own Your Impact," May 10, 2022, https://www.ibm.com/thought-leadership/institute-business-value/en-us/report/2022-ceo.

3. Florian V. Eppink, Matthew Winden, Will C. C. Wright, and Suzie Greenhalgh, "Non-Market Values in a Cost-Benefit World: Evidence from a Choice Experiment," *PLoS ONE* 11, no. 10 (October 2016): e0165365, https://doi.org/10.1371/journal.pone.0165365.

4. D. A. DiGerolamo, "Simple Stoic Advice," The Stoic Within (blog), March 18, 2021, https://medium.com/the-stoic-within/simple-stoic-advice-b22b07849d97.

5. "Chick-fil-A's Closed-on-Sunday Policy," 2009, https://web.archive.org/web/20110708145427/https://www.chick-fil-a.com/media/pdf/closedonsunday policy.pdf.

6. Chick-fil-A, "Who We Are," accessed July 30, 2022, https://www.chick-fil-a.com/about/who-we-are.

7. Rogelio Oliva and James Quinn, "Interface's Evergreen Services Agreement," Harvard Business School Case 603-112, February 2003.

Chapter 2

1. Minimalist Quotes, "Marcus Aurelius Quote: Look beneath the Surface; Let Not the Several Quality of a Thing nor Its Worth Escape Thee," February 20, 2021, https://minimalistquotes.com/marcus-aurelius-quote-21247.

2. Thomas Filk, "It Is the Theory Which Decides What We Can Observe (Einstein)," in *Contextuality from Quantum Physics to Psychology*, Vol. 6, ed. Ehtibar Dzhafarov, Scott Jordan, Ru Zhang, and Victor Cervantes (Hackensack, NJ: World Scientific, 2015), 77–92, https://doi.org/10.1142/9789814730617_0005.

3. Melissa Connolly, "The Trouble with Excess Inventory—A Quick Primer," Process Excellence Network, January 20, 2012, https://www.processexcellence network.com/lean-six-sigma-business-performance/articles/the-trouble-with -inventory-a-quick-primer.

Chapter 3

1. Avril Haines, "DNI Haines Remarks at the 2021 Leaders Summit on Climate," 2021 Leaders Summit on Climate, April 22, 2021, https://www.dni.gov /index.php/newsroom/speeches-interviews/speeches-interviews-2021/item /2208-dni-haines-remarks-at-the-2021-leaders-summit-on-climate.

2. Dan Murtaugh, Rajesh K. Singh, and Naureen S. Malik, "A Hot, Deadly Summer Is Coming, with Frequent Blackouts," Bloomberg, May 23, 2022, https://www.autoblog.com/2022/05/23/summer-electricity-shortages.

3. Kaori Kohyama, "Japanese Insurers Sell Heatstroke Coverage during Sizzling Summer," July 25, 2022, https://www.bloomberg.com/news/articles/2022-07-25 /japan-insurers-sell-heatstroke-coverage-during-sizzling-summer.

4. Shoko Oda, "Peaking Tokyo Heat Sees Residents Urged to Save Power Again," Bloomberg, June 29, 2022, https://www.bloomberg.com/news/articles /2022-06-29/peaking-tokyo-heatwave-sees-residents-urged-to-save-power-again.

5. Damian Carrington, "Revealed: How Climate Breakdown Is Supercharging Toll of Extreme Weather," *The Guardian*, August 4, 2022, https://www.the guardian.com/environment/2022/aug/04/climate-breakdown-supercharging -extreme-weather.

6. Henry Fountain and Mira Rojanasakul, "The Last 8 Years Were the Hottest on Record," *New York Times*, January 10, 2023, https://www.nytimes.com /interactive/2023/climate/earth-hottest-years.html.

7. Jeff Berardelli, "100.4 Degree Arctic Temperature Record Confirmed as Study Suggests Earth Is Warmest in at Least 12,000 Years," CBS News, July 1, 2020, https://www.cbsnews.com/news/arctic-temperature-record-100-4-degrees-earth -warmest-12000-years.

8. Berardelli, "100.4 Degree Arctic Temperature Record Confirmed."

9. Andy Pitman, Anna Ukkola, and Seth Westra, "What Is a One-in-100 Year Weather Event? And Why Do They Keep Happening So Often?" UNSW Newsroom, March 24, 2021, https://newsroom.unsw.edu.au/news/science-tech/what -one-100-year-weather-event-and-why-do-they-keep-happening-so-often

10. Pitman, Ukkola, and Westra, "What Is a One-in-100 Year Weather Event?"

11. Erin X. Wong, "Last Month Was the Hottest August Yet in North America and Europe," Bloomberg, September 15, 2022, https://www.bloomberg.com /news/articles/2022-09-15/last-month-was-the-hottest-august-yet-in-north -america-and-europe#xj4y7vzkg.

12. William Wilkes, Jack Wittels, and Irina Vilcu, "Historic Drought Threatens to Cripple European Trade," Bloomberg, August 10, 2022, https://www.bloom berg.com/news/features/2022-08-10/europe-s-low-water-levels-threaten-rhine -river-hit-80b-trade-lifeline.

13. Leo Sands, "Pakistan Floods: One Third of Country Is under Water— Minister," BBC News, August 30, 2022, https://www.bbc.com/news/world -europe-62712301.

14. Brian K. Sullivan and Sybilla Gross, "The World Has a $1 Trillion La Nina Problem," Bloomberg, September 15, 2022. https://www.bloomberg.com /graphics/2022-la-nina-weather-risk-global-economies.

15. David I. Armstrong McKay, Arie Staal, Jesse F. Abrams, Ricarda Winkelmann, Boris Sakschewski, Sina Loriani, Ingo Fetzer, Sarah E. Cornell, Johan Rockström, and Timothy M. Lenton, "Exceeding 1.5°C Global Warming Could Trigger Multiple Climate Tipping Points," Science 377, no. 6611 (September 9, 2022): eabn7950, https://doi.org/10.1126/science.abn7950.

16. Sasha Stashwick, "Buy Clean Takes Center Stage at US DOT and Other Agencies," NRDC, September 15, 2022, https://www.nrdc.org/experts/sasha -stashwick/buy-clean-takes-center-stage-dot-and-other-agencies.

17. Ryan T. Beckwith and Bill Allison, "Five US States Will Decide If the 2024 Election Can Be Stolen," Bloomberg, August 7, 2022, https://www.bloomberg .com/graphics/us-election-risk-index/about.

18. Zenger News, "Extreme Temperatures Linked to Rise in Hate Tweets, Study Shows," Newsweek, September 19, 2022, https://www.newsweek.com/extreme -temperatures-linked-rise-hate-tweets-study-shows-1744122.

19. Jianghao Wang, Nick Obradovich, and Siqi Zheng, "A 43-Million-Person Investigation into Weather and Expressed Sentiment in a Changing Climate," *One Earth* 2, no. 6 (June 2020): 568–577, https://doi.org/10.1016/j.oneear.2020.05.016.

20. Jessie Yeung, "US Bans Imports from China's Xinjiang Region over Forced Labor Concerns," CNN, June 22, 2022, https://www.cnn.com/2022/06/21/us/us-import-ban-xinjiang-goods-forced-labor-china-intl-hnk/index.html.

21. Foo Y. Chee, "Exclusive: EU Aims to Ban Products, Imports Made with Forced Labour," *Reuters*, September 9, 2022, https://www.reuters.com/markets/europe/exclusive-eu-seeks-ban-products-made-with-forced-labour-document-2022-09-09.

22. Lucy Wallace and Alicia Bayly, "US Inflation Hit 40-Year High in June, Driven by Record Gas Prices," CNN, July 13, 2022, https://www.cnn.com/2022/07/13/economy/cpi-inflation-june/index.html.

23. Statista, "EU Inflation Rate 2022," accessed December 13, 2022, https://www.statista.com/statistics/685943/cpi-inflation-rate-europe.

24. "Climate Litigation Spikes, Giving Courts an 'Essential Role' in Addressing Climate Crisis," *UN News*, accessed May 11, 2023, https://news.un.org/en/story/2021/01/1083032.

25. Combined total of US and global cases listed in the Climate Change Litigation Database of Sabin Center for Climate Change Law at Columbia Law School, as of May 11, 2023, http://climatecasechart.com.

26. Isabella Kaminski, "Why 2023 Will Be a Watershed Year for Climate Litigation," *The Guardian*, January 4, 2023, https://www.theguardian.com/environment/2023/jan/04/why-2023-will-be-a-watershed-year-for-climate-litigation.

27. Seth Borenstein, "Warming-Stoked Tides Eating Huge Holes in Greenland Glacier," *Los Angeles Times*, May 8, 2023, https://www.latimes.com/world-nation/story/2023-05-08/warming-stoked-tides-eating-huge-holes-in-greenland-glacier; Chris Mooney and Brady Dennis, "Seas Have Drastically Risen Along Southern US Coast in Past Decade," *Washington Post*, April 10, 2023, https://www.washingtonpost.com/climate-environment/2023/04/10/sea-level-rise-southern-us.

28. Olivia White, Kevin Buehler, and Sven Smith, "The Russia-Ukraine Crisis: Twelve Global Disruptions," McKinsey, May 9, 2022, https://www.mckinsey.com/business-functions/strategy-and-corporate-finance/our-insights/war-in-ukraine-twelve-disruptions-changing-the-world.

29. White, Buehler, and Smith, "The Russia-Ukraine Crisis."

30. Matt Lindner (@mattlindner), "The CEO of Dick's Sporting Goods on LinkedIn," Twitter, June 24, 2022, 11:56 a.m., https://twitter.com/mattlindner /status/1540363274910171137.

31. Karen R. Harper, "Texas Abortion Foes Use Legal Threats and Propose More Laws to Increase Pressure on Providers and Their Allies," *Texas Tribune*, July 18, 2022, https://www.texastribune.org/2022/07/18/texas-abortion-laws-pressure -campaign.

32. Caroline Kitchener and Devlin Barrett, "Antiabortion Lawmakers Want to Block Patients from Crossing State Lines," *Washington Post*, June 30, 2022, https://www.washingtonpost.com/politics/2022/06/29/abortion-state-lines; Saul Loeb, "Missouri Lawmakers Propose Banning Getting Abortions in Other States," NBC News, accessed August 12, 2022, https://www.nbcnews.com/news /us-news/missouri-lawmakers-propose-banning-obtaining-abortion-another -state-rcna20465.

33. Cat Zakrzewski, "South Carolina Bill Outlaws Websites That Tell How to Get an Abortion," *Washington Post*, July 22, 2022, https://www.washingtonpost .com/technology/2022/07/22/south-carolina-bill-abortion-websites.

34. Adam Wren (@adamwren), "Eli Lilly and Co.—among Indiana's largest employers—on the state's new near-total abortion ban: 'Given this new law, we will be forced to plan for more employment growth outside our home state.'" Twitter, August 6, 2022, 8:30 a.m., https://twitter.com/adamwren/status /1555894094244741120.

35. Michael J. Broyde, and Timothy R. Holbrook, "Opinion: Marriage Equality Laws and Roe's Reversal," *The Atlanta Journal-Constitution*, July 7, 2022.

36. Peter Dazeley, "Birth Control Restrictions Could Follow Abortion Bans, Experts Say," NBC News, June 24, 2022. https://www.nbcnews.com/health /health-news/birth-control-restrictions-may-follow-abortion-bans-roe-rcna35289.

37. David Gelles, "How Republicans Are 'Weaponizing' Public Office Against Climate Action," *New York Times*, August 5, 2022, https://www.nytimes.com /2022/08/05/climate/republican-treasurers-climate-change.html.

38. Lauren Giella, "Norwegian Cruise Line Balks at Florida Banning Businesses from Requiring COVID Vaccines," *Newsweek*, May 7, 2021, https://www.news week.com/norwegian-cruise-line-balks-florida-banning-businesses-requiring -covid-vaccines-1589712.

39. Greg Sargent (@theplumlinegs). This segment also features a comically perfect example of Ron DeSantis confessing right out in the open that his governmental actions against Disney were designed to retaliate against the company for its "views and ideology," Twitter, May 5, 2023, 7:51 a.m., https://twitter.com/ThePlumLineGS/status/1654453798528532482.

40. IBM, "Building an Equal Opportunity Workforce," IBM100, March 7, 2012, http://www-03.ibm.com/ibm/history/ibm100/us/en/icons/equalworkforce.

41. IBM, "Building an Equal Opportunity Workforce."

Chapter 4

1. Richard J. Leider, *The Power of Purpose: Find Meaning, Live Longer, Better*, 3rd ed. (San Francisco: Berrett-Koehler Publishers, 2015).

2. Munteanu C. Cătălin and Pagalea Andreea, "Brands as a Mean of Consumer Self-Expression and Desired Personal Lifestyle," *Procedia—Social and Behavioral Sciences*, 109 (January 2014): 103–107, https://doi.org/10.1016/j.sbspro.2013.12.427.

3. Paul Krugman, "How to Destroy a Brand, Musk Style," *New York Times*, December 30, 2022, https://www.nytimes.com/2022/12/30/opinion/elon-musk-tesla-democrats.html.

4. Daniel Ladik, Francois Carrillat, and Mark Tadajewski, "Belk's (1988) 'Possessions and the Extended Self' Revisited," *Journal of Historical Research in Marketing* 7, no. 2 (January 2015): 184–207, https://doi.org/10.1108/JHRM-06-2014-0018.

5. Enrique P. Becerra, Lorena Carrete, and Pilar Arroyo, "A Study of the Antecedents and Effects of Green Self-Identity on Green Behavioral Intentions of Young Adults," *Journal of Business Research* 155 (January 2023): 113380, https://doi.org/10.1016/j.jbusres.2022.113380.

6. Natalie Lacey, "Global Trends 2020: Understanding Complexity," Ipsos, February 27, 2020, https://www.ipsos.com/sites/default/files/ct/publication/documents/2020-02/ipsos-global-trends-2020-understanding-complexity.pdf.

7. For example, Sustainable Brands 2022 conference sponsors included companies such as Nestle and Target. See Sustainable Brands, "Sponsors & Partners," accessed June 16, 2022, https://sustainablebrands.com/conferences/sustainablebrands/sponsors-partners.

8. Porter Novelli, "Purpose Perception Implicit Association Study," February 2021, https://www.porternovelli.com/wp-content/uploads/2021/02/Purpose-Perception-2021-Porter-Novelli-Implicit-Association-Study.pdf.

9. Adeline Diab and Gina M. Adams, "ESG Assets May Hit $53 Trillion by 2025, a Third of Global AUM," Bloomberg Intelligence, February 23, 2021, https://www.bloomberg.com/professional/blog/esg-assets-may-hit-53-trillion-by-2025-a-third-of-global-aum.

10. MSCI, "Explore 30 Years of ESG," accessed June 6, 2022, https://www.msci.com/esg/30-years-of-esg. The first index, introduced in 1990, was the Domini 400 Social Index, now called the MSCI KLD 400 Social Index.

11. Dennis Green, "How Whole Foods Went from a Hippie Natural Foods Store to Amazon's $13.7 Billion Grocery Weapon," Business Insider, May 2, 2019, https://www.businessinsider.com/whole-foods-timeline-from-start-to-amazon-2017-9. Whole Foods CEO John Mackey opened a smaller natural foods store in 1978, which was not called Whole Foods.

12. "How Many Advertisements Do We See Each Day?" What's Working in Marketing (blog), April 15, 2014, https://blog.telesian.com/how-many-advertisements-do-we-see-each-day; Ron Marshall, "How Many Ads Do You See in One Day? Get Your Advertising Campaigns Heard," Red Crow Marketing, September 10, 2015, https://www.redcrowmarketing.com/2015/09/10/many-ads-see-one-day.

13. Zeno, "Unveiling the 2020 Zeno Strength of Purpose Study," June 17, 2020, https://www.zenogroup.com/insights/2020-zeno-strength-purpose.

14. Marketing Charts, "Most Americans Report Being More Likely to Trust a Purpose-Led Company," June 14, 2019, https://www.marketingcharts.com/brand-related/csr-108861.

15. Marketing Charts, "Purpose Pays, Consumers Say," June 6, 2018, https://www.marketingcharts.com/brand-related/csr-83626.

16. Eleanore Adams, "Analysis: High Amazon Star Rating Ups Conversion," Pattern, January 23, 2020, https://pattern.com/blog/analysis-high-amazon-star-rating-ups-conversion-sales-and-sessions.

17. Michael Luca, "Reviews, Reputation, and Revenue: The Case of Yelp.Com," Working paper 12-016, Harvard Business School, 2011, https://www.hbs.edu/ris/Publication%20Files/12-016_a7e4a5a2-03f9-490d-b093-8f951238dba2.pdf.

18. Instacart, "$10 for You, $10 for a Friend," https://www.instacart.com/store/referrals.

19. Genevieve Northup, "9 Types of Referral Bonuses," Indeed Career Guide, updated March 15, 2023, https://www.indeed.com/career-advice/pay-salary/referral-bonus.

20. Edelman, "In Brands We Trust?" Edelman Trust Barometer Special Report, 2019, https://www.edelman.com/sites/g/files/aatuss191/files/2019-07/2019_edelman_trust_barometer_special_report_in_brands_we_trust.pdf.

21. Marketing Charts, "So Informative Content Helps. But What Kind of Information?" April 16, 2018, https://www.marketingcharts.com/brand-related-83041.

22. Edelman, "2022 Special Report: The Geopolitical Business," accessed June 7, 2023, https://www.edelman.com/trust/2022-trust-barometer/special-report-geopolitical-business.

23. Maggie Koerth, "How Natural Disasters Can Change a Politician," Five ThirtyEight, September 30, 2022, https://fivethirtyeight.com/features/how-natural-disasters-can-change-a-politician.

24. Mark Strassman, "North Carolina Faces Business Boycott over Anti-LGBT Law," CBS News, March 30, 2016, https://www.cbsnews.com/news/north-carolina-faces-business-boycott-over-anti-lgbt-law.

25. Oliver Darcy, "Advertisers Abandon Fox News Host Tucker Carlson's Show over Anti-Immigration Comments," CNN, December 18, 2018, https://www.cnn.com/2018/12/18/media/tucker-carlson-fox-news-advertisers/index.html.

26. Eliza Relman, "Tucker Carlson Embraces White-Supremacist 'replacement' Conspiracy Theory, Claiming Democrats Are 'Importing' Immigrants to 'Dilute' American Voters," Business Insider, April 9, 2021, https://www.businessinsider.com/tucker-carlson-endorses-white-supremacist-replacement-conspiracy-theory-2021-4.

27. Jay Peters, "New T-Mobile CEO Tweets 'Bye-Bye, Tucker Carlson,' Won't Sponsor Him Anymore," The Verge, June 12, 2020, https://www.theverge.com/2020/6/11/21288661/t-mobile-ceo-tweets-tucker-carlson-advertising.

28. IBM, "2022 Sustainability Consumer Research: Sustainability and Profitability," April 2022, https://www.ibm.com/thought-leadership/institute-business-value/en-us/report/2022-sustainability-consumer-research.

29. Tara Burns, "COVID-19 Increasing Consumers' Focus on 'Ethical Consumption,' Accenture Survey Finds," Accenture, May 4, 2020, https://newsroom .accenture.com/news/covid-19-increasing-consumers-focus-on-ethical-con sumption-accenture-survey-finds.htm.

30. IBM, "2022 Consumer Study: Consumers Want It All," January 2022, https://www.ibm.com/thought-leadership/institute-business-value/en-us /report/2022-consumer-study.

31. Maryn Liles, "101 Iconic Baseball Quotes, Sayings & 'Yogi-Isms' from the One and Only Yogi Berra," Parade, September 20, 2020, https://parade.com /1087007/marynliles/yogi-berra-quotes.

32. Marketing Charts, "So Informative Content Helps. But What Kind of Information?"

33. Paul J. Lavrakas, "Social Desirability," in *Encyclopedia of Survey Research Methods*, ed. Paul J. Lavrakas (Thousand Oaks, CA: SAGE Publications, 2008), 826–826, https://dx.doi.org/10.4135/9781412963947.n537.

34. IRI, "Sustainability and the Consumer," accessed May 7, 2023, https:// www.iriworldwide.com/IRI/media/Library/IRI-NYU-Sustainability-2022-PDF .pdf.

35. McKinsey & Company, "Do ESG Claims on Packaging Help Products Sell Better?," accessed February 11, 2023. https://www.mckinsey.com/industries /consumer-packaged-goods/our-insights/consumers-care-about-sustainability -and-back-it-up-with-their-wallets.

36. Mintel, "Parents Drive Natural and Organic Personal Care Market," March 20, 2017, https://www.mintel.com/press-centre/beauty-and-personal-care/parents -drive-natural-and-organic-personal-care-market.

37. Michael Harris, "Neuroscience Proves: We Buy on Emotion and Justify with Logic—But with a Twist," Medium (blog), June 15, 2015, https://medium .com/@salesforce/neuroscience-proves-we-buy-on-emotion-and-justify-with -logic-but-with-a-twist-4ff965cdeed8.

38. Tanya Gazdik, "Discover Card, Avis, Google Tops in Customer Loyalty," MediaPost, February 7, 2019, https://www.mediapost.com/publications/article /331635/discover-card-avis-google-tops-in-customer-loyal.html.

39. Ben & Jerry's, "Silence Is NOT an Option," accessed October 3, 2022, https://www.benjerry.com/about-us/media-center/dismantle-white-supremacy.

40. Maxine P. Brewing, "#JustBrands: To Push Cultural Change, Brands Must Unpack Their 'BAGS.'" Sustainable Brands, August 21, 2020, https://sustainablebrands.com/read/organizational-change/justbrands-to-push-cultural-change-brands-must-unpack-their-bags.

41. BusinessWeek (@BW), ""If we share values on climate, same-sex marriage rights, racism, I think that's a deeper bond than sugar and fat." This is how Ben & Jerry's perfected the delicate recipe for corporate activism," Twitter, July 25, 2020, https://twitter.com/bw/status/1287074006722580480.

Chapter 5

1. Tanya Gazdik, "Discover Card, Avis, Google Tops in Customer Loyalty," MediaPost, February 7, 2019, https://www.mediapost.com/publications/article/331635/discover-card-avis-google-tops-in-customer-loyal.html.

2. Connor Brooke, "Brand Trust Is More Important than Ever for Consumers," Business2Community, August 9, 2019, https://www.business2community.com/branding/brand-trust-is-more-important-than-ever-for-consumers-02229321.

3. Gazdik, "Discover Card, Avis, Google Tops in Customer Loyalty."

4. Antoine Harary and Tonia Ries, "Competence Is Not Enough," Edelman, accessed June 6, 2022, https://www.edelman.com/research/competence-not-enough.

5. Harary and Ries, "Competence Is Not Enough."

6. Goodreads, "Daring Greatly Quotes (Page 3 of 25)," accessed June 6, 2022, https://www.goodreads.com/work/quotes/19175758-daring-greatly-how-the-courage-to-be-vulnerable-transforms-the-way-we-l?page=3. Brown also notes that we find it hard to be open and truthful ourselves; perhaps this makes it all the more powerful when we see others doing it. She says, "We love seeing raw truth and openness in other people, but we're afraid to let them see it in us. Here's the crux of the struggle: I want to experience your vulnerability but I don't want to be vulnerable."

7. Porter Novelli, "Purpose Pays, Consumers Say," Marketing Charts (blog), June 6, 2018, https://www.marketingcharts.com/brand-related/csr-83626.

8. Harary and Ries, "Competence Is Not Enough."

9. Dora C. Lau, Jun Liu, and Ping P. Fu, "Feeling Trusted by Business Leaders in China: Antecedents and the Mediating Role of Value Congruence," *Asia*

Pacific Journal of Management 24, no. 3 (September 1 2007): 321–340, https://doi.org/10.1007/s10490-006-9026-z.

10. Arthur W. Page Society, "The Dynamics of Public Trust in Business—Emerging Opportunities for Leaders," accessed June 6, 2022, https://knowledge.page.org/report/the-dynamics-of-public-trust-in-business-emerging-opportunities-for-leaders.

11. Matt Petronzio, "90% of Americans More Likely to Trust Brands That Back Social Causes," Mashable, January 11, 2015, https://mashable.com/archive/corporate-social-causes.

12. Bob Helbig, "The Importance of Trust and Values in Workplace Culture," Energage, December 8, 2015, https://www.energage.com/the-importance-of-trust-and-values-in-workplace-culture.

13. CNN Money, "America's Biggest Rip-Offs—Movie Theater Popcorn—900% Markup," last updated February 2, 2010, https://money.cnn.com/galleries/2010/news/1001/gallery.americas_biggest_ripoffs/2.html.

14. CNN Money, "America's Biggest Rip-Offs."

15. "Food Waste Statistics: The Reality of Food Waste," Quest, August 8, 2019, https://www.questrmg.com/2019/08/08/food-waste-statistics-the-reality-of-food-waste.

16. "Our Vision Is to Power the Waste-Free Economy - Spoiler Alert," accessed May 10, 2023, https://www.spoileralert.com/about-us.

17. "Spoiler Alert Raises $11M to Accelerate CPG Waste Prevention," accessed May 10, 2023, https://www.spoileralert.com/resources/series-a-fundraising.

18. Berkeley Lab, "Indoor Air Quality: Performance Summary," n.d, https://iaqscience.lbl.gov/performance-summary.

Chapter 6

1. Winston, Andrew, George Favaloro, and Tim Healy, "Energy Strategy for the C-Suite," *Harvard Business Review*, January 1, 2017, https://hbr.org/2017/01/energy-strategy-for-the-c-suite.

2. Winston, Favaloro, and Healy, "Energy Strategy for the C-Suite."

3. Alissa J. Rubin, Ben Hubbard, Josh Holder, Noah Throop, Emily Rhyne, Jeremy White, James Glanz, Josh Williams, Sarah Almukhtar, and Rumsey

Taylor, "Extreme Heat Will Change Us," *New York Times*, November 18, 2022, https://www.nytimes.com/interactive/2022/11/18/world/middleeast/extreme-heat.html.

4. We Mean Business Coalition, "The Climate Has Changed," September 2014, p. ix, https://www.wemeanbusinesscoalition.org/wp-content/uploads/2017/08/The-Climate-Has-Changed_3.pdf.

5. Ravi Jagannathan, Iwan Meier, and Vefa Tarhan, "The Cross-Section of Hurdle Rates for Capital Budgeting: An Empirical Analysis of Survey Data," NBER working paper 16770, 2011.

6. We Mean Business Coalition, "The Climate Has Changed," 4.

7. We Mean Business Coalition, "The Climate Has Changed," 5.

8. Unilever, "Journey to Zero Waste," February 8, 2016, https://www.unilever.com/news/news-search/2016/Unilever-announces-new-global-zero-non-hazardous-waste-to-landfill-achievement.

9. Materials that are recycled don't count as having gone to landfill, and in some cases materials that are burned to produce energy also are not considered to have gone to landfill.

10. Olivia Burton, "How Ethical and Sustainable Are Your Favourite Sportswear Brands?" The Green Hub, September 18, 2019, https://thegreenhubonline.com/2019/09/18/how-ethical-and-sustainable-are-your-favourite-sportswear-brands.

11. Brad Kennedy, "Green Spot: 3P at 3M," Industry Week, April 15, 2008, https://www.industryweek.com/the-economy/environment/article/22007795/green-spot-3p-at-3m.

12. 3M, "Our Global Impact: Sustainability/ESG," accessed September 8, 2022, https://www.3m.com/3M/en_US/sustainability-us/environmental/waste.

13. 3M News Center, "3M Marks 35 Years of Pollution Prevention Pays," April 22, 2010, https://news.3m.com/2010-04-22-3M-Marks-35-Years-of-Pollution-Prevention-Pays.

14. Joann Muller, "How GM Makes $1 Billion a Year by Recycling Waste," *Forbes*, February 21, 2013, https://www.forbes.com/sites/joannmuller/2013/02/21/how-gm-makes-1-billion-a-year-by-recycling-waste.

15. Wayne Labs, "A Lean and Green Approach to Reduce Waste, Improve Quality," Food Engineering, May 20, 2019, https://www.foodengineeringmag.com

/articles/98301-a-lean-and-green-approach-to-reduce-waste-improve-quality. Emphasis is in the original.

16. Charles Fishman, "Why GE, Coca-Cola, and IBM Are Getting into the Water Business," Fast Company, April 11, 2011, https://www.fastcompany.com /1739772/why-ge-coca-cola-and-ibm-are-getting-water-business.

17. Fishman, "Why GE, Coca-Cola, and IBM Are Getting into the Water Business."

18. Fishman, "Why GE, Coca-Cola, and IBM Are Getting into the Water Business."

19. Fishman, "Why GE, Coca-Cola, and IBM Are Getting into the Water Business."

20. Staples, "Sustainable Products," accessed June 6, 2022, https://www.staples .com/sbd/cre/marketing/about_us/corporate-responsibility/environment /sustainable-products.

21. Sustainable Business Council, "Moving Missoula toward Zero Waste Guide," April 1, 2015, https://issuu.com/sustainablebusinesscouncil/docs/toward zerowasteguide-final.

22. UPS, "Cube Optimization," https://www.ups.com/media/en/CubeOptimi zationSalesSheet.pdf.

23. Simha Mummalaneni, and Jonathan Z. Zhang, "Maximizing the Benefits of B2B Supplier Diversification," MIT Sloan Management Review, 2020.

24. Michael Schrage, "10 Three Scenarios to Guide Your Global Supply Chain Recovery," MIT Sloan Management Review, 2020.

25. Winston, Favaloro, and Healy, "Energy Strategy for the C-Suite."

26. Robert G. Eccles and Svetlana Klimenko, "The Investor Revolution," Harvard Business Review, May 1, 2019, https://hbr.org/2019/05/the-investor -revolution.

27. US Securities and Exchange Commission, "Proposed Rule," 2022, https:// www.sec.gov/rules/proposed/2022/33-11042.pdf.

28. Peter R. Orszag and Zachery Halem, "Investors Are Punishing the Polluters. Here's Proof," Washington Post, December 1, 2021, https://www.washington post.com/business/energy/investors-are-punishing-the-polluters-heres-proof /2021/12/01/b627b31e-52a6-11ec-83d2-d9dab0e23b7e_story.html.

Chapter 7

1. Scott B. Kaufman, "Does Creativity Require Constraints?" *Psychology Today*, August 30, 2011, https://www.psychologytoday.com/us/blog/beautiful-minds /201108/does-creativity-require-constraints.

2. Joel Makower, "How Sustainability Leadership Drives Innovation," Green-Biz, October 28, 2013, https://www.greenbiz.com/article/how-sustainability -leadership-drives-innovation.

3. Makower, "How Sustainability Leadership Drives Innovation."

4. Marc Stoiber, "For Brilliant Innovation, Start with Beautiful Constraint," Unreasonable (blog), accessed June 6, 2022, https://unreasonablegroup.com /articles/for-brilliant-innovation-start-with-beautiful-constraint.

5. Derick Ruiz, "The Nike Atsuma Reduces Material Waste by Increasing Pattern Efficiency," Modern Notoriety, December 23, 2019, https://www.modern -notoriety.com/nike-atsuma-release-date.

6. Nike, "Purpose Moves Us: FY18 NIKE Impact Report," 2018, https://s3-us -west-2.amazonaws.com/purpose-cms-production01/wp-content/uploads/2019 /05/20194957/FY18_Nike_Impact-Report_Final.pdf.

7. Nike, "Purpose Moves Us."

8. Harvard Business Review and EY, "The Business Case for Purpose," 2015, https://assets.ey.com/content/dam/ey-sites/ey-com/en_gl/topics/digital/ey-the -business-case-for-purpose.pdf.

9. Chin-Lung Lin and Shih-Kuan Chiu, "The Impact of Shared Values, Corporate Cultural Characteristics, and Implementing Corporate Social Responsibility on Innovative Behavior," *International Journal of Business Research and Management* 8, no. 2 (2017). http://www.cscjournals.org/manuscript/Journals /IJBRM/Volume8/Issue2/IJBRM-239.pdf.

10. Allison Holzer, Jen G. Baron, and Sandra Spataro, *Dare to Inspire: Sustain the Fire of Inspiration in Work and Life*, illustrated edition (Boston: Da Capo Lifelong Books, 2019).

11. Meril Sakaria, "Forbes: How Passion and Purpose Spark Innovation," MIT Office of Innovation, October 25, 2021, https://innovation.mit.edu/news-article /forbes-how-passion-and-purpose-spark-innovation.

12. Peter F. Drucker, "The Discipline of Innovation," *Harvard Business Review*, August 1, 2002, https://hbr.org/2002/08/the-discipline-of-innovation.

13. Rosabeth Moss Kanter, "Seven Truths about Change to Lead By and Live By," *Harvard Business Review*, August 23, 2010, https://hbr.org/2010/08/seven -truths-about-change-to-l.

14. Yang Yang, Tanya Y. Tian, Teresa K. Woodruff, Benjamin F. Jones, and Brian Uzzi, "Gender-Diverse Teams Produce More Novel and Higher-Impact Scientific Ideas," *Proceedings of the National Academy of Sciences* 119, no. 36 (September 6, 2022): e2200841119, https://doi.org/10.1073/pnas.2200841119.

15. Yang, Tian, Woodruff, Jones, and Uzzi, "Gender-Diverse Teams Produce More Novel and Higher-Impact Scientific Ideas."

16. Cristian L. Dezso and David G. Ross, "Does Female Representation in Top Management Improve Firm Performance? A Panel Data Investigation," *Strategic Management Journal* 33, no. 9 (2012): 1072–1089.

17. Dezso and Ross, "Does Female Representation in Top Management Improve Firm Performance?"

18. Rocío Lorenzo, Nicole Voigt, Karin Schetelig, Annika Zawadzki, Isabelle Welpe, and Prisca Brosi, "The Mix That Matters," Boston Consulting Group, April 26, 2017, https://www.bcg.com/publications/2017/people-organization -leadership-talent-innovation-through-diversity-mix-that-matters.

19. Rocío Lorenzo, Nicole Voigt, Miki Tsusaka, Matt Krentz, and Katie Abouzahr, "How Diverse Leadership Teams Boost Innovation," Boston Consulting Group, January 23, 2018, https://www.bcg.com/publications/2018/how -diverse-leadership-teams-boost-innovation.

20. Richard B. Freeman, and Wei Huang, "Collaboration: Strength in Diversity," *Nature* 513, no. 7518 (September 2014): 305, https://doi.org/10.1038 /513305a; Richard Freeman, and Wei Huang, "Collaborating with People Like Me: Ethnic Coauthorship within the United States," updated July 7, 2015, https://scholar.harvard.edu/freeman/publications/collaborating-people-me -ethnic-coauthorship-within-united-states.

21. Roger C. Mayer, Richard S. Warr, and Jing Zhao, "Do Pro-Diversity Policies Improve Corporate Innovation?" *Financial Management* 47, no. 3 (September 2018): 617–650, https://doi.org/10.1111/fima.12205.

22. Sylvia A. Hewlett, Melinda Marshall, and Laura Sherbin, "How Diversity Can Drive Innovation," *Harvard Business Review*, December 1, 2013, https://hbr .org/2013/12/how-diversity-can-drive-innovation

23. Hewlett, Marshall, and Sherbin, "How Diversity Can Drive Innovation."

24. Deloitte Review, "The Diversity and Inclusion Revolution: Eight Powerful Truths," January 22, 2018, https://www2.deloitte.com/uk/en/insights/deloitte -review/issue-22/diversity-and-inclusion-at-work-eight-powerful-truths.html.

25. Tata Consultancy Services, "TCS 2021 Global Leadership Study," 2021, https://www.tcs.com/insights/perspectives/articles/tcs-2021-global-leadership -study-how-leaders-are-balancing-inno.

26. Yang, Tian, Woodruff, Jones, and Uzzi, "Gender-Diverse Teams Produce More Novel and Higher-Impact Scientific Ideas."

27. Tata Consulting Services, "TCS 2021 Global Leadership Study."

Chapter 8

1. "APA Dictionary of Psychology," accessed August 27, 2022, https://diction ary.apa.org.

2. Paul Gompers and Silpa Kovvali, "The Other Diversity Dividend," *Harvard Business Review*, July 1, 2018, https://hbr.org/2018/07/the-other-diversity -dividend.

3. According to McKinsey, women represented 48 percent of entry-level employees versus 26 percent of the C-suite, while women of color represented 19 percent of entry-level employees and 5% of the C-suite. McKinsey, "Women in the Workplace 2022," accessed May 14, 2023, https://www.mckinsey.com /featured-insights/diversity-and-inclusion/women-in-the-workplace#.

4. Gompers and Kovvali, "The Other Diversity Dividend."

5. Gompers and Kovvali, "The Other Diversity Dividend."

6. Sundiatu Dixon-Fyle, Kevin Dolan, Dame V. Hunt, and Sara Prince, "How Diversity, Equity, and Inclusion (DE&I) Matter," May 19, 2020, https://www .mckinsey.com/featured-insights/diversity-and-inclusion/diversity-wins-how -inclusion-matters.

7. Dixon-Fyle, Dolan, Hunt, and Prince, "How Diversity, Equity, and Inclusion (DE&I) Matter."

8. Credit Suisse, "Credit Suisse Gender 3000 Report Shows Women Hold Almost a Quarter of Board Room Positions Globally," September 28, 2021, https://www.credit-suisse.com/about-us-news/en/articles/media-releases/credit -suisse-gender-3000-report-shows-women-hold-almost-a-quart-202109.html.

9. Investopedia, "Alpha," accessed August 30, 2022, https://www.investopedia.com/terms/a/alpha.asp.

10. Kent Thune, "What Is the Average Return of the Stock Market?" Seeking Alpha, January 2, 2023, https://seekingalpha.com/article/4502739-average-stock-market-return.

11. Mengsteab T. Beraki, Mussie T. Tessema, Parag Dhumal, Kathryn J. Ready, and Sebhatleab Kelati, "Exploring the Correlation between Diversity and Financial Performance: An Empirical Study," *International Journal of Business Performance Management* 23, no. 1–2 (January 2022): 206–223, https://doi.org/10.1504/IJBPM.2022.119578.

12. Jeremiah Green, and John R. M. Hand, "Diversity Matters/Delivers/Wins Revisited in S&P 500® Firms," Working paper, Texas A&M and UNC–Chapel Hill, August 2021, https://doi.org/10.2139/ssrn.3849562.

13. McKinsey, "Women in the Workplace 2022."

14. Frank Dobbin, and Alexandra Kalev, "Why Diversity Training Doesn't Work: The Challenge for Industry and Academia," *Anthropology Now* 10, no. 2 (2018): 48–55.

15. Deloitte Australia and Victorian Equal Opportunity and Human Rights Commission, "Waiter, Is That Inclusion in My Soup? A New Recipe to Improve Business Performance," 2013, accessed May 10, 2023, https://www2.deloitte.com/content/dam/Deloitte/au/Documents/human-capital/deloitte-au-hc-diversity-inclusion-soup-0513.pdf.

16. Yixuan Li, Jaclyn Koopmann, Klodiana Lanaj, and John R. Hollenbeck, "An Integration-and-Learning Perspective on Gender Diversity in Self-Managing Teams: The Roles of Learning Goal Orientation and Shared Leadership," *The Journal of Applied Psychology* 107, no. 9 (September 2022): 1628–1639, https://doi.org/10.1037/apl0000942.

17. Emily Hemming, "The Wharton School, Moody's and DiversityInc Release New DEI Study," News (blog), May 19, 2021, https://news.wharton.upenn.edu/press-releases/2021/05/the-wharton-school-moodys-and-diversityinc-release-new-dei-study. (For the full study, see https://www.wharton.upenn.edu/wp-content/uploads/2021/05/Applied-Insights-Lab-Report.pdf.)

18. Paul Ingram and Yoonjin Choi, "What Does Your Company Really Stand For?" *Harvard Business Review*, November 1, 2022, https://hbr.org/2022/11/what-does-your-company-really-stand-for.

19. Hemming, "The Wharton School, Moody's and DiversityInc Release New DEI Study."

20. Scott Page, *The Difference: How the Power of Diversity Creates Better Groups, Firms, Schools, and Societies—New Edition* (Princeton, NJ: Princeton University Press, 2008).

21. Sarah E. Gaither, Evan P. Apfelbaum, Hannah J. Birnbaum, Laura G. Babbitt, and Samuel R. Sommers, "Mere Membership in Racially Diverse Groups Reduces Conformity," *Social Psychological and Personality Science* 9, no. 4 (May 2018): 402–410, https://doi.org/10.1177/1948550617708013.

22. Gaither, Apfelbaum, Birnbaum, Babbitt, and Sommers, "Mere Membership in Racially Diverse Groups Reduces Conformity."

23. Sheen S. Levine, Evan P. Apfelbaum, Mark Bernard, Valerie L. Bartelt, Edward J. Zajac, and David Stark, "Ethnic Diversity Deflates Price Bubbles," *Proceedings of the National Academy of Sciences* 111, no. 52 (December 30, 2014): 18524–18529, https://doi.org/10.1073/pnas.1407301111.

24. ScienceDaily, "Racial Diversity Improves Group Decision Making in Unexpected Ways, According to Tufts University Research," April 10, 2006, https://www.sciencedaily.com/releases/2006/04/060410162259.htm.

25. Samuel R. Sommers, "On Racial Diversity and Group Decision Making: Identifying Multiple Effects of Racial Composition on Jury Deliberations," *Journal of Personality and Social Psychology* 90, no. 4 (April 2006): 597–612, https://doi.org/10.1037/0022-3514.90.4.597.

26. Denise L. Loyd, Cynthia S. Wang, Katherine W. Phillips, and Robert B. Lount, "Social Category Diversity Promotes Premeeting Elaboration: The Role of Relationship Focus," *Organization Science* 24, no. 3 (June 2013): 757–772, https://doi.org/10.1287/orsc.1120.0761.

27. Anthony L. Antonio, Mitchell J. Chang, Kenji Hakuta, David A. Kenny, Shana Levin, and Jeffrey F. Milem, "Effects of Racial Diversity on Complex Thinking in College Students," *Psychological Science* 15, no. 8 (August 2004): 507–510, https://doi.org/10.1111/j.0956-7976.2004.00710.x.

28. Katherine W. Phillips, Gregory B. Northcraft, and Margaret A. Neale, "Surface-Level Diversity and Decision-Making in Groups: When Does Deep-Level Similarity Help?" *Group Processes & Intergroup Relations* 9, no. 4 (October 2006): 467–482, https://doi.org/10.1177/1368430206067557.

29. Katherine W. Phillips, "How Diversity Makes Us Smarter," *Scientific American*, October 1, 2014, https://doi.org/10.1038/scientificamerican1014-42.

30. Phillips, Northcraft, and Nealem "Surface-Level Diversity and Decision-Making in Groups"

31. Phillips, "How Diversity Makes Us Smarter."

32. Phillips, "How Diversity Makes Us Smarter."

33. Novartis webinar on their sustainability materiality process, February 9, 2021.

34. Jie Chen, Woon S. Leung, Wei Song, and Marc Goergen, "Why Female Board Representation Matters: The Role of Female Directors in Reducing Male CEO Overconfidence," *Journal of Empirical Finance* 53 (September 2019): 70–90, https://doi.org/10.1016/j.jempfin.2019.06.002.

35. Chen, Leung, Song, and Goergen, "Why Female Board Representation Matters."

36. Linda H. Chen, Jeffrey Gramlich, and Kimberly A. Houser, "The Effects of Board Gender Diversity on a Firm's Risk Strategies," *Accounting and Finance* 59, no. 2 (June 2019): 991–1031, https://doi.org/10.1111/acfi.12283.

37. Chen, Gramlich, and Houser, "The Effects of Board Gender Diversity on a Firm's Risk Strategies."

38. Michael Landel, "Gender Balance and the Link to Performance," McKinsey Quarterly, February 1, 2015, https://www.mckinsey.com/featured-insights/leadership/gender-balance-and-the-link-to-performance.

39. Landel, "Gender Balance and the Link to Performance."

40. Sodexo, "Why Diversity Shows Up in Profit Margins & How to Make It Happen," accessed May 11, 2023, https://www.sodexo.com/en/en/blog/our-everyday-stories/business-stories/2020/gender-diversity-in-profits.

41. Sodexo Group, "Sodexo's Gender Balance Study 2018: Expanded Outcomes over 5 Years," accessed May 15, 2023, https://cn.sodexo.com/files/live/sites/com-wwd/files/02%20PDF/Case%20Studies/2018_Gender-Balance-Study_EN.pdf.

42. Erik Larson, "New Research: Inclusive Decision Making Increases Performance of Diverse Global Companies," Cloverpop, September 19, 2017, https://www.cloverpop.com/blog/new-research-inclusive-decision-making-increases-performance-of-diverse-global-companies.

43. Sodexo Group, "Sodexo's Gender Balance Study 2018."

Part IV

1. Evan Ratliff, "We Can Protect the Economy from Pandemics. Why Didn't We?" Wired, June 16, 2020, https://www.wired.com/story/nathan-wolfe-global -economic-fallout-pandemic-insurance.

2. Jack Freund, *Measuring and Managing Information Risk: A FAIR Approach* (Amsterdam: Butterworth-Heinemann, 2015).

Chapter 9

1. Brian Kennedy, "Remembering the Dot-Com Office Chair," *New York Magazine*, September 16, 2006, https://nymag.com/news/intelligencer/21364.

2. Raina Kelley, "How James Dyson Revolutionized the Vacuum," *Newsweek*, January 13, 2011, https://www.newsweek.com/how-james-dyson-revolution ized-vacuum-67039.

3. Emma Clark, "Dyson's Domestic Dilemma," BBC News, October 2, 2003, http://news.bbc.co.uk/2/hi/business/3113002.stm.

4. Rebecca Smithers, "Dyson Sues Rival Vax over Vacuum Cleaner Design," *The Guardian*, January 27, 2010, https://www.theguardian.com/business/2010 /jan/27/dyson-sues-vax.

5. Cambridge Dictionary, "Hoovering," accessed June 6, 2022, https:// dictionary.cambridge.org/us/dictionary/english/hoovering.

6. Porter Novelli, "Addressing Social Justice & Diversity in Communications," Purpose Tracker, January 6, 2021, https://www.porternovelli.com/wp-content /uploads/2021/01/06_Porter-Novelli-Purpose-Tracker-Wave-VII-Addressing -Social-Justice-Diversity-in-Communications.pdf.

7. Roger McNamee, "Platforms Must Pay for Their Role in the Insurrection," Wired, January 7, 2021, https://www.wired.com/story/opinion-platforms-must -pay-for-their-role-in-the-insurrection.

8. Todd Spangler, "Unilever Will Halt US Ad Spending on Facebook, Instagram and Twitter through at Least End of 2020," Variety (blog), June 26, 2020, https://variety.com/2020/digital/news/unilever-pulling-ads-facebook-twitter -instagram-1234691368.

9. Spangler, "Unilever Will Halt US Ad Spending on Facebook, Instagram and Twitter through at Least End of 2020."

10. Jonathan Vanian, "Facebook Scrambles to Escape Stock's Death Spiral as Users Flee, Sales Drop," CNBC, September 30, 2022, https://www.cnbc.com /2022/09/30/facebook-scrambles-to-escape-death-spiral-as-users-flee-sales-drop .html.

11. Vanian, "Facebook Scrambles to Escape Stock's Death Spiral as Users Flee, Sales Drop."

12. Taylor Telford, "MyPillow CEO Says Bed Bath & Beyond, Kohl's, Wayfair Are Dropping His Products," *Washington Post*, January 19, 2021. https://www .washingtonpost.com/business/2021/01/19/my-pillow-ceo-lindell. Lindell later suggested that he wasn't talking to Trump about how he should declare martial law rather than recognize his defeat by Joe Biden, but photographs of his notes as he walked into the White House proved otherwise.

13. Travis M. Andrews, "Some Trump Backers Are Getting Hit with One-Star Online Reviews—Including MyPillow and Real Estate Agent Jenna Ryan," *Washington Post*, January 20, 2021, https://www.washingtonpost.com/tech nology/2021/01/20/mypillow-yelp-amazon-jenna-ryan.

14. Telford, "MyPillow CEO Says Bed Bath & Beyond, Kohl's, Wayfair Are Dropping His Products."

15. Telford, "MyPillow CEO Says Bed Bath & Beyond, Kohl's, Wayfair Are Dropping His Products."

16. Andrews, "Some Trump Backers Are Getting Hit with One-Star Online Reviews."

17. Discussion at a Sustainable Brands member meeting, 2021.

18. Statista, "Top Liquid Laundry Detergent Brands in the United States," 2021, https://www.statista.com/statistics/188716/top-liquid-laundry-detergent-brands -in-the-united-states.

19. Watt Poultry, "Walmart to Establish Sustainability Standards," Egg Produc-tion, November 24, 2010, https://www.wattagnet.com/articles/7584-walmart -to-establish-sustainability-standards.

20. Walmart Sustainability Hub, "THESIS Index," September 6, 2017, accessed May 11, 2023, https://www.walmartsustainabilityhub.com/reporting/thesis-index.

21. Benjamin Romano, "REI Rolls Out Rigorous New Sustainability Standards for Suppliers," *Seattle Times*, August 12, 2020, https://www.seattletimes.com /business/retail/rei-rolls-out-rigorous-new-sustainability-standards-for-suppliers.

22. Romano, "REI Rolls Out Rigorous New Sustainability Standards for Suppliers."

23. Tara Burns, "COVID-19 Increasing Consumers' Focus on 'Ethical Consumption,' Accenture Survey Finds," Accenture, May 4, 2020, https://newsroom .accenture.com/news/covid-19-increasing-consumers-focus-on-ethical-con sumption-accenture-survey-finds.htm.

24. Katherine Latham, "Has Coronavirus Made Us More Ethical Consumers?" BBC News, January 14, 2021, https://www.bbc.com/news/business-55630144.

25. Natalie Babbage, "#WhoCares? Who Does?" Kantar, September 2020, https://kantar.turtl.co/story/whocares-who-does-2020-p.

26. Burns, "COVID-19 Increasing Consumers' Focus on 'Ethical Consumption.'"

27. Burns, "COVID-19 Increasing Consumers' Focus on 'Ethical Consumption.'"

28. Burns, "COVID-19 Increasing Consumers' Focus on 'Ethical Consumption.'"

29. BBMG, "Radically Better Future," December 2020, https://globescan.com /wp-content/uploads/2020/12/BBMG_GlobeScan_Radically-Better-Future -Report_2020.pdf.

30. WeSpire, "Behavior Change to Drive Employee Engagement for Impactful and Purposeful Work," accessed June 6, 2022, https://www.wespire.com. The success of WeSpire, which counts among its clients companies such as Novartis, Caesars Entertainment, and BASF, is itself a sign of the changing dynamics of business. The company says, "The WeSpire platform, driven by proven behavioral science, encourages the entire workforce to make a positive impact at work and in their communities."

31. WeSpire, "WeSpire GenZ," 2018, https://www.wespire.com/wp-content /uploads/2018/07/WeSpire_GenZ-2.pdf.

32. Student Scholarships, "Retail Salespersons and Sales Clerks—What Do Retail Salespersons and Sales Clerks Do?," accessed June 6, 2022, https:// studentscholarships.org/salary_ca/87/retail_salespersons_and_sales_clerks.php.

33. WSI at the Aspen Institute, "Reinventing Low Wage Work," accessed May 11, 2023, http://www.aspenwsi.org/wordpress/wp-content/uploads/RetailOver view.pdf.

34. WeSpire, "WeSpire GenZ, 2018."

35. Sustainable Brands, "Brands Take Note: Gen Z Is Putting Its Money Where Its Values Are," May 8, 2018, https://sustainablebrands.com/read/walking-the -talk/brands-take-note-gen-z-is-putting-its-money-where-its-values-are.

36. Bloomberg, "CEO Who Jumped the COVID Vaccine Line Is Out of a Job," Fortune, January 25, 2021, https://fortune.com/2021/01/25/ceo-jumped -covid-vaccine-line-rod-baker-great-canadian-gaming.

37. Stuart Braun, "The Spin Machine Upending the Climate Consensus," DW, September 3, 2020, https://www.dw.com/en/trump-climate-change-denial -emissions-environment-germany-fake-heartland-seibt/a-52688933.

Chapter 10

1. William Wilkes, Jack Wittels, and Irina Vilcu, "Historic Drought Threatens to Cripple European Trade," Bloomberg, August 10, 2022, https://www.bloom berg.com/news/features/2022-08-10/europe-s-low-water-levels-threaten-rhine -river-hit-80b-trade-lifeline.

2. Hanna Ziady, "The Ever Given Is Finally Leaving the Suez Canal," CNN, July 7, 2021, https://www.cnn.com/2021/07/07/business/ever-given-suez-canal /index.html.

3. Kat Eschner, "Backlog at the Port of Vancouver Is a Sign of Supply-Chain Disruption to Come," Fortune, December 1, 2021, https://fortune.com/2021/12 /01/port-of-vancouver-flooding-supply-chain-disruption-logistics.

4. Tripp Mickle, Chang Che, and Daisuke Wakabayashi, "Apple Built Its Empire with China. Now Its Foundation Is Showing Cracks," New York Times, November 7, 2022, https://www.nytimes.com/2022/11/07/business/apple-china-ymtc .html.

5. Mickle, Che, and Wakabayashi, "Apple Built Its Empire with China."

6. Adam Ward, "Intense Flooding, Mudslides Cause Evacuations in BC," CTVNews, November 15, 2021, https://www.ctvnews.ca/canada/intense-flood ing-mudslides-cause-evacuations-in-b-c-1.5667216.

7. Aya E. Murphy, Amy Simonson, and Paul P. Murphy, "One of the Largest Ports in North America Is Experiencing Big Delays Due to Flooding in Pacific Northwest, Officials Say," CNN, November 18, 2021, https://www.cnn.com /2021/11/18/weather/pacific-northwest-flooding-thursday/index.html.

8. Ian Austen, and Vjosa Isai, "Vancouver Is Marooned by Flooding and Besieged Again by Climate Change," *New York Times*, November 21, 2021, https://www.nytimes.com/2021/11/21/canada-flooding-climate-change.html.

9. Eschner, "Backlog at the Port of Vancouver Is a Sign of Supply-Chain Disruption to Come."

10. Jesus Jiménez, "New York City Faces the First 'Flash Flood Emergency' in Its History," *New York Times*, September 2, 2021, https://www.nytimes.com /2021/09/02/nyregion/new-york-city-faces-the-first-flash-flood-emergency-in -its-history.html.

11. Yossi Sheffi, "What Everyone Gets Wrong about the Never-Ending COVID-19 Supply Chain Crisis," *MIT Sloan Management Review*, October 25, 2021, https://sloanreview.mit.edu/article/what-everyone-gets-wrong-about-the-never -ending-covid-19-supply-chain-crisis.

12. Sheffi, "What Everyone Gets Wrong about the Never-Ending COVID-19 Supply Chain Crisis."

13. Jon Jackson, "What Did Kanye West Say That Was Antisemitic, and Has He Apologized?" *Newsweek*, October 25, 2022, https://www.newsweek.com /kanye-west-apologize-antisemitic-remarks-1754608.

14. Glenn Rowley, "Kanye West Loses Billionaire Status after Adidas Cuts Ties over His Antisemitic Comments," *Billboard* (blog), October 25, 2022, https:// www.billboard.com/music/music-news/kanye-west-loses-billionaire-status -adidas-cuts-ties-1235160917.

15. Annika Stechemesser, Anders Levermann, and Leonie Wenz, "Temperature Impacts on Hate Speech Online: Evidence from 4 Billion Geolocated Tweets from the USA," *The Lancet Planetary Health* 6, no. 9 (September 2022): e714–725, https://doi.org/10.1016/S2542-5196(22)00173-5.

16. Jianghao Wang, Nick Obradovich, and Siqi Zheng, "A 43-Million-Person Investigation into Weather and Expressed Sentiment in a Changing Climate," *One Earth* 2, no. 6 (June 2020): 568–577, https://doi.org/10.1016/j.oneear.2020 .05.016.

17. Laura Millan, "Climate Change Is Making People Angrier Online," Bloomberg, September 13, 2022, https://www.bloomberg.com/news/articles/2022-09 -13/climate-change-is-making-people-angrier-online.

18. Wang, Obradovich, and Zheng, "A 43-Million-Person Investigation into Weather and Expressed Sentiment in a Changing Climate."

19. Magdalena Hirsch, "Becoming Authoritarian for the Greater Good? Authoritarian Attitudes in Context of the Societal Crises of COVID-19 and Climate Change," *Frontiers in Political Science* 4 (2022), https://www.frontiersin .org/articles/10.3389/fpos.2022.929991.

20. Sustainable Brands, "US Consumers More Concerned about Ocean Plastic than Climate Change," June 20, 2019, https://sustainablebrands.com/read /waste-not/us-consumers-more-concerned-about-ocean-plastic-than-climate -change.

21. Arne Gast, Pablo Illanes, Nina Probst, Bill Schaninger, and Bruce Simpson, "Corporate Purpose: Shifting from Why to How," *McKinsey Quarterly*, April 22, 2020, https://www.mckinsey.com/business-functions/people-and-organizational -performance/our-insights/purpose-shifting-from-why-to-how.

22. Witold Henisz, Tim Koller, and Robin Nuttall, "Five Ways That ESG Creates Value," *McKinsey Quarterly*, November 14, 2019, https://www.mckinsey .com/business-functions/strategy-and-corporate-finance/our-insights/five-ways -that-esg-creates-value.

23. Kamala Kelkar, "Paris, Madrid, Athens and Mexico City Are Quitting Diesel," PBS NewsHour, December 3, 2016, https://www.pbs.org/newshour /world/cities-quit-diesel-environment.

24. Karryon, "Plastic No More! Accor to Eliminate Single-Use Plastic by 2022," February 4, 2020, https://karryon.com.au/industry-news/plastic-no-more-accor -to-eliminate-single-use-plastic-by-2022/.

25. European Circular Economy Stakeholder Platform, "A French Act of Law against Waste and for a Circular Economy," February 27, 2020, https://circu lareconomy.europa.eu/platform/en/strategies/french-act-law-against-waste-and -circular-economy.

26. Hospitality Net. "Single-Use Plastic in the Guest Experience Makes Way for Sustainable Alternatives in the Maldives," accessed May 10, 2023, https://www .hospitalitynet.org/news/4115255.html.

27. Danielle Garrand, "Macy's Announces It Will Stop Selling Fur by End of 2020 Fiscal Year," CBS News, October 22, 2019, https://www.cbsnews.com /news/macys-fur-macys-announces-it-will-stop-selling-fur-end-of-2020-fiscal -year.

28. Kate Gibson, "Nordstrom to Stop Selling Fur and Exotic Animal Skin Products," CBS News, September 29, 2020, https://www.cbsnews.com/news /nordstrom-fur-exotic-animal-skin-to-stop-selling-products.

29. Allison Gatlin, "Eli Lilly Dives on Twitter Chaos, Taking Novo, Sanofi with It," Investor's Business Daily, November 11, 2022, https://www.investors.com /news/technology/lly-stock-dives-taking-novo-sanofi-with-it-after-fake-twitter -account-promises-free-insulin.

30. Annie Lowrey, "The Small-Business Die-Off Is Here," The Atlantic, May 4, 2020, https://www.theatlantic.com/ideas/archive/2020/05/bridge-post-pandemic -world-already-collapsing/611089.

31. Chetty Friedman, "The Economic Tracker," Opportunity Insights Economic Tracker, April 15, 2022, https://tracktherecovery.org.

32. Chetty Friedman, "Track the Economic Impacts of COVID-19 on People, Businesses, and Communities across the United States in Real Time," Opportunity Insight Economic Tracker, April 15, 2022, https://tracktherecovery.org.

33. Wilkes, Wittels, and Vilcu, "Historic Drought Threatens to Cripple European Trade," Bloomberg, August 10, 2022, https://www.bloomberg.com/news /features/2022-08-10/europe-s-low-water-levels-threaten-rhine-river-hit-80b -trade-lifeline.

34. Eschner, "Backlog at the Port of Vancouver Is a Sign of Supply-Chain Disruption to Come."

35. Jasmine Andersson, and Doug Faulkner, "Heatwave: Fires Blaze after UK Passes 40C for First Time," BBC News, July 19, 2022, https://www.bbc.com /news/uk-62217282.

36. Michael Kolodny, and Lora Wayland, "GM Temporarily Suspends Advertising on Twitter Following Elon Musk Takeover," CNBC, October 28, 2022, https://www.cnbc.com/2022/10/28/gm-temporarily-suspends-advertising-on -twitter-following-elon-musk-takeover.html.

37. Ted Cruz (@tedcruz), "The Fortune 100 have become the economic enforcers for the radical Left. The Dems support censorship & Big Business is in bed with them trying to silence Americans. If you value your liberties, fight back," Twitter, November 4, 2022, 11:19 a.m., https://twitter.com/tedcruz /status/1588596717838299136.

38. Josh Holmes (@HolmesJosh), "This is a helpful list of brands who are begging to sit in front of a House panel next year to discuss their company's participation in leftist corporate extortion," Twitter, November 4, 2022, 1:17 p.m., https://Twitter.Com/Holmesjosh/Status/1588626474327760904.

39. Rich Lowry (@RichLowry), "I feel so stupid. I felt sure that Elon Musk's acquisition of Twitter was sure to deliver robust Republican majorities in the House and Senate," Twitter, November 9, 2022, 6:41 a.m., https://Twitter.Com /Richlowry/Status/1590353882919899142.

40. Statista, "Number of Coworking Spaces US 2017 Statistic," accessed June 6, 2022, https://www.statista.com/statistics/797546/number-of-coworking-spaces-us.

41. US Securities and Exchange Commission, "FORM S-1," 1933, https://www .sec.gov/Archives/edgar/data/1533523/000119312519220499/d781982ds1.htm #toc781982_2.

42. Joe Shute, "Bill Gates: 'My Biggest Fears about What's Coming next for This World,'" Yahoo Finance, September 18, 2018, https://finance.yahoo.com /news/bill-gates-super-successful-held-041636204.html.

43. Nick Leiber, "Preparing Businesses for Uncertainty," Bloomberg, August 2020, https://www.bloomberg.com/news/articles/2020-08-04/small-business-pre paring-and-planning-for-uncertainty.

44. Leiber, "Preparing Businesses for Uncertainty."

45. Homsar, "Outrun," eBaum's World, June 30, 2018, https://www.ebaums world.com/jokes/outrun/699332.

46. Paul Michelman, "Leading with Crisis as Your Copilot," *MIT Sloan Management Review*, December 20, 2020, https://sloanreview.mit.edu/article/leading -with-crisis-as-your-copilot.

47. Arthur M. Schneiderman, "Are There Limits to Total Quality Management?" strategy+business, April 1, 1998, https://www.strategy-business.com/article /16188.

48. "Zeno's paradox" notwithstanding, that doesn't mean you never get to the finish line, of course. Many companies have.

49. Veronica Poole and Kristen Sullivan, "Tectonic Shifts: How ESG Is Changing Business, Moving Markets, and Driving Regulation," Deloitte Insights, October 29, 2021, https://www2.deloitte.com/us/en/insights/topics/strategy/esg -disclosure-regulation.html.

50. Fortune, "Doomsayers Predicted Trillions in COVID Relief Spending Would Trigger Epic Inflation. What Happened?," August 25, 2020, https://fortune .com/2020/08/25/trillions-coronavirus-spending-inflation/.

51. Henisz, Koller, and Nuttall, "Five Ways That ESG Creates Value."

52. Walmart, "Walmart Policies and Guidelines," November 7, 2017, https://corporate.walmart.com/policies.

53. Jackson Family Wines presentation at Sustainable Brands conference in San Diego in 2014.

54. Giulia McDonnell Nieto del Rio, Nicholas Bogel-Burroughs, and Ivan Penn, "His Lights Stayed on During Texas' Storm. Now He Owes $16,752," *New York Times*, February 21, 2021, https://www.nytimes.com/2021/02/20/us/texas-storm-electric-bills.html.

55. Diana Mitlin, Victoria A. Beard, David Satterthwaite, and Jillian Du, "Unaffordable and Undrinkable: Rethinking Urban Water Access in the Global South," WRI, August 13, 2019. https://www.wri.org/research/unaffordable-and-undrinkable-rethinking-urban-water-access-global-south.

56. Brad Plumer, "A Glimpse of America's Future: Climate Change Means Trouble for Power Grids," *New York Times*, February 16, 2021, https://www.nytimes.com/2021/02/16/climate/texas-power-grid-failures.html.

57. Mathew Nelson, "How Can Climate Change Disclosures Protect Reputation and Value?" EY, April 27, 2020, https://www.ey.com/en_gl/climate-change-sustainability-services/how-can-climate-change-disclosures-protect-reputation-and-value.

58. Nelson, "How Can Climate Change Disclosures Protect Reputation and Value?"

59. Nelson, "How Can Climate Change Disclosures Protect Reputation and Value?"

60. NASA, "2020 Tied for Warmest Year on Record, NASA Analysis Shows," January 14, 2021, https://climate.nasa.gov/news/3061/2020-tied-for-warmest-year-on-record-nasa-analysis-shows.

61. Henry Fountain and Mira Rojanasakul, "The Last 8 Years Were the Hottest on Record," *New York Times*, January 10, 2023, https://www.nytimes.com/interactive/2023/climate/earth-hottest-years.html.

62. Dan Murtaugh, Rajesh K. Singh, and Naureen S. Malik, "A Hot, Deadly Summer Is Coming, with Frequent Blackouts," Bloomberg, May 23, 2022, https://www.autoblog.com/2022/05/23/summer-electricity-shortages.

63. While not a record, one example is Saint Louis, which had a high temperature of 19°F on February 17 (low of 7) and a high of 66 degrees six days later (low of 43).

64. Nelson, "How Can Climate Change Disclosures Protect Reputation and Value?"

65. Business Wire, "Announcing the 100 Best Workplaces for Diversity," December 20, 2019, https://www.businesswire.com/news/home/2019122000 5112/en/Announcing-the-100-Best-Workplaces-for-Diversity.

66. Business Wire, "Announcing the 100 Best Workplaces for Diversity."

67. Business Wire, "Announcing the 100 Best Workplaces for Diversity."

68. Examples include Sustainalytics, Moody's ESG, S&P Global, Refinitiv, MSCI, and the international ISO standard for social responsibility, ISO 26000.

69. Miki Tsusaka, Martin Reeves, and Stephanie Hurder, "Diversity at Work," Boston Consulting Group, July 18, 2020, https://www.bcg.com/en-us/publica tions/2017/diversity-at-work.

Chapter 11

1. Arne Gast, Pablo Illanes, Nina Probst, Bill Schaninger, and Bruce Simpson, "Corporate Purpose: Shifting from Why to How," *McKinsey Quarterly*, April 22, 2020, https://www.mckinsey.com/business-functions/people-and-organizational -performance/our-insights/purpose-shifting-from-why-to-how.

2. Pentland Analytics and Aon, "Reputation Risk Study—Impact of Social Media and Cyber Attacks on Shareholder Brand Value," accessed December 4, 2022. http://www.aon.com/reputation-risk-cyber-social-media-pentland-analytics -aon/index.html. The full report is available at https://aon.io/reprisk2018 -download.

3. Pentland Analytics and Aon, "Reputation Risk in the Cyber Age," Pentland Analytics, 2018, https://aon.io/reprisk2018-download.

4. Pentland Analytics and Aon, "Reputation Risk in the Cyber Age: The Impact on Shareholder Value."

5. Gast, Illanes, Probst, Schaninger, and Simpson, "Corporate Purpose: Shifting from Why to How."

6. Aon, "Wellbeing Is Top of Employee Agendas—How Does Your Business Fare? Aon Rising Resilient," accessed June 8, 2022, https://www.aon.com /risingresilient/self-assessment-tool.

7. Jessica Dolcourt, "Samsung Galaxy Note 7 Recall: Everything You Still Need to Know about What's Coming Next," CNET, April 16, 2017, https://www.cnet .com/tech/mobile/samsung-galaxy-note-7-return-exchange-faq.

8. Pete Pachal, "Samsung Rises Again: Can the Galaxy S8 Erase the Disastrous Note 7?" Mashable, March 29, 2017, https://mashable.com/feature /samsung-galaxy-s8-forget-note-7.

9. Andrew Martonik, "Galaxy S8 Pre-Orders Were 30% Higher than Galaxy S7's Record Number," Android Central, April 24, 2017, https://www.androidcentral .com/galaxy-s8-pre-orders-were-30-larger-galaxy-s7s-record-number.

10. Pentland Analytics and Aon, "Reputation Risk in the Cyber Age."

11. Pachal, "Samsung Rises Again."

12. Pentland Analytics and Aon, "Reputation Risk in the Cyber Age."

13. Neal E. Boudette, "Volkswagen Sales in US Rebound After Diesel Scandal," *New York Times*, November 1, 2017, https://www.nytimes.com/2017/11/01 /business/volkswagen-sales-diesel.html.

14. Wilfried Eckl-Dorna, "Auto Wichert Insolvenz: So leiden VW-Händler unter Leasing-Diesel, Elektroautos," *Manager Magazine*, February 20, 2020, https://www.manager-magazin.de/unternehmen/autoindustrie/auto-wichert -insolvenz-vw-haendler-stuerzen-ueber-leasing-diesel-elektroautos-a-1304894 .html.

15. William Boston, "VW to Receive Dieselgate Settlement from Former CEO, Executives," *Wall Street Journal*, June 9, 2021, https://www.wsj.com/articles/vw -to-receive-dieselgate-settlement-from-former-ceo-executives-11623248510.

16. Sean O'Kane, "VW Executive Given the Maximum Prison Sentence for His Role in Dieselgate," The Verge, December 6, 2017, https://www.theverge .com/2017/12/6/16743308/volkswagen-oliver-schmidt-sentence-emissions -scandal-prison.

17. Aon, "The Rising Resilient: How Workforce Resilience Will Enable Businesses to Survive," 2020, p. 5, https://risingresilient.s3.eu-west-2.amazonaws .com/aon-rising-resilient-report-en.pdf.

18. Pentland Analytics and Aon, "Reputation Risk in the Cyber Age."

19. ACORE, "Renewable Energy in America 2006," Herman Scheer, November 30, 2006, http://www.hermannscheer.de/en/index.php/press-mainmenu-20/speeches-mainmenu-23/152-renewable-energy-in-america-2006.

20. First Street Foundation, "As the Seas Have Been Rising, Tri-State Home Values Have Been Sinking," August 23, 2018, https://firststreet.org/press/as-the-seas-have-been-rising-tri-state-home-values-have-been-sinking.

21. Alissa J. Rubin, Ben Hubbard, Josh Holder, Noah Throop, Emily Rhyne, Jeremy White, James Glanz, Josh Williams, Sarah Almukhtar, and Rumsey Taylor, "Extreme Heat Will Change Us," *New York Times*, November 18, 2022, https://www.nytimes.com/interactive/2022/11/18/world/middleeast/extreme-heat.html.

22. US Customs and Border Protection, "Uyghur Forced Labor Prevention Act," accessed November 16, 2022, https://www.cbp.gov/trade/forced-labor/UFLPA.

23. Comments at the WSJ Risk and Compliance Forum, "WSJ Risk & Compliance Forum," November 16, 2022, 23:05, https://riskforum.wsj.com.

24. Comments at the WSJ Risk and Compliance Forum, "WSJ Risk & Compliance Forum," 2:35.

25. Comments at the WSJ Risk and Compliance Forum, "WSJ Risk & Compliance Forum," 28:30.

26. US Climate Resilience Toolkit, "Managing Climate Risk in the US Financial System," October 2020, https://toolkit.climate.gov/reports/managing-climate-risk-us-financial-system.

27. Swiss Re, "World Economy Set to Lose up to 18% GDP from Climate Change if No Action Taken, Reveals Swiss Re Institute's Stress-Test Analysis," accessed December 12, 2022, https://www.swissre.com/media/press-release/nr-20210422-economics-of-climate-change-risks.html.

28. Ioannis Ioannou and George Serafeim, "The Impact of Corporate Social Responsibility on Investment Recommendations: Analysts' Perceptions and Shifting Institutional Logics: CSR and Investment Recommendations," *Strategic Management Journal* 36, no. 7 (July 2015): 1053–1081, https://doi.org/10.1002/smj.2268.

29. Etihad, "The Future of Aviation Is Sustainable," *Reuters*, November 7, 2022, https://www.reuters.com/sponsored/article/the-future-of-aviation-is-sustainable.

30. Henry Fountain, "Climate Change Is Making Hurricanes Stronger, Researchers Find," *New York Times*, May 18, 2020, https://www.nytimes.com /2020/05/18/climate/climate-changes-hurricane-intensity.html.

31. Kelly Levin, Sophie Boehm, and Rebecca Carter, "6 Big Findings from the IPCC 2022 Report on Climate Impacts, Adaptation and Vulnerability," WRI, February 27, 2022, https://www.wri.org/insights/ipcc-report-2022-climate -impacts-adaptation-vulnerability.

32. David G. Victor, Sadie Frank, and Eric Gesick, "We're Not Ready for the Next Big Climate Disasters," *New York Times*, May 14, 2021, https://www .nytimes.com/2021/05/14/opinion/climate-disasters.html.

33. Masrur Jamaluddin, Heather Chen, and Angus Watson, "Indonesia Bans Sex Outside Marriage as Parliament Passes Sweeping New Criminal Code," CNN, December 6, 2022, https://www.cnn.com/2022/12/05/asia/indonesia -new-code-passed-sex-cohabitation-intl-hnk/index.html.

34. Associated Press, "Report: Authoritarianism on the Rise as Democracy Weakens," VOA, November 30, 2022, https://www.voanews.com/a/report -authoritarianism-on-the-rise-as-democracy-weakens/6856151.html.

35. National Intelligence Council, *Global Trends 2040: A More Contested World* (Washington, DC: National Intelligence Council, 2021), https://www.dni.gov /files/ODNI/documents/assessments/GlobalTrends_2040.pdf.

36. CDP, "Engaging the Chain: Driving Speed and Scale,"2021, https://www .cdp.net/en/research/global-reports/engaging-the-chain.

37. Kate Abnett, and Jake Spring, "EU Agrees Law Preventing Import of Goods Linked to Deforestation," *Reuters*, December 6, 2022, https://www.reuters.com /business/environment/eu-agrees-law-preventing-import-goods-linked-defor estation-2022-12-06.

Chapter 12

1. John Wooden, quoted in Quotefancy.com, accessed December 16, 2022, https://quotefancy.com/quote/844855/John-Wooden-Good-values-are-like-a -magnet-they-attract-good-people.

2. Richard Morgan, "The Average Manufacturer's Gross Profit Percent," Chron, accessed June 9, 2022, https://smallbusiness.chron.com/average-manufacturers -gross-profit-percent-15827.html. For a sample of about four thousand listed

companies, gross profit was higher, over 40 percent on average. See Ready Ratios, "Industry Ratios (Benchmarking): Gross Margin," accessed June 9, 2022, https://www.readyratios.com/sec/ratio/gross-margin/.

3. For simplicity's sake, I won't be addressing questions such as does this change if the sales representative doesn't meet their sales target—those complexities do change things but not enough to affect the conclusion of my example.

4. WeSpire, "WeSpire GenZ," 2018, https://www.wespire.com/wp-content /uploads/2018/07/WeSpire_GenZ-2.pdf.

5. WeSpire, "WeSpire GenZ."

6. Pat Auger, Timothy M. Devinney, Grahame R. Dowling, Christine Eckert, and Nidthida Lin, "How Much Does a Company's Reputation Matter in Recruiting?" *MIT Sloan Management Review*, March 19, 2013, https://sloanreview.mit .edu/article/how-much-does-a-companys-reputation-matter-in-recruiting. The salary was in Australian dollars; however, when the study was conducted, the exchange rate between the Australian dollar and US dollar was close to 1:1.

7. Seb Murray, "MBA Careers: Companies Invest in Sustainability to Recruit Executive Talent," *Business Because*, June 3, 2015, https://www.businessbecause .com/news/mba-careers/3299/mba-careers-companies-invest-in-sustainability.

8. Murray, "MBA Careers: Companies Invest in Sustainability to Recruit Executive Talent."

9. Richard Fry, "Millennials Are the Largest Generation in the US Labor Force," Pew Research Center (blog), April 4, 2018, https://www.pewresearch.org/fact -tank/2018/04/11/millennials-largest-generation-us-labor-force.

10. Nuremberg Institute for Market Decisions, "The Next Generation of Leaders Is Aware of Its Strengths and Demands Respect," May 8, 2015, https://www.nim .org/en/press/next-generation-leaders-aware-its-strengths-and-demands-respect.

11. Murray, "MBA Careers: Companies Invest in Sustainability to Recruit Executive Talent."

12. Andrea Ucini, "What Companies Are for," *The Economist*, August 22, 2019, https://www.economist.com/leaders/2019/08/22/what-companies-are-for.

13. Nuremberg Institute for Market Decisions, "The Next Generation of Leaders Is Aware of Its Strengths and Demands Respect."

14. IBM, "Sustainability at a Turning Point," 2021, https://www.ibm.com /downloads/cas/WLJ7LVP4.

15. Rebecca Picciotto, "Workers and Consumers Say They're Likely to Favor Pro-LGBTQ Businesses, New Study Says," CNBC, December 13, 2022, https://www.cnbc.com/2022/12/13/workers-consumers-prefer-pro-lgbtq-brands-glaad-study.html.

16. Reid Hoffman, "How Being Values-Driven Rather than Profit-Driven Helped Howard Schultz Make Starbucks More Profitable," LinkedIn, March 9, 2018, https://www.linkedin.com/pulse/how-being-values-driven-rather-than-profit-driven-helped-reid-hoffman.

17. Jennifer Rubin, "Distinguished Persons: Unions Break through in 2022," *Washington Post*, December 18, 2022, https://www.washingtonpost.com/opinions/2022/12/18/distinguished-persons-labor-unions-2022.

18. Hoffman, "How Being Values-Driven Rather than Profit-Driven Helped Howard Schultz Make Starbucks More Profitable."

19. Hoffman, "How Being Values-Driven Rather than Profit-Driven Helped Howard Schultz Make Starbucks More Profitable." Note that China has government-provided health insurance, which individuals can supplement with private plans.

20. EY, "EY Research Reveals Less than Half of Full-Time Workers Surveyed Globally Trust Their Employer, Boss or Colleagues a Great Deal," June 21, 2016, https://www.prnewswire.com/news-releases/ey-research-reveals-less-than-half-of-full-time-workers-surveyed-globally-trust-their-employer-boss-or-colleagues-a-great-deal-300287869.html.

21. EY, "EY Research Reveals Less than Half of Full-Time Workers Surveyed Globally Trust Their Employer, Boss or Colleagues a Great Deal."

22. EY, "EY Global Generations 3.0: A Global Study of Trust in the Workplace," 2016, http://ccnews.pl/wp-content/uploads/2016/09/report_global_generations_3.0.pdf.

23. Responsabilidad Social y Sustentabilidad, "CEMEX México, lider en RSE por segundo año," November 4, 2015, https://responsabilidadsocial.net/cemex-mexico-lider-en-rse-por-segundo-ano.

24. Boston Consulting Group, "CEMEX's Lorenzo H. Zambrano on Building the Future," November 26, 2012, https://www.bcg.com/publications/2012/leadership-management-two-speed-economy-zambrano-lorenz-cemex-ceo-on-building-the-future.

25. Rosabeth Moss Kanter, "SuperCorp: Values as Guidance System," HBS Working Knowledge, August 24, 2009, http://hbswk.hbs.edu/item/supercorp -values-as-guidance-system.

26. Sustainable Brands, "#BusinessCase: REI Proves Values-First Approach Leads to Longevity," Sustainable Brands, July 13, 2017, https://sustainable brands.com/read/walking-the-talk/businesscase-rei-proves-values-first-approach -leads-to-longevity.

27. KPMG, "Consolidated Financial Statements," December 28–29, 2018, https://www.rei.com/assets/about-rei/financial-information/rei-fy19-issued -financial-statements/live.pdf.

28. MarketWatch, "Dick's Sporting Goods Inc. Annual Income Statement," accessed June 9, 2022, https://www.marketwatch.com/investing/stock/dks /financials.

29. Sustainable Brands, "#BusinessCase: REI Proves Values-First Approach Leads to Longevity."

30. Jeffrey R. Edwards and Daniel M. Cable, "The Value of Value Congruence," *Journal of Applied Psychology* 94, no. 3 (2009): 654–677, doi: 10.1037/a0014891.

31. Ting Ren, "Value Congruence as a Source of Intrinsic Motivation," *Kyklos* 63, no. 1 (February 2010): 94–109, https://doi.org/10.1111/j.1467-6435.2010 .00462.x.

32. Ren, "Value Congruence as a Source of Intrinsic Motivation."

33. Bea Boccalandro, "Increasing Employee Engagement through Corporate Volunteering," Voluntare, January 2019, https://www.beaboccalandro.com /wp-content/uploads/2019/01/Engagement-Report-Voluntare_eng_04122018-2 .pdf.

34. Boccalandro, "Increasing Employee Engagement through Corporate Volunteering."

35. Daniel M. Cable and Virginia S. Kay, "Striving for Self-Verification during Organizational Entry," *Academy of Management Journal* 55, no. 2 (April 2012): 360–380, https://doi.org/10.5465/amj.2010.0397.

36. Jessica Amortegui, "5 Reasons You Need to Instill Values in Your Orga- nization," Fast Company, March 27, 2014, https://www.fastcompany.com /3028201/5-reasons-you-need-to-instill-values-in-your-organization.

37. Anna Sutton, "Living the Good Life: A Meta-Analysis of Authenticity, Well-Being and Engagement," *Personality and Individual Differences* 153 (January 2020): 109645, https://doi.org/10.1016/j.paid.2019.109645.

38. Sutton, "Living the Good Life."

39. Julie Coffman, Elyse Rosenblum, Andrea D'Arcy, and Laura Thompson Love, "10 Proven Actions to Advance Diversity, Equity, and Inclusion," Bain, August 11, 2021, https://www.bain.com/insights/10-proven-actions-to-advance -diversity-equity-and-inclusion.

40. Dana Chandler, and Adam Kapelner, "Breaking Monotony with Meaning: Motivation in Crowdsourcing Markets," *Journal of Economic Behavior & Organization* 90 (June 2013): 123–133, https://doi.org/10.1016/j.jebo.2013.03.003.

41. Chandler and Kapelner, "Breaking Monotony with Meaning: Motivation in Crowdsourcing Markets."

42. Emma Seppälä and Kim Cameron, "Proof That Positive Work Cultures Are More Productive," *Harvard Business Review*, December 1, 2015, https://hbr .org/2015/12/proof-that-positive-work-cultures-are-more-productive.

43. Leslie Brokaw, "Does Sustainability Change the Talent Equation?" *MIT Sloan Management Review*, October 1, 2009, https://sloanreview.mit.edu/article /does-sustainability-change-the-talent-equation.

44. Boston Consulting Group, "CEMEX's Lorenzo H. Zambrano on Building the Future," November 26, 2012, https://www.bcg.com/publications/2012 /leadership-management-two-speed-economy-zambrano-lorenz-cemex-ceo-on -building-the-future.

45. Murray, "MBA Careers: Companies Invest in Sustainability to Recruit Executive Talent."

46. Morning Consult, "How to Attract Top Talent," 2018, https://morning consult.com/form/how-to-attract-top-talent.

47. Arne Gast, Pablo Illanes, Nina Probst, Bill Schaninger, and Bruce Simpson, "Corporate Purpose: Shifting from Why to How," *McKinsey Quarterly*, April 22, 2020, https://www.mckinsey.com/business-functions/people-and-organizational -performance/our-insights/purpose-shifting-from-why-to-how.

48. Helene Cavalli, "Sharing An Employer's Core Values Is Leading Driver to Boost Employee Engagement," accessed January 30, 2023, https://www.hr .com/en/app/blog/2009/10/sharing-an-employers-core-values-is-leading-driver _g1duzaye.html.

Chapter 13

1. Jim Harter, "US Employee Engagement Slump Continues," Gallup, April 25, 2022, https://www.gallup.com/workplace/391922/employee-engagement -slump-continues.aspx.

2. Bea Boccalandro, "Increasing Employee Engagement through Corporate Volunteering," Voluntare, January 2019, p. 8, https://www.beaboccalandro.com /wp-content/uploads/2019/01/Engagement-Report-Voluntare_eng_04122018-2 .pdf.

3. US Department of Defense. "Dept. of Defense IG Group Employee Engagement Survey and Analysis Tool," Corporate Leadership Council, 2008, p. 6, https://media.defense.gov/2018/Aug/16/2001954995/-1/-1/1/DEPTOFDEFEN SEIGGROUP.PDF. The foundation of the analysis wasn't restricted to military employees; the Department of Defense used the Corporate Leadership Council's assessment, which has also been used by numerous civilian companies such as Caterpillar.

4. Stuart Hearn, "How Does Employee Engagement Affect Performance?" Clear Review, July 26, 2015, https://www.clearreview.com/how-does-employee -engagement-impact-performance.

5. Gallup, "State of American Workplace," 2017, p. 16, https://www.gallup .com/workplace/238085/state-american-workplace-report-2017.aspx.

6. State of California Employment Development Department, "Paid Family Leave: 10 Years of Helping Californians in Need," 2014, https://www.edd.ca .gov/disability/pdf/Paid_Family_Leave_10_Year_Anniversary_Report.pdf.

7. Lydia Dishman, "The Real Cost Of Paid Parental Leave For Business," Fast Company, January 28, 2016, https://www.fastcompany.com/3055977/the-real -cost-of-paid-parental-leave-for-business.

8. Bock writes that "the attrition rate for women after childbirth was twice our average attrition rate . . . After making the change in leave, the difference in attrition rates vanished . . . The cost of having a mom out of the office for an extra couple of months was more than offset by the value of retaining her expertise and avoiding the cost of finding and training a new hire."

9. Wayne Huang, John Mitchell, Carmel Dibner, Andrea Ruttenberg, and Audrey Tripp, "How Customer Service Can Turn Angry Customers into Loyal Ones," *Harvard Business Review*, January 16, 2018, https://hbr.org/2018/01/how -customer-service-can-turn-angry-customers-into-loyal-ones.

10. The average was $38.66 per month, according to the Tax Foundation (Tax Foundation, "Cell Phone Taxes and Fees in 2018," December 11, 2018, https://taxfoundation.org/cell-phone-taxes-2018).

11. Jessica M. Warnell, "Engaging Millennials for Ethical Leadership What Works for Young Professionals and Their Managers," Business Expert Press, 2015, http://45.114.134.178:9000/digi/IG01/2015/IG01T0000374/IG01T0000374.pdf.

12. Daniel Korschun, C. B. Bhattacharya, and Scott D. Swain, "CSR and the Frontline Context: How Social Programs Improve Customer Service," Nuremberg Institute for Market Decisions, June 29, 2016, https://www.nim.org/en/publications/gfk-marketing-intelligence-review/all-issues/responsible-marketing/csr-and-frontline-context-how-social-programs-improve-customer-service.

13. Daniel Korschun, C. B. Bhattacharya, and Scott D. Swain, "CSR and the Frontline Context: How Social Programs Improve Customer Service," *GfK Marketing Intelligence Review* 8, no. 1 (May 2016): 24–29, https://doi.org/10.1515/gfkmir-2016-0004.

14. Rebecca Koenig, "5 Years Since Starbucks Offered to Help Baristas Attend College, How Many Have Graduated?—EdSurge News," EdSurge, July 25, 2019, https://www.edsurge.com/news/2019-07-25-5-years-since-starbucks-offered-to-help-baristas-attend-college-how-many-have-graduated.

15. Bruce N. Pfau, "How an Accounting Firm Convinced Its Employees They Could Change the World," *Harvard Business Review*, October 6, 2015, https://hbr.org/2015/10/how-an-accounting-firm-convinced-its-employees-they-could-change-the-world.

16. Work well-being is displayed when searching company reviews. For example, as of May 15, 2023, reviews of Indeed are located at https://www.indeed.com/cmp/Indeed.

17. M. Esther García-Buades, José M. Peiró, María Isabel Montañez-Juan, Malgorzata W. Kozusznik, and Silvia Ortiz-Bonnín, "Happy-Productive Teams and Work Units: A Systematic Review of the 'Happy-Productive Worker Thesis.'" *International Journal of Environmental Research and Public Health* 17, no. 1 (January 2020): 69, https://doi.org/10.3390/ijerph17010069.

18. Sustainable Brands, "Study: More 'Human' Companies Outperform Business-as-Usual Competitors," September 29, 2017, https://sustainablebrands.com/read/marketing-and-comms/study-more-human-companies-outperform-business-as-usual-competitors.

19. Sustainable Brands, "Study: More 'Human' Companies Outperform Business-as-Usual Competitors."

20. Richard Levick, "It's War: The New Dilemma for Corporations and Social Issues," ChiefExecutive (blog), April 9, 2021, https://chiefexecutive.net/its -war-the-new-dilemma-for-corporations-and-social-issues.

21. Peter Burke, "DeSantis Bashes 'Woke' Disney after CEO Voices Opposition to 'Don't Say Gay' Bill," WPTV West Palm Beach, March 11, 2022, https:// www.wptv.com/news/political/desantis-bashes-woke-disney-after-ceo-voices -opposition-to-dont-say-gay-bill.

22. David Gelles and Andrew R. Sorkin, "Hundreds of Companies Unite to Oppose Voting Limits, but Others Abstain," *New York Times*, April 14, 2021, https://www.nytimes.com/2021/04/14/business/ceos-corporate-america-voting -rights.html.

23. Kate Gibson, "Eli Lilly Pushes Back against Indiana's New Abortion Law," CBS News, August 8, 2022, https://www.cbsnews.com/news/abortion-indiana -eli-lilly-cummins-roche.

24. Amy Walters, "Existential Threat—Or Politics as Usual?" Cook Political, April 7, 2021, https://www.cookpolitical.com/analysis/national/national-politics /existential-threat-or-politics-usual.

25. Walters, "Existential Threat—Or Politics as Usual?"

26. Edelman, "2019 Edelman Trust Barometer: Global Report," 2019, https:// www.edelman.com/sites/g/files/aatuss191/files/2019-02/2019_Edelman_Trust _Barometer_Global_Report.pdf.

27. Edelman, "2019 Edelman Trust Barometer: Global Report."

28. Edelman, "2019 Edelman Trust Barometer: Global Report."

29. Nathan Layne, "Explainer: Big Changes under Georgia's New Election Law," *Reuters*, June 14, 2021, https://www.reuters.com/world/us/big-changes -under-georgias-new-election-law-2021-06-14/.

30. Todd C. Frankel, "More than 100 Corporate Executives Hold Call to Discuss Halting Donations and Investments to Fight Controversial Voting Bills," *Washington Post*, April 11, 2021, https://www.washingtonpost.com/business /2021/04/11/companies-voting-bills-states.

31. Reid J. Epstein and Trip Gabriel, "As Michigan G.O.P. Plans Voting Limits, Top Corporations Fire a Warning Shot," *New York Times*, April 13, 2021, https://

www.nytimes.com/2021/04/13/us/politics/michigan-voting-rights-republicans
.html.

32. Gelles and Sorkin, "Hundreds of Companies Unite to Oppose Voting
Limits, but Others Abstain."

33. Gelles and Sorkin, "Hundreds of Companies Unite to Oppose Voting
Limits, but Others Abstain."

34. Alex Kingsbury, "Who Is Financing Trump's 'Big Lie' Caucus? Corporations You Know," *New York Times*, June 15, 2022, https://www.nytimes.com
/2022/06/15/opinion/jan6-companies-donate.html.

35. Erb Institute, "Corporate Political Responsibility: The Missing Link in Companies' ESG Strategies," February 18, 2021, https://erb.umich.edu/2021/02/18
/corporate-political-responsibility-the-missing-link-in-companies-esg-strategies.

36. Thomas Lyon, "Beyond ESG—Corporate Political Responsibility," Corporate Counsel Business Journal, October 19, 2021, https://ccbjournal.com/articles
/beyond-esg-corporate-political-responsibility (comment at 7:20 into the
episode).

37. Cliff Rothman, "A Welcome Mat for Gay Customers," *New York Times*,
August 17, 2001, https://www.nytimes.com/2001/08/17/automobiles/a-welcome
-mat-for-gay-customers.html.

38. Rothman, "A Welcome Mat for Gay Customers."

39. Rothman, "A Welcome Mat for Gay Customers."

40. Edelman, "2019 Edelman Trust Barometer: Global Report."

41. Edelman, "Edelman Trust Barometer 2020 Ethics Competence Business
Can Only Build Trust by Doing the Right Thing Not Just Saying It," January
20, 2020, https://belongingworks.com/2020/01/20/edelman-trust-barometer
-2020-ethics-competence-business-can-only-build-trust-by-doing-the-right
-thing-not-just-saying-it.

42. "WeSpire's 2023 State of Employee Engagement in Impact," accessed May
11, 2023, https://8353230.fs1.hubspotusercontent-na1.net/hubfs/8353230/State
%20of%20ESG%20Employee%20Engagement%202023.pdf.

43. Eagle Hill Consulting, "Nearly Half of US Workforce Unsure of Employers'
Core Values," December 1, 2016, https://www.eaglehillconsulting.com/news
/half-us-workforce-unsure-employers-core-values.

44. Techniques to accomplish this are covered in Sean Fath, Richard P. Larrick, Jack Bl Soll, and Susan Zhu, "Why Putting on Blinders Can Help Us See More Clearly," *MIT Sloan Management Review*, June 8, 2021.

45. Robin J. Fly and Irene Padavic, "What's Really Holding Women Back?" *Harvard Business Review*, March 1, 2020, https.//hbr.org/2020/03/whats-really -holding-women-back.

46. Frank Dobbin and Alexandra Kalev. 2018, "Why Diversity Training Doesn't Work: The Challenge for Industry and Academia," *Anthropology Now* 10 (2): 48–55.

47. Dobbin and Kalev, "Why Diversity Training Doesn't Work."

48. David A. Thomas and Robin J. Ely, "Making Differences Matter: A New Paradigm for Managing Diversity," *Harvard Business Review*, September 1, 1996, https://hbr.org/1996/09/making-differences-matter-a-new-paradigm-for-man aging-diversity.

Part VI

1. Actor, director, and TV host LeVar Burton, interviewed during "The One Thing," Leadercast.com, May 4, 2022.

Chapter 14

1. Sunnie Giles, "The Most Important Leadership Competencies, According to Leaders around the World," *Harvard Business Review*, March 15, 2016, https:// hbr.org/2016/03/the-most-important-leadership-competencies-according-to -leaders-around-the-world.

2. Hal E. Hershfield, "Future Self-Continuity: How Conceptions of the Future Self Transform Intertemporal Choice," *Annals of the New York Academy of Sciences* 1235 (October 2011): 30–43, https://doi.org/10.1111/j.1749-6632.2011.06201.x.

3. Paul Ingram, "The Forgotten Dimension of Diversity," *Harvard Business Review*, January 1, 2021, https://hbr.org/2021/01/the-forgotten-dimension-of-diversity.

4. Luigi Guiso, Paola Sapienza, and Luigi Zingales, "The Value of Corporate Culture," NBER working paper, October 2013, https://doi.org/10.3386/w19557.

5. Guiso, Sapienza, and Zingales, "The Value of Corporate Culture."

6. Guiso, Sapienza, and Zingales, "The Value of Corporate Culture."

7. Lolly Daskal, "30 Quotes on Trust That Will Make You Think," Inc.com, February 5, 2015, https://www.inc.com/lolly-daskal/trust-me-these-30-quotes -about-trust-could-make-a-huge-difference.html.

8. Book of Threes, "Ethos, Pathos, Logos—A General Summary of Aristotle's Appeals," October 10, 2014, https://www.bookofthrees.com/ethos-pathos-logos -a-general-summary-of-aristotles-appeals.

9. Christopher Sirk, "Ethos, Pathos, Logos: The Three Modes of Persuasion," CRM.org, June 2, 2020, https://crm.org/articles/ethos-pathos-logos-the-three -modes-of-persuasion.

10. Simon Sinek, "How Great Leaders Inspire Action," accessed May 7 2023, https://www.ted.com/talks/simon_sinek_how_great_leaders_inspire_action.

11. Sinek, How Great Leaders Inspire Action.

12. Victoria Sakal, "Bigger than the Boardroom: Evolving Expectations of Today's CEOs," Morning Consult (blog), June 10, 2020, https://morningcon sult.com/2020/06/10/bigger-than-the-boardroom-evolving-expectations-of -todays-ceos.

13. Aliza Astrow, "Resolving the Progressive Paradox with Professor Robb Willer," Third Way, March 30, 2022, https://www.thirdway.org/interview /resolving-the-progressive-paradox-with-professor-robb-willer.

14. Jan G. Voelkel and Matthew Feinberg, "Morally Reframed Arguments Can Affect Support for Political Candidates," *Social Psychological and Personality Science* 9, no. 8 (2017).

15. Matthew Feinberg and Robb Willer, "The Moral Roots of Environmental Attitudes," *Psychological Science* 24, no. 1 (January 2013): 56–62, https://doi .org/10.1177/0956797612449177.

16. Melissa De White, "The Power of Dressing Progressive Economic Policies in Conservative Clothes," Stanford Business Insights, June 6, 2019, https://www .gsb.stanford.edu/insights/power-dressing-progressive-economic-policies -conservative-clothes.

17. Jack Brittain and Sim Sitkin. "Carter Racing," Delta Leadership, June 2006, https://execed.poole.ncsu.edu/wp-content/uploads/2020/06/Carter-Racing -A.pdf.

18. Jennifer Agiesta, "Behind the Numbers—On Eve of Execution, Virginians Broadly Support Penalty," *Washington Post*, November 9, 2009, http://voices

.washingtonpost.com/behind-the-numbers/2009/11/on_eve_of_execution_virginians.html.

19. Death Penalty Information Center, "State Polls and Studies," accessed June 10, 2022, https://deathpenaltyinfo.org/facts-and-research/public-opinion-polls/state-polls-and-studies.

20. Agiesta, "Behind the Numbers."

21. Caryle Murphy, "Catholicism, Politics a Careful Mix for Kaine," *Washington Post*, October 31, 2005, http://www.washingtonpost.com/wp-dyn/content/article/2005/10/30/AR2005103001314.html.

22. Murphy, "Catholicism, Politics a Careful Mix for Kaine."

23. Murphy, "Catholicism, Politics a Careful Mix for Kaine."

24. Marc Fisher, "Maryland & Virginia Go Separate Ways on Death Penalty—Raw Fisher," *Washington Post*, January 2009, http://voices.washingtonpost.com/rawfisher/2009/01/maryland_virginia_go_separate.html.

25. Daniel Druckman, Benjamin J. Broome, and Susan H. Korper, "Value Differences and Conflict Resolution: Facilitation or Delinking?" *Journal of Conflict Resolution* 32, no. 3 (September 1988): 489–510, https://doi.org/10.1177/0022002788032003005.

26. Innovarsity, "Steve Jobs Quotes," accessed June 10, 2022, http://www.innovarsity.com/coach/quotes_a_jobs.html.

27. Nicole A. Gillespie and Leon Mann, "Transformational Leadership and Shared Values: The Building Blocks of Trust," *Journal of Managerial Psychology* 19, no. 6 (January 2004): 588–607, https://doi.org/10.1108/02683940410551507.

28. Gillespie and Mann, "Transformational Leadership and Shared Values."

29. Thomas A. Stewart and Joyce E. Davis, "Why Value Statements Don't Work," *Fortune Magazine*, June 10, 1996.

30. Chaoping Li and Yuanjie Bao, "Ethical Leadership and Positive Work Behaviors: A Conditional Process Model," *Journal of Managerial Psychology*, 2020, https://www.emerald.com/insight/content/doi/10.1108/JMP-10-2018-0475/full/html.

31. Vanessa Burbano, "Getting Gig Workers to Do More by Doing Good: Field Experimental Evidence from Online Platform Labor Marketplaces," *Organization and Environment* 34, no. 3 (2019). http://www.vanessaburbano.com/uploads/2/5/0/4/25049117/performancepaper_20170418_name.pdf.

32. Min-Jik Kim and Byung-Jik Kim, "The Performance Implication of Corporate Social Responsibility: The Moderating Role of Employee's Prosocial Motivation," *International Journal of Environmental Research and Public Health* 18, no. 6 (January 2021): 3128, https://doi.org/10.3390/ijerph18063128.

33. Inyong Shin and Won-Moo Hur, "How Are Service Employees' Perceptions of Corporate Social Responsibility Related to Their Performance? Prosocial Motivation and Emotional Labor as Underlying Mechanisms," *Corporate Social Responsibility and Environmental Management* 27, no. 6 (2020): 2867–2878, https://ideas.repec.org/a/wly/corsem/v27y2020i6p2867-2878.html.

34. Naina Dhingra, Andrew Samo, Bill Schaninger, and Matt Schrimper, "Help Your Employees Find Purpose—or Watch Them Leave," McKinsey, April 15, 2021, https://www.mckinsey.com/business-functions/people-and-organizational -performance/our-insights/help-your-employees-find-purpose-or-watch-them -leave.

35. Nick Bloom (@I_Am_NickBloom), "The shift to WFH is the largest shock to labor markets in decades. Pre-pandemic WFH was trending towards 5% of days by 2022. Now WFH is now stabilizing at 30%, a 6-fold jump. In America alone this is saving about 200 million hours and 6 billion miles of commuting a week," Twitter, August 29, 2022, 5:59 a.m., https://twitter.com/i_am_nickbloom /status/1564236320259461120.

36. Emma Jacobs, "Employers Beware: Hybrid Work Weakens Loyalty," *Financial Times*, February 6, 2022.

Index